LETTERS *to* YOUNG SCHOLARS:
An Introduction to Christian Thought

By William Carey Ringenberg

Published by the
Taylor University Press
236 West Reade Avenue
Upland, Indiana 46989

Published by Taylor University Press
236 West Reade Avenue
Upland, Indiana 46989-1001
For additional copies call 765-998-5216
or consult www.taylor.edu/bookstore.com

Dedicated
with appreciation
for the common quest
to my students
of the
past, present, and future.

TABLE OF CONTENTS

FOREWARD

The challenge of Christian education in the ultimate sense is to assist students to develop a Christian worldview. All people, whether they know it or not, conduct their lives on the basis of their view of the world (i.e. the picture that they hold in their minds of how things work; how things relate to each other; what those things mean; what is most important; and what constitutes duty, loyalty, patriotism, faith, meaning and a thousand other ideas in the lexicon of human existence).

"As a man thinketh in his heart, so is he" (Prov. 23: 7 KJV). Most do not have a name for their worldview, and many have only informally and with inconsistency cobbled together a philosophy of living that lurches from crisis to crisis and adapts to convenience, survival needs, whims, and various personal, family, religious and political values. Sadly, many Christians, after securing their personal salvation with the knowledge of certain biblical passages and confidence in the "Amazing Grace of Jesus Christ", live lives largely uninformed by Christian theology, the Bible, and the wisdom of the ages derived from the careful examination of the thoughts and experiences of both secular and pious people who have struggled deeply with the foundational issues of existence.

The picture that guides our lives is called by many names: a synoptic, a road map, a philosophy of life, a meta-narrative, and among youth, a lifestyle. It can be 1) a well defined and subtly shaded great master-piece, 2) a crude, legalistic paint-by-the-numbers effort, 3) a mosaic of pieces collected from often unrelated and incompatible sources, or 4) in worst cases, an angry portrait of splashes, blobs, runs and mixtures that mirror a life of despair, emptiness and nihilism. All paintings start with an idea; some work and some do not. This book is about the pre-suppositions that inspire the synoptic and then the implications of the choices selected for the pallet of experience. Each chapter teaches an important question that humans face. This book argues for the logic and reason behind an evangelical Christian worldview.

William Carey Ringenberg has spent a lifetime in the classroom and is in intimate contact with students over these issues. His book is a guide, a can opener, a discussion starter to assist young minds (older minds will find it useful as well) to ask the right questions, and then, at the level that their ability, motivation, or interests direct them, to explore these issues in depth. Each chapter has a suggested set of questions to "prime the pump" and also a suggested reading list that will take the student to the depth that their current state of development can tolerate. The book list is not exhaustive but rather selective and representative. The bibliography in each of the suggested readings will lead the learner to the best that is available on each topic. This book can be a valuable asset to the individual reader, but it is best used as a guide to small group discussion or as an outline for a course in Christian thought or the Christian worldview. Ringenberg helps us think "Christianly" and employs some of the best secular as well as Christian thinkers to assist us. The book covers the classical as well as the contemporary and the questions and conflicts as well as the answers and dilemmas. He does not seek closure on all issues because it is not always possible. He does not lead the students to comforting shortcuts that only provide a temporary comfort that will destroy them in the end; but with humility and honesty he presents both the Christian view and also the sincere and difficult questions and conclusions that remain within the human condition.

A discussion of these topics will not solve all of our problems; however, for the sincere seeker these chapters will begin a confident quest in the right direction—one that will not lead to dogmatism but rather to a confident faith informed by the best of Christian thought.

The genius of the book is that the chapters can be studied in any order and stand independently of each other. They fit together in a mosaic but can be arranged according to the interest and perceived relevance to each student or group.

I am excited about this book and will use it extensively as I try to instill in young and old minds alike our examined Christian worldview.

Jay Kesler
Chancellor, Taylor University

PREFACE

So little trouble do men take in the search after truth; so readily do they accept whatever comes first to hand.

—Thucydides

You will seek me and find Me, when you search for Me with all your heart.

—Jeremiah 29:13

Ask and it will be given to you; seek and you will find; knock and it will be opened to you. For everyone who asks receives, and he who seeks finds, and to him who knocks it will be opened.

—Matthew 7:7-8

And you shall know the truth, and the truth shall make you free.

—John 8:32

I search after truth, by which man never yet was harmed.

—Marcus Aurelius

They who know the truth are not equal to those who love it, and they who love it are not equal to those who delight in it.

—Confucius

...the discovery of truth depends on the heart and will, not just the head and mind. This is why the prime requisite for finding any great truth...is love, passion, questing, and questioning.... Answers are not as hard to come by as we think; and questions, real questioning, is a lot more rare and precious than we think! Finding is not the problem, seeking is.

—Peter Kreeft

It is no doubt an evil to be full of faults, but it is a still greater evil to be full of them and unwilling to recognize them, since this entails the further evil of deliberate self-delusion.

—Blaise Pascal

In defense of his conclusion he was willing to cheat in the evidence—a habit more usual to religious writers than to historical.
—Charles Williams on Lawrence Wentworth,
a character in his <u>Descent into Hell</u>.

...he did not want to speak to her. He wanted to be alone with his fantasies.

—Charles Williams on Lawrence Wentworth

...to hate the truth is even more horrible than to hate a person, for if we love the truth but hate a person, the truth will tell us that persons are not to be hated. But if we hate the truth, there is no more hope for us to find the true way....

—Peter Kreeft

Deliberate self-delusion may even be "the unforgivable sin," for once we shut out our souls to the light, we shut them to God, for God is light. We can repent of any sin if only we see the light; refusing light (truth) makes repentance impossible.

—Peter Kreeft

What kind of truth is it which has these mountains as its boundary and is a lie beyond them?

—Montaigne

This preface is both an introduction to the book and also, in some limited ways, the first essay of the book. The above quotations and the remainder of this paragraph suggest the three working foci of the book, namely 1) the search for truth, 2) intellectual honesty, and 3) the primacy of universal truth. *The search for truth* is the passionate quest for ultimate reality. *Intellectual honesty* is the commitment to remove the blinders, no matter how painful the process, which keep us from seeing the truth. The assumption of both the relentless journey to find truth and the attitude of intellectual honesty is that ultimate truth is ultimate goodness. *The primacy of universal truth* emphasizes that central truth should not be confused with secondary convictions.

This book is an outgrowth of an Honors course which for many years I have offered to Taylor University freshmen. The most recent title of this interdisciplinary course is Foundations of Christian Thought. The course is designed to introduce students to the general education (liberal arts) portion of a Christian college education. It gives major emphasis to the humanities and social sciences disciplines, the integration of the Christian faith with these disciplines, and the application of Christian thought to daily living (applied Christianity). It seeks to challenge the students to become broader in perspective and appreciation, more compassionate toward all of God's creatures, and more confident and committed as they develop their world views and personal values. The course asks these basic questions: 1) How can we know God? 2) How can we best understand ourselves? and 3) How can we human beings best live together on this earth where God has placed us?

The book reflects the general scope and working principles of the course, although some of the specific content differs. Like the course, *Letters to Young Scholars* is intended as a stimulus to individual and group thinking on many of life's most important issues. The book is merely one person's contribution to the ongoing human dialogue.

When, in the chapter essays, I speak with strong conviction, it is only *my* strong conviction. Each person, with the aid of multiple sources of input including ultimately the voice of the Holy Spirit, must reach his or her own conclusions; otherwise, what you call your views are not really that. All that any of us can do for one another is to share our experiences, love each other, and point one another to the ultimate source of knowledge and guidance. We learn together and from each other as we share our thoughts; and as truth-seekers when we receive new understanding, we gladly accept it and improve our thinking. Thus, although this book is part apologia, part testimony, and part intellectual biography, ultimately it is an invitation to dialogue. It seeks to be an opening word, not the last word, on the many subjects of ultimate concern which it considers.

Furthermore the book assumes that in the pursuit of ultimate reality, one can find truth anywhere and thus must seek it broadly. This explains why the format of each chapter includes not only an essay but also an intentionally comprehensive opening series of related quotations from classical and recent literature and a concluding bibliographical list of suggestions for further reading. The purpose of the quotations is not primarily to illustrate the main ideas of the essay (which is the purpose of chapter-opening quotations in many books), but rather to broaden the base of the dialogue, exposing the readers to multiple — and sometimes contradictory — ideas in readily accessible form from seminal thinkers, some of whom may not yet fully recognize that our common quest is the pursuit of the person and mind of our Maker.

The Biblical quotations used in the book come, unless otherwise noted, from the *New King James Version*. The other quotations have come from a broad variety of sources with the authors usually identified. Quotation reference books which I found especially helpful included Frank S. Mead, ed, *The Encyclopedia of Religious Quotations*; George Seldes, ed., *The Great Thoughts*; Elizabeth Knowles, ed., *The Oxford*

Essential Quotations Dictionary, American edition; and Eugene Ehrlich and Marshall DeBruhl, eds., *The International Thesaurus of Quotations,* 1996 edition.

One of the more difficult issues facing modern writers is the development of a workable approach to gender-related phrasing. At times the choice appears to be among being 1) grammatically incorrect, 2) socially insensitive, or 3) wordy and awkward in expression—not a happy set of options! My plan has been to seek to avoid the above dilemmas whenever possible by employing alternate word forms or using plural expressions (e.g. "People...their" rather than "one...he or she"). When the aforementioned trilemma seems inescapable, I have sought to choose what for the specific context is the least unsatisfactory option.

Many people contributed to the making of the book. Thanks to faculty colleagues and Dean Dwight Jessup for semester sabbatical and January term leaves to prepare the text. Also I am grateful for the helpful suggestions and encouragement of David Allison, Stephen Bedi, Clarence (Bud) Bence, Christopher Bennett, Daniel Bowell, Stanley Burden, Daryl Charles, Lenore Chernenko, Winfried Corduan, JoAnn Cosgrove, Mark Cosgrove, Richard Ehresman, Barbara Heavilin, Stephen Hoffmann, Dwight Jessup, Jay Kesler, Robert Lay, Matthew Mendham, Steven Messer, Robert Moore-Jumonville, David Neuhouser, Roger Phillips, Jeffrey Rediger, Loyal Ringenberg, Matthew Ringenberg, Rebecca Ringenberg, David Ritchie, Paul Robbins, John Sanders, Frederick Schulze, James Spiegel, Andrew Whipple, and Ryan Woods. Daniel Jordan and Roger Judd contributed very meaningfully to the publication process; they also designed the cover. Darlene Jordan, Rebecca Ringenberg, and Lishauna Taylor typed the manuscript. Robert Moore-Jumonville graciously provided a "trial run" for the book by using it as a complementary text in two of his classes.

WCR

THE HUMAN CONDITION

1. THE REMOTENESS OF GOD

Verily Thou art a God that hidest Thyself....

—Isaiah 45:15a (KJV)

...the basic source of man's existential anguish...arises not because of <u>his existence</u> but because of <u>his separated existence</u>.

—William Johnston

The soul knows for certain...that it is hungry. ...the danger is not lest the soul should doubt whether there is any bread, but lest, by a lie, it should persuade itself that it is not hungry.

—Simone Weil

We all know that there is no true good here below, that everything that appears to be good in this world is finite, limited, wears out, and once worn out, leaves necessity exposed in all its nakedness.

—Simone Weil

We are each born with a secret, a secret we try to hide every second of our lives by a million clever devises, both internal and external. The secret is that each of us is terribly alone, each finds that loneliness unendurable, each reaches out desperately to overcome it in those million ways, [but] never fully succeeds....

—Peter Kreeft

What can be seen on earth indicates neither the total absence, nor the manifest presence of divinity, but the presence of a hidden God. Everything bears this stamp....

—Blaise Pascal

If there were no obscurity man would not feel his corruption; if there were no light man could not hope for a cure. Thus it is not only right but useful for us that God should be partly concealed and partly revealed, since it is equally dangerous for man to know God without knowing his own wretchedness as to know his wretchedness without knowing God.

—Blaise Pascal

"They say that there is a God who made the whole world including me, and I believe it, also. But while I find this belief comforting, I don't find it comforting enough. This God who is behind the world, why does He have to be so far behind it that I can't see Him or feel Him? I would like Him to come to my house and touch me and put His arm around me and tell me He loves me and that all will be well for me always. I would not like it if my human father, who lived in another state or country, while calling me periodically, never came to visit me. If God is a God of love, why is He so distant from those He loves?"

Such is the common human complaint. It is not always articulated very well, nor always even understood very clearly, but it is universally sensed—and often to the core of one's being. The fact is, of course, that God is indeed hidden, but only partially. Similarly he is revealed but not fully, not enough to completely satisfy, not enough to prevent us from longing for more of Him.

We want more closeness to God than is available in this life; we all do, Christians and non-Christians alike. The latter many deny the fact or seek its fulfillment in less than divine objects, but even Christians who have found the One who fulfills lament the limited degree of fulfillment available in this life. As expressed by Gerard Manley Hopkins in the beginning verses of his poem, "Nondum", the sensitive Christian, when focusing upon the incomplete part of divine revelation, cries in a deeply felt even if overstated manner:

4

God though to Thee our psalm we raise
No answering voice comes from the skies;
To Thee the trembling sinner prays
But no forgiving voice replies;
Our prayer seems lost in desert ways,
Our hymn in the vast silence dies.
We see the glories of the earth
But not the hand that wrought them all:
Night to a myriad world gives birth,
Yet like a lighted empty hall
Where stands no host at door or hearth
Vacant creation's lamps appal.

Why does God appear so remote? The many possible explanations include the following:

1. God appears remote because He is not there; He simply does not exist. "Then why do we cry for Him so?" is the obvious response to this view.

2. A universal driving force or first cause or oversoul is greater and better than are we and like a magnet compels us to seek and identify with and perhaps even become absorbed in it. In this very impersonal and amoral view (somewhere between nothingness and theism), the feeling of remoteness and dis-ease is less significant than the compelling attraction which pulls us toward wholeness. The latter facilitates a completing of our existence.

3. God is playing games with us or is like the absentee Father who chooses to distance Himself from His children. If this view is true, then we live in dire circumstances, no better than the perceived situation of the Ancient Greeks and Romans in their relationships with their moody and unpredictable deities.

4.   Somehow, even apart from the issue of sin, the sense of the distance from God is a divinely-intentioned testing to facilitate our maturing as humans.

5.   The hiddenness of God is a necessary factor in the condition of human freedom with which God made us. While freedom is of utmost importance in God's plan for His human creatures, it carries with it such grave risks (i.e., the possibility of choosing against God) that God chooses to give us the insecurity and sense of neediness that follow His distancing Himself from us to compel (not force) us to seek Him. Thus the hiddenness that leads to longing is a marvelous gift of God for a being that possesses the power of moral choice.

6.   The human sense of distance from God is a direct result of the Fall. Created originally in innocence and perfect harmony and fellowship, this idyllic state in the garden ended when humans chose not to live in obedience to God, thus destroying the face-to-face relationship. Therefore, the reason that God appears remote is that we humans have distanced ourselves from Him. Eden was lost—for now—because of sin. This past choice haunts us, but God offers us another opportunity (redemptive grace) which may be realized partially in the present order and perfectly in the future. There is no greater human pain than the sense of separation from God. This in itself suggests hope for restoration, as surely a loving God would not make us miserable for nothing.

Christians disagree on whether by inheritance the sins of Adam and Eve made sinners of us all ("In Adam's fall, we sinned all"). Some support this "doctrine of original sin;" others argue that humans are separated from God, not by the actions of our forebears but by their own volitional, sinful choices. There are intellectual difficulties with either view. For example if an individual, who did not ask to be born, is a condemned sinner merely by birth and before being able to make a moral choice, then there exists a real or perceived problem of fairness. On the other hand, if one accepts the idea that "all have sinned" (Romans 3:23) but not the idea that all inherited the status of sinners from our first parents, then there exists the question of the reality of human "choice." How does a genuine choice exist between A and B when arguably all who have ever lived have chosen B. Has A really been a viable option? In a sense this conflict between original sin advocates and choice-only proponents is essentially a theoretical problem. For, in practice, virtually all Christians believe that if one really wants and seeks God, then God will restore His fellowship with that person.

QUESTIONS FOR REFLECTION AND DISCUSSION:

1. What is your best understanding of the widely-perceived sense of alienation or distancing from God?

2. To what extent do you accept the idea of original sin (i.e., we fell with Adam and Eve regardless of any choice of our own)?

SUGGESTIONS FOR FURTHER READING:

1. William Barrett, *Irrational Man: A Study in Existential Philosophy*

2. The Book of Ecclesiastes

3. Peter Kreeft, *Christianity for Modern Pagans: Pascal's Pensees*

4. John of the Cross, *Dark Night of the Soul*

5. William Johnston, ed., *The Cloud of Unknowing*

6. Chaim Potok, *The Chosen*

2. LONGING

As the deer pants for the water brooks,
So pants my soul for you, O God.

—Psalm 42:1

...the entire life of a good Christian is nothing less than holy desire.

—Augustine

Thou hast made us for Thyself, and our hearts are restless until they rest in Thee.

—Augustine

...He is not far from each of us;

—Acts 17:27b

Speak to Him, thou, for He hears,
and Spirit with Spirit can meet—
Closer is He than breathing,
and nearer than hands and feet.

—Alfred, Lord Tennyson

If Father points to ultimate reality and Son supplies the clue to the divine mystery, Spirit epitomizes the nearness of the power and presence of God.

—Clark Pinnock

I am beginning now to see how radically the character of my spiritual journey will change when I no longer think of God as hiding out and making it as difficult as possible for me to find Him, but, instead, as the One who is looking for me while I am doing the

9

hiding. When I...discover God's joy at my coming home, then my life may become less anguished and more trusting.

—Henry Nouwen

The true Christian is in all countries a pilgrim and a stranger.

—George Santayana

If I find in myself a desire which no experience in this world can satisfy, the most probable explanation is that I was made for another world.

—C. S. Lewis

Man's highest perfection is union with God in consummate love....

—unknown author of The Cloud of Unknowing

To be made for eternity and forced to dwell in time is for mankind a tragedy of huge proportions. All within us cries for life and permanence, and everything around us reminds us of mortality and change. Yet that God has made us of the stuff of eternity is both a glory and a prophecy, a glory yet to be realized and a prophecy yet to be fulfilled.

—A. W. Tozer

For now we see in a mirror, dimly, but then face to face. Now I know in part, but then I shall know just as I also am known.

—I Corinthians 13:12

Immortal, invisible, God only wise,
In light inaccessible hid from our eyes,...
All praise we would render—O help us to see
'Tis only the splendor of light hideth Thee!

—Walter Chalmers Smith

This essay on Longing could almost be a part of the previous chapter on the Remoteness of God; certainly the two are closely related. The essay on Remoteness described a major aspect of the human problem, while this one on Longing describes the beginning of the solution to the human problem. The feeling of remoteness is prerequisite to longing. Longing is preliminary to finding; it leads to seeking, and seeking leads to finding. The statement of Jesus, "seek, and you will find," (Matthew 7:7) is one of the most important declarations in the Bible; it refers to much more than praying narrowly defined, as one can and should see all of the questing life as one grand prayer.

Knowingly or otherwise, everyone is lonely, everyone feels inadequate, everyone longs for something more. This universal sense bespeaks a human separateness, an existence of partiality rather than unity. We are made for God, but we are not totally united to Him. This inherent need for passionate attachment to something greater than ourselves is one of the most empirically verifiable evidences of the existence of God. Those who deny or reject this basic desire are fighting against their basic instincts. Those who embrace this longing are greatly blessed because of that to which the longing can lead.

Longing is so universal and intense that we seek to find a solution to it somewhere, somehow, even when our seeking is misguided (i.e., directed toward objects which are only imitations—and sometimes very cheap ones—of the real solution). While these substitute solutions can provide some fulfillment, they are always incomplete and even downright disappointing in the end.

Many of the substitute solutions involve things which are not bad in and of themselves but become false gods when we seek to find ultimate happiness through them. This they are not able to give us, and we are foolish to place such high expectations upon them. Many of these are gifts of God (e.g. key people in our lives like family members, friends, or inspiring political or cultural figures; financial resources; personal influence or even power; personal talents; a fulfilling career; or an able mind). Of course, only the giver of these gifts can provide us with the ultimate gift, that ultimate fulfillment which comes not only from Him but in Him.

Sometimes we pursue noble causes which seek to promote the divine purposes of peace, justice, and human dignity in the world but then come to identify with the movement or organization and its humanly defined success more than the One who gives meaning to the cause. Specific examples of these causes could include economic opportunity for the deprived, world hunger, world peace, relief and development, political liberation, sacredness of life, and even the local church or institutional religion in general.

Then there are the ways of seeking satisfaction which appear to be blatantly evil. In many cases, however, even these are less inherently wicked than representing the pursuit of good (i.e., fulfillment) in counterproductive or destructive ways. Prostitution and promiscuity often represent a search for love, acceptance, and meaning; the active pursuit of power and popularity for their own sake frequently stem from a quest for acceptance; the focus on the acquisition of large sums of money sometimes reflects the search for security. Of course love, acceptance, dignity, meaning, and security are good things, and the desire for them is a God-given blessing designed to draw us to Him. But so often we take the wrong path in our search for Him.

The practitioners of non-Christian religions often have an advantage over those followers of the aforementioned substitute solutions to the problem of longing. For they are more likely to be sincere seekers of God, a status to which Jesus offers great hope (Matthew 7:7; also see Deuteronomy 4:29). We must not too quickly judge people on the basis

12

of their organizational affiliation. Jesus also tells us that Judgment Day will offer many surprises (Matthew 7:21-23, 8:11-12).

Another non-Christian view that has much to commend it is the pessimistic variety of existential philosophy. Its primary virtue is its commitment to intellectual honesty; it is a very courageous half-truth. It clearly sees the problem of human loneliness and the barrenness of the previously discussed substitute solutions, but it stops short of finding and embracing the ultimate solution. The natural consequence is despair. The near greatness of this view is also its awfulness. Few can tolerate facing with honesty the misery of our fallen state unless this is coupled with an immediate prospect of relief and redemption. Peter Kreeft has described well the intolerable pain of non-Theistic existentialism, noting that Freidrich Nietzsche and John-Paul Sartre, arguably the two most influential advocates of this view, have "driven more skeptics screaming into the arms of the priests than any preacher of our time."

The ultimate solution to the problem of loneliness is to recognize and fully embrace the idea that we were made for nothing less than intimate fellowship with God both now in this imperfect order and eternally in His new order. In our present search for God, it is of great comfort to know that God is also searching for us (for example, see Revelation 3:20). He wants us to find Him; He is not hiding. But He wants us to seek Him freely because He respects and values our freedom. To help us in our search for Him in this life, He has come to us in the second and third members of the Trinity. Jesus in the Incarnation not only provided for our restoration to God but also revealed to us more fully the nature of God ("if you have seen Me you have seen the Father"). Then as he prepared to leave this earth, He promised that the Holy Spirit would come in a new way as a permanent divine helper, comforter, and teacher.

Nevertheless, even Christians long for something more, and well they should. God has always revealed Himself progressively, and we modern believers have a fuller understanding of the nature and purposes of God than did the pre-Christian era people. Thus our knowledge of the New Testament record can mitigate our sense of void and help us to see it as a sign of love and as a promise of a future era of ultimate fulfillment. Thus, ironically, the people who have found God continue to pursue Him.

Gerard Manley Hopkins' poem, "Nondum," appeared in its beginning verses in the previous chapter as a complaint of the remoteness of God. Now the same poem in its culminating verses expresses the hope and faith that our longings will find their ultimate fulfillment in the next life:

> Oh! Till Thou givest that sense beyond,
> To show Thee that Thou art, and near,
> Let patience with her chastening wand
> Dispel the doubt and dry the tear;
> And lead me child-like by the hand
> If still in darkness not in fear.
>
> Speak! Whisper to my watching heart
> One word—as when a mother speaks
> Soft, when she sees an infant start,
> Till dimpled joy steals o'er its cheeks.
> Then to behold Thee as Thou art,
> I'll wait till morn eternal breaks

QUESTIONS FOR REFLECTION AND DISCUSSION:

1. Does every genuine seeker of God find Him? If not, what did the Incarnate One mean by His statement, "Seek, and you will find"?

2. Do you agree with the sweeping statement that "Knowingly or otherwise, everyone is lonely, everyone feels inadequate, everyone longs for something more"?

SUGGESTIONS FOR FURTHER READING:

1. Harry Emerson Fosdick, *The Meaning of Prayer*

2. Julian of Norwich, *Revelation of Love*

3. William Johnstone, ed., *The Cloud of Unknowing*

4. Morton Kelsey, *Reaching: The Journey to Fulfillment*

5. Peter Kreeft, *Christianity for Modern Pagans: Pascal's Pensees*

6. C. S. Lewis, *Surprised by Joy*

7. C. S. Lewis, "The Weight of Glory," chapter one in *The Weight of Glory and other Addresses*

8. A. W. Tozer, *The Pursuit of God*

9. Simone Weil, *Waiting for God*

3. THE INEVITABILITY OF DEATH

...of the tree of the knowledge of good and evil you shall not eat,
for in the day that you eat of it you shall surely die. For dust you
are, and to dust you shall return.

—Genesis 2:17, 3:19b

The days of our lives are seventy years;
And if by reason of strength they are eighty years,
Yet their boast is only labor and sorrow;
For it is soon cut off, and we fly away.

—Psalm 90:10

Anyone can stop a man's life, but no one his death; a thousand
doors open on to it.

—Seneca the Younger

The boast of heraldry, the pomp of pow'r,
And all that beauty, all that wealth e'er gave,
Awaits alike th' inevitable hour,
The paths of glory lead but to the grave.

—Thomas Gray

The last enemy that will be destroyed is death.

—I Corinthians 15:26

Death remains a fearful and cruel monster.

—Paul Tournier

Without God, death is horrific. With God, death is still fearsome,
but it can be seen to have a meaning and purpose and a hope.

—Paul Johnson

Shrinking away from [death]...is something unhealthy and abnormal which robs the second half of life of its purpose.

—*Carl Jung*

Do not seek death. Death will find you. But seek the road which makes death a fulfillment.

—*Dag Hammarskjold*

That...He might...release those who through fear of death were all their lifetime subject to bondage.

—*Hebrews 2:14-15*

The gospel...is fundamentally a story about [the] conquest of death.... The "good news" of Christianity claims to answer the "bad news" of death.

—*Peter Kreeft*

One short sleep past, we wake eternally
And death shall be no more; death, thou shalt die.

—*John Donne*

The best of all is God is with us.

—*John Wesley*
(on his deathbed)

What the bereaved man needs is not the comfort of some platitudes about death; what he needs is a living faith in the Living God, and then he can comfort himself.

—*Elton Trueblood*

The elegance of death is the eloquence of human poverty coming face to face with the riches of divine mercy.

—*Thomas Merton*

Far though from out our bourne of time and place
The flood may bear me far,
I hope to see my pilot face to face
When I have crossed the bar.

—*Alfred Lord Tennyson*

Death is always sad, I suppose to us who look forward to it; I expect
it will seem very different when we can look back upon it.

—*Lewis Carroll*

What happens after death is so unspeakably glorious that our
imaginations and our feelings do not suffice to form even an ap-
proximate conception of it....

—*Carl Jung*
(after a near-death experience)

It may appear strange to include the subject of death in a series of essays addressed primarily to young people, for during the early years
death often seems so far away and there are many other pressing issues
and interests to consider and experience. Nevertheless, death is an
ever-present reality for people of all ages. While, as Jim Elliott stated,
"The old must die, and the young may die," it is also true that the young
will die sooner or later. Furthermore, few young people survive the
youthful years without experiencing the death of a family member or
friend. Therefore, all people, regardless of age, best prepare for living
by preparing well for dying.

Do you remember when you first realized the inevitability of death?
My moment of awakening came at about age nine when one morning I
asked my father, "Are dying and the second coming of Christ the only
ways that a person can leave this life?" I probably was hoping that there

was some less traumatic option. When he answered in the affirmative, a dawn of sobering realism replaced my age of innocence.

Another shocking moment for many—usually much later in life—comes with the realization that death is not only inevitable but also imminent. Samuel Johnson once noted "...when a man knows he is to be hanged in a fortnight, it concentrates his mind wonderfully." Here is a haunting question: "If we never died and knew we would never die, would we ever seek God?" Perhaps this rhetorical question more than the idea of punishment explains the reason for death.

It is not so much the inescapability of death as the dread of this unavoidable phenomenon that so disturbs us. This fear of death in concert with the sense of distance—or even alienation—from God is the ultimate source of human anxiety. The general consensus among Christians today is that physical death as well as spiritual death is the result of the Fall. If the Fall did not introduce physical death, it probably at least introduced its dread (see I Corinthians 15:56a).

While strong faith should lessen the fear of death, it does not preclude it. One can identify noteworthy saints who experienced great angst when contemplating death. Apparently the degree of concern depends more upon temperament than upon spirituality. An emphasis upon the absence of emotion over one's death is more Stoic, Platonic, or Epicurean than Christian. Note the great trauma experienced by Jesus just before and during his death (Mark 14:32-36; Luke 22:39-42; Matthew 26:36-42; 27:46); if the Incarnate One, in becoming like us, did not escape the anxiety of death, we should not be surprised that it continues as the great existential issue for us mortals.

One of the greatest of all Biblical themes—and the testimony of countless believers—is the idea of the existence of special grace for special needs. Time and time again at the moment of death—as well as during those many crises of life ("mini-deaths" in a psychological sense)—the trusting individual receives extraordinary divine assistance. It happened to Jesus in the Garden of Gethsemane: "Then an angel appeared to Him from heaven, strengthening Him" (Luke 22:43).

The ultimate Christian solution to the problem of death is not avoidance or denial but direct confrontation of the enemy and triumph through trust in the One who overcomes death. The greater the realization of the profundity of the difficulty, the greater the ability to rely upon our ultimate source of help. For me a helpful image of dying is that of crawling into the back seat of the car and lying down, relaxing, and going to sleep as God drives the vehicle home, in this case to the ultimate home in the ultimate place with our ultimate friend to experience the ultimate adventure.

During the last third of the twentieth century we have acquired what appears to be significant, new—or more verifiable—information on the subject of life after death. In many ways this information could be encouraging to those who want God in their lives, although some Christians in some ways find it threatening. The development of cardiopulmonary resuscitation means that emergency medical practice can bring many more people back from the brink of death. Therefore, we have more people who can tell of their "near-death" experiences (NDEs). Furthermore, since the pioneering work of researcher Raymond Moody, we have an increasing number of systematic studies of this experience.

There is a remarkable uniformity to the stories told by the NDE people interviewed by the researchers. "All of the people who go through this come away believing that the most important thing in their life is love," Moody reports. "For most of them, the second most important thing in life is knowledge." Love and knowledge, they learn, are the two things that we can take with us at death, and they return transformed with a value system that emphasizes more than ever before loving relationships and an enhanced quest for learning. In addition, the NDEers report experiencing some or all of the following: an initial resistance which gives way to the pleasantness of surrender, a sense of being outside of one's body with the ability to move rapidly from place to place including into the heavens, the passing through a tunnel, meeting deceased friends and relatives, meeting a being of great light, a concentrated life review as if there were a merger of time and space, a sense of great peace and a reluctance to return to this life, and a border or limit beyond which they cannot pass.

Some Christians have been resistant of these reports because 1) in some ways they appear to overlap with New Age teachings, 2) some interpretations of their experiences by individual NDEers appear to be subjective and even speculative, and 3) perhaps most significantly, the reports talk much more about heaven-like scenes than about hell-like ones. The important thing, of course, is neither to under-emphasize nor exaggerate the significance of the NDE reports. They do tell us something important and new, but there is much more that they do not tell us. For one thing none of the NDEers fully died, at least not permanently; almost certainly there is more to dying than what any of them has yet experienced.

So the question remains as to how much the NDE phenomenon provides new empirical evidence of the next life and how much it represents a self-fulfilling prophecy whereby people who believe that they may be dying see dramatic visions of what they expect and/or hope to see when they do die. Much about death continues to be a mystery, and for each of us that likely will not change in this life. Meanwhile, we do not despair but trust in the One who conquered death and promised to lead us through it to a glorious future.

QUESTIONS FOR REFLECTION AND DISCUSSION:

1. Did the Fall introduce physical death, as well as spiritual death? If your answer is yes, then if there had been no Fall and thus no death, how would there be enough space for all of us?

2. How do you explain the growing phenomena of people reporting near-death experiences?

SUGGESTIONS FOR FURTHER READING:

1. Larry DenBesten, "The Dying Experience," *The Reformed Journal*, November, 1978

2. Paul Johnson, "The Four Last Things: Death," Chapter 12 in *The Quest for God*

3. Peter Kreeft, *Love Is Stronger Than Death*

4. George Eldon Ladd, *The Last Things*

5. Raymond A. Moody, Jr., *Life After Life*

6. Raymond A. Moody, Jr., *The Light Beyond*

7. Karlis Osis and Erlendur Harraldsson, *At The Hour of Death*

8. Leo Tolstoy, *The Death of Ivan Ilyich*

9. D. Elton Trueblood, "Death," in *The Common Ventures of Life*

4. THE BLESSEDNESS
OF NEEDINESS

The basis of all Christianity is an imperious sense of need...
—William Barclay

I take pleasure in infirmities, in reproaches, in needs, in persecutions, in distresses for Christ's sake. For when I am weak, then I am strong.
—II Corinthians 12:10

Christianity... has nothing (as far as I know) to say to people who do not know that they have anything to repent of and who do not feel they need any forgiveness.
—C.S. Lewis

Very few of us seek God's love and power simply because we are pure, devoted and religious. Generally we seek the Resurrected One because we are forced to—because we stand against the night of evil within us and around us.
—Morton Kelsey

I am convinced that without a gut-level experience of our profound spiritual emptiness it is not possible to encounter the living God.
—Brennan Manning

We are absolutely dependent upon God, everyone of us all of the time. There are no exceptions. Few absolute statements are true, but this one is. The essay title above refers less to the human condition per se than to an accurate perception of this condition. When one realizes even

25

for a moment how utterly incapable he or she is, then God can begin to do something noble for that person.

Now we have many God-given abilities. (But these are all and always derivative.) Even so there are times and circumstances when we say to ourselves: "I don't see any way through this situation; I don't have the answer; I desperately need God's help." Our very sense of despondency can lead to our blessedness as we call upon our Creator-God for power beyond ourselves. The antennae of our perceptive skills becomes heightened ("To truly hear you must get near" reads an old African proverb), and we are likely to hear God through our needfulness.

Swiss "doctor of the whole person," Paul Tournier, wrote in one of his many helpful books, *The Strong and the Weak*, "All men, in fact, are weak. All are weak because all are afraid. They are all afraid of being trampled underfoot. They are all afraid of their inner weaknesses being discovered. They all have secret faults; they all have a bad conscience on account of certain acts which they would like to keep covered up. They are all afraid of other men and of God, of themselves, of life, and of death.... So, then, there are not as the world thinks, weak persons on the one hand, and on the other hand strong. There are, on the one hand, weak persons, who are aware of their weaknesses, who know the vanity of all psychological compensations, and who in the last resort count only on the grace of God. And there are, on the other hand, weak persons who believe in the value of their strong reactions, or their doctrines, their successes, and their virtues." For the latter, God can do nothing but patiently, lovingly wait for them to acknowledge their neediness and seek Him. For the former, even now, he offers His riches: "Blessed are the poor in spirit, for theirs is the Kingdom of Heaven" (Matthew 5:3).

For those of us who choose to deal with our weakness by receiving God's grace and listening to His voice, we will find that He can speak His love to us through anything. Just as Satan is likely to work on us through our most vulnerable areas, so also God is likely to speak to us through the ways in which we best perceive and most naturally think. For me a common such avenue is improbability. When I am desperately seeking God, I frequently hear through a combination of related circumstances (coincidences) that in the aggregate would be highly unlikely to occur at random. These may include, for example, several of the following: 1) a voice on the radio, television or telephone, 2) the minister's unusually focused words or prayers, 3) the inner voice in meditation, 4) an especially vivid dream that responds to an intensely expressed need, or 5) a highly telling passage in a book, all exquisitely timed and with a sense of assuredness and even awe. Various people have referred to these expressions as "synchronicity," "holy luck," and "God's winks." However God speaks to a given person, we all have the assurance that as we earnestly seek Him in a spirit of dependancy, we find Him, and He brings us into eternal, loving fellowship with Him.

QUESTIONS FOR REFLECTION AND DISCUSSION:

1. What do you think that Paul means by his statement, "When I am weak, then I am strong" (II Corinthians 12:10b)?

2. Do you ever/frequently /always feel inferior or inadequate? Is it a relief to discover that almost everybody else does also, whether they recognize it consciously or not? Explain your reaction to these questions.

3. Does God speak to you? If so, what are the most natural ways that He does so?

SUGGESTIONS FOR FURTHER READING:

1. Paul Clasper, "Holy Luck," in *Theological Ferment*

2. Paul Tournier, *The Strong and the Weak*

5. HOPE

Never despair.

—Horace

Say not the struggle naught availeth.

—Arthur Hugh Clough

Work without hope draws nectar
in a sieve,
And hope without an object
cannot live.

—Samuel Taylor Coleridge

When you say a situation or a person is hopeless, you are slamming
the door in the face of God.

—Charles L. Allen

Who would have thought my shriveled heart could have recovered
greenness?

—George Herbert

The fact of the religious vision, and its history of persistent expan-
sion, is our one ground for optimism. Apart from it, human life is
a flash of occasional enjoyments lighting up a mass of pain and
misery, a bagatelle of transient experience.

—Alfred North Whitehead

No matter how ruined man and his world may seem to be, and no matter how terrible man's despair may become, as long as he continues to be a man his very humanity continues to tell him that life has a meaning.

—Thomas Merton

Hope springs eternal in the human breast:
Man never Is, but always To Be blest.

—Alexander Pope

For those who believe in Christ, there is no sorrow that is not mixed with hope—no despair. There is only a constant being born again, a constant going from darkness to light.

—Vincent Van Gogh

Little ones, no ill can chance;
Fear ye not, but sing and dance;
Though the high-heaved heaven should fall
God is plenty for us all:
God is love and strength!

—George Macdonald

Hope is the wish and even expectation that what one wants to happen will happen. The concept of Christian hope usually refers to the idea that life continues beyond death and in a better form. Hope contrasts with faith in that it is more general and more elementary. Essentially, hope is foundational for faith; if neediness is the parent of hope, hope is the parent of faith.

Lack of hope is nearly the worst thing a human can experience. Job did not lose all hope despite his lament, "My days are swifter than a weaver's shuttle and are spent without hope." (Job 7:6). Later he proclaimed in one of the most powerful Old Testament statements of ultimate trust, "For I know that my Redeemer lives, and He shall stand at last on the earth; and after my skin is destroyed, this I know, that in my flesh I shall see God." By contrast, Judas, the betraying disciple, so despaired that he hanged himself.

While Job temporarily may have lost hope for this life, he did not lose ultimate hope. Judas, whether with realistic perception or not, lost all hope, period. Judas's situation illustrates one form of hopelessness, namely the conviction that one has so completely failed the personal God that he or she cannot or should not find redemption.

A second type of hopelessness develops from a belief that existence is meaningless, ends with death, and involves no personal God. It finds perhaps its most poignant modern expression in the atheistic variety of existentialism, including the novels of Jean-Paul Sartre and Albert Camus which starkly and vividly describe a world with nothing beyond our temporal, individual selves. Note for example the sense of meaninglessness and despair in the experience of Antoine Roquentin in Sartre's carefully named novel, *Nausea*: "I was just thinking...that here we sit, all of us eating and drinking to preserve our precious existence and really there is nothing, nothing, absolutely no reason for existing."

While the Christian believers by definition do not experience the ultimate despair expressed above, they do fully experience the existential anxiety which is endemic in the human race. "All anxiety," psychologist Paul Tournier reminds us, "is reduced to anxiety about death." Is anxiety about death sinful? Not necessarily. Christ himself experienced it (Matthew 26:37-44; 27:46). Lack of anxiety regarding death is more Epicurean and Stoic than Christian; it usually involves repressed feeling more than courage. We do well to face fully the fact that death—and the life-long knowledge of our mortality—is extremely traumatic for nearly all of us; it is our "last enemy" (1 Corinthians 15:26).

For Christians, our hope for our future throughout this life, at death, and for the next life becomes so intensely related to our relationship with Jesus that it becomes faith as well as hope. We say with Paul, " I know whom I have believed and am persuaded that He is able to keep what I have committed to Him until that day" (II Timothy 1;12b); and with the writer to the Hebrews, "This hope we have as an anchor of the soul, both sure and steadfast..."(Hebrews 6:19 a).

QUESTIONS FOR REFLECTION AND DISCUSSION:

1. Which of the following are true about human anxiety: a) it would exist even if the human race had not yet sinned, b) it is a result of sin, c) it is an act of sin, d) it is a blessing meant to lead us to God, e) hope in God reduces it, f) hope in God should eliminate it.

2. Is any expression of hope an inherently religious act?

SUGGESTIONS FOR FURTHER READING:

1. William Barrett, *Irrational Man: A Study in Existential Philosophy*

2. Paul Boyer, *When Time Shall Be No More*

3. Victor Frankl, *Man's Search for Meaning*

4. George Eldon Ladd, *The Blessed Hope*

5. George Eldon Ladd, *The Last Things*

6. Jürgen Moltmann, *Theology of Hope*

7. Paul Tournier, *Learn to Grow Old*

6. THE OMNIPOTENCE OF GOD

I believe in God the Father Almighty, maker of heaven and earth;
                                              —The Apostles' Creed

*The Lord has established His throne in heaven, and His Kingdom
rules over all.*
                                              —Psalm 103:19

God...works all things according to the counsel of His will...
                                              —Ephesians 1:3a, 11b

*God is over all things, under all things; outside all; within but
not enclosed; without but not excluded; above but not raised up;
below but not depressed; wholly above, presiding; wholly beneath,
sustaining; wholly without, embracing; wholly within, filling.*
                                              —Hildebert of Lavardin

*God is great, and therefore He will be sought; He is good, and
therefore He will be found.*
                                              —Anonymous

The omnipotence of God is one of the central ideas of Christian theism.
The Lord of Lords is Creator of all, Sustainer of all, Ordainer of all.
What about the existence of human free will? That too is a central idea
in Christian thinking, but human freedom—and thus human responsibility—exists only by decree of the Sovereign God. It is derivative.
We humans have nothing and are nothing but what is given to us. God
in His wisdom determined that it was good for humans, created in His
image, to be made free moral agents who could choose for or against
Him and for or against good. Such choices and their consequences

are the essence of human history. Calvinists, Arminians, and other Christians debate the exact degree and meaning of the human freedom provided by a Sovereign God, but with few exceptions, accept—in practice if not always in theory—its reality. Sometimes such debates on the details of God's gift of freedom are highly productive; at other times they provide a prime example of how humans can choose against God in the graceless ways that they attempt to argue for Him.

Omnipotence is one major description of God's nature; love is the ultimate description of His essence. In other words, God uses His power to dispense His love. Fritz Guy, in *The Grace of God and the Will of Man*, has appropriately emphasized the importance of integrating the Old Testament idea of the power of God with Jesus' teaching and demonstration of the love of God: "To the person who takes seriously Jesus' claim 'He who has seen Me has seen the Father' (John 14:9), it is obvious that divine power is expressed not by decreeing and controlling (in the fashion of an ancient despot or a feudal lord), but by self-giving and enabling."

QUESTIONS FOR REFLECTION AND DISCUSSION:

1. What do you think of the question: "Could God make a rock so big that He could not throw it?"

2. Do Calvinists believe more completely in the sovereignty of God than do Arminians?

SUGGESTIONS FOR FURTHER READING:

1. James Boice, *The Sovereign God*

2. Emil Brunner, *The Christian Doctrine of God*

3. John Calvin, *Institutes of the Christian Religion*

4. Carl F. H. Henry, *God, Revelation, and Authority*

5. J. I. Packer, *Evangelism and the Sovereignty of God*

6. Clark H. Pinnock, ed., *The Grace of God and the Will of Man*

7. A.W. Tozer, *The Knowledge of the Holy*, especially chapters 12 and 22

7. HUMAN FREEDOM

Liberty is so holy a thing that God was forced to permit Evil that it might exist.

> —Lord John Acton
> (in Gertrude Himmelfarb, <u>Lord Acton</u>)

A Robin Red Breast in a Cage
Puts all Heaven in a Rage

> —William Blake

I know why the caged bird sings, ah me,
When his wing is bruised and his bosom sore, —
When he beats his bars and would be free;
It is not a carol of joy or glee,
But a prayer that he sends from his heart's deep core,
But a plea, that upward to Heaven, he flings —
I know why the caged bird sings.

> —Paul Laurence Dunbar

There is nothing men more readily give themselves to than pushing their own beliefs. When ordinary means fail, they add commandment, violence, fire and sword.

> —Michel de Montaigne

Despots themselves do not deny that freedom is excellent; only they desire it for themselves alone, and they maintain that everyone else is altogether unworthy of it.

> —Alexis de Tocqueville

We prefer self-government with danger to servitude with tranquility.

—*Kwame Nkrumah*

None who have always been free can understand the terrible fascinating power of the hope of freedom to those who are not free.

—*Pearl Buck*

The Spirit of God first imparts love; he next inspires hope, and then gives liberty; and that is about the last thing we have in many of our churches.

—*Dwight L. Moody*

Religion itself is outraged when outrage is done in its name.

–*Mohandas Gandhi*

As God has created our independence so that we should have the possibility of renouncing it out of love, we should for the same reason wish to preserve the independence of our fellows. He who is perfectly obedient sets an infinite price upon the faculty of free choice in all men.

—*Simeon Weil*

None can love freedom heartily, but good men; the rest love not freedom, but license.

—*John Milton*

Liberty means responsibility, that is why most men dread it.
—*George Bernard Shaw*

We humans passionately seek and need both large amounts of freedom and large amounts of security. God gives us love and freedom, and, as we wish it, security; we best act out Jesus' commandments to love God and our neighbors when we give the same to others. When Christians debate theology, perhaps the greatest point of agreement is the idea of discipleship—we are to seek to be as much as possible like the God-man himself. This concept is expressed in the title of two of the most read Christian classics, Thomas a' Kempis' *The Imitation of Christ* and Charles Sheldon's *In His Steps*. The heart of imitating Christ is this: Just as He emptied Himself of some of His power to create and empower us as free moral agents, so also we are to use this freedom and power both to give ourselves back to Him and to freely empower those fellow creatures who in some way need part of our strength. Historically, humans have less clearly seen the idea of a God who lovingly shares his power and calls His followers to do the same than they have the idea of a God who exerts His power to the maximum. Truly loving, giving, Christian individuals, churches, and even states use their power to help people move away from an immature dependency to the appropriation of the self-respect given to us all by a loving God. By contrast, the drive for power over others, whether emanating from an individual, a church, or a state, stands in contrast to both the example and formula given us by the Son of Man.

Unfortunately, much of human history is the story of a person or persons trying to control another person or persons, and of the latter seeking to resist the former. This control/resist dynamic is a significant factor, if not the dominant one, in arguably the majority of wars, internal revolts, church fights, husband-wife arguments, parent-child struggles, and labor-management conflicts. Why is humanity's need to control so consuming? Part of the desire to control stems from our intuitive belief that there are right and wrong ways of doing things, and as, presumably, we want others to do the right, we therefore seek to assure that they will do it by controlling their circumstances. With few exceptions such as the appropriate parental direction in the development of children and governmental restraint of the wicked, such control is usually self-defeating in that it is contrary to the principle of individual choice with which God has endowed us. Other reasons for seeking to control others are less noble: to exercise willfulness, to demonstrate superiority, or to act out sadistic feelings.

If the desire to control others is due largely to sinfulness, including perhaps a quest to be like a false image of God or even to replace God, the desire to be free from control stems from the way that God made us all not merely as free moral beings but as creatures who value this freedom to an inestimable degree. For no other reason than to protect themselves from human threats to their God-given freedom have people been so willing to die prematurely. This passionate valuing of freedom by people everywhere at all times is the best proof of its existence as a prime factor in the human condition.

Freedom, no less than power, can be misused. A person abusing power seeks to control others; a person abusing freedom ignores others and their needs. Freedom is never an end in itself, but is a gift to allow us to choose voluntarily the collective good for ourselves and others, namely, union with God and one another. In exercising our freedom, we can ignore people one by one or as collective entities. If, in the twentieth century, Communist and Fascist systems have often sinned in exercising tyranny over their subjects, then Western systems of capitalism have often erred by emphasizing the importance of production and industrialism over assuring minimum security for large numbers of their peoples. As Richard Emrich reminds us, "Our responsibility does not cease when our neighbor confronts us, not as an individual, but in the shape of millions of slum dwellers and tenant farmers. To love God means to...never...rest content while a social order condemns millions to insecurity. Christian individualism, then, is a social individualism, and we can only be bound to God if we are bound to our fellows with their very practical needs."

In the class on Christian Thought from which this book has developed, the aspect of human freedom which most engages the students is the question of the extent to which individuals are free to choose and retain personal salvation. They argue for and against election (predestination), free will (the ability to choose for or against God and salvation), original sin (the idea that each person is born a sinner rather than in a morally neutral state), and "eternal security" or "perseverance of the saints" (the belief that once a person becomes a Christian that status cannot change). Here are a few thoughts to contribute to this discussion:

1. We do well to begin our consideration of this and all other subjects by trying to understand how much God loves us. If his love is not absolute, then why did He create us?

2. We must, early in our deliberations, reflect on the extent of human freedom and why a sovereign God would endow his creatures with any meaningful measure of it. If we do not possess decisive moral freedom, why then does God allow evil to be so rampant in the world, and why do we humans so deeply sense that a moral law is incumbent upon us to obey?

3. The Bible clearly talks about election (e.g. Matthew 24:24; John 6:37a, 6:39a; Romans 8:29-30, 33; 9:6ff; 11:5, 7, 28; Ephesians 1:4; Colossians 3:12), and the Bible clearly talks about free will (e.g. Deuteronomy 30:19; Joshua 24:15; Isaiah 55:1; Jeremiah 11:7-8; Matthew 23:37; Luke 11:2,4; 13:34; John 7:17; I Peter 5:2). Is it not possible that both concepts are true—that they somehow are complementary rather than contradictory? Is it possible that everyone is predestined to grace and will have it when he or she is willing to receive it?

4. If God gives the free will to choose for or against Him, and we choose Him, does He then take away our free will to leave Him again? If so, why would He at that point take away the freedom that was so important for Him to give us in the first place? If a Christian can choose to stop being a Christian, is this not done only by reversing the act of commitment that made him or her a Christian initially?

In your thinking about the divine and human roles in the salvation process—as in your thinking about all issues—do not be limited by traditional human categories or options. Read the Bible with an open mind and recognize that equally devout, thoughtful, and honest people reach quite different conclusions in their study of it. Note that throughout church history, official spokespersons and groups, including preachers, bishops, denominations, and councils have often felt compelled to take strong, explicit positions on issues, sometimes for political or organizational reasons. Always value the truth more than the official proclamation of any human organization.

QUESTIONS FOR REFLECTION AND DISCUSSION:

1. How much do Calvinists and Arminians differ in concept and how much merely in emphasis?

2. Nearly all of us want a meaningful degree of both freedom and security. Which is more important to you and where do you place yourself on the freedom/security continuum (F— —/— —S)?

SUGGESTIONS FOR FURTHER READING:

1. John Acton, *Essays on Freedom and Power*

2. John Acton, *History of Freedom*

3. Mortimer J. Adler, "Liberty," ch. 47 in *The Great Ideas*

4. Roland H. Bainton, *The Travail of Religious Liberty*

5. Jonathan Edwards, *Freedom of the Will*

6. Jacques Ellul, *The Ethics of Freedom*

7. Charles G. Finney, "Natural Ability," "Gracious Ability," and "The Notion of Inability" in *Lectures on Systematic Theology*

8. Gustavo Gutierrez, *A Theology of Liberation*

9. C. S. Lewis, "On Special Providences," Appendix B in *Miracles*

10. C. S. Lewis, "Time and Beyond Time," Book IV, Chapter 3, in *Mere Christianity*

11. John Stuart Mill, *On Liberty*

12. Clark Pinnock, ed., *The Grace of God and the Will of Man*

13. B. F. Skinner, *Beyond Freedom and Dignity*

14. Nathanial Taylor, *Concio ad Clerum: On Human Nature, Sin, and Freedom*

15. G. Weston, *The Free Church Through the Ages*

ENCOUNTERING THE DIVINE

8. INTELLECTUAL OPENNESS

He said: Who then are the true philosophers?
Those, I said, who are lovers of the vision of truth.

—*Socrates*

Man with the burning soul
Has but an hour of breath.
To build a ship of Truth
In which his soul may sail,
Sail on the sea of death,
For death takes toll
Of beauty, courage, youth,
Of all but Truth.

—*John Masefield*

...the object of opening the mind, as of opening the mouth, is to shut it again on something solid.

—*G. K. Chesterton*

...let every man be swift to hear,...

—*James 1:19*

One truth discovered, one pang of regret at not being able to express it, is better than all the fluency and flippancy in the world.

—*William Hazlitt*

An honest heart being the first blessing, a knowing head is the second.

—*Thomas Jefferson*

Truth may sometimes come out of the Devil's mouth.

—*Thomas Fuller*

Whenever we both, Christian and Jew, care more for God Himself than for our images of God, we are united in the feeling that our Father's house is differently constructed than our human models take it to be.

—*Martin Buber*

O Lord, if there is a Lord, save my soul, if I have a soul.

—*Ernest Renan*

There lives more faith in honest doubt,
Believe me, than in half the creeds.

—*Lord Tennyson*

We are least open to precise knowledge concerning the things we are most vehement about.

—*Eric Hoffer*

...the moment that you desire something or fear something, your heart will consciously or unconsciously get in the way of your thinking.

—*Anthony de Mello*

How strange it is to see with how much passion
People see things only in their own fashion!

—*Moliere*

In most discussions, each man has some point to maintain and his object is to justify his own thesis and disprove his neighbor's. He may have originally adopted his thesis because of some sign of

truth in it, but his mode of supporting it is generally to block up
every cranny in his soul at which more truth might enter.

—George MacDonald

...[Bascombe's] mind was only directed at finding holes in another's
consistency rather than seeing whether truth had anything to teach
his own self.

—George MacDonald

It is with narrow-souled people as with narrow-necked bottles:
the less they have in them, the more noise they make in pouring it
out.

—Alexander Pope

Minds that have nothing to confer
Find little to perceive.

—William Wordsworth

The problem of the closed mind has been with us ever since—beginning with the Fall—humankind has had something to hide. Jesus compared the closed mind to impacted soil in His parable of the sower (Matthew 13). In the story the farmer's seed, representing the light of the Kingdom of God, when planted met with four results, three of which were negative. In two cases it found short-term reception until the rocky soil (i.e., belief that the cost of maintenance is too high) or the competition of weeds (i.e., the perception that the side shows are more appealing than the central reality) prevented it from growing. The hardest soil, by contrast, didn't even allow the seed to germinate.

It is a dangerous thing to reject light. Physically, without light we could not see and would have no food to eat, air to breathe, nor heat to keep sufficiently warm. Intellectually, without light we would have no knowledge, no awareness of truth, and no ability to perceive God. In addition to the statement "God is love" (See chapter 13 on "The Love of God"), the only other such sweeping Biblical description of a characteristic of God is "God is light" (I John 1:5). Love and truth, then, are the most basic and most essential descriptions of God; other characteristics derive from these two (e.g. mercifulness, justice, and holiness).

Closed-mindedness is a result of willfulness or fear. The former involves a rejection of the sovereignty of God, at least for the person. The latter involves inadequate or incomplete knowledge, with the solution being more light regarding the love, goodness, or power of God. Surely God looks more approvingly at the person who is very slow to embrace new light because of a fear of displeasing Him than the one who is open to change merely because of an admiring enjoyment of engaging one's mind. Open-mindedness in the abstract is not necessarily helpful; it is meaningful only inasmuch as it indicates that we are pursuing truth, which, to the degree that it is done purely, means that we are pursuing God.

In the pursuit of God with an open mind, let me suggest the following principles:

1. Do not be discouraged if you find it difficult to be intellectually open. Few people achieve this goal easily. Self-deception is a universal disease; overcoming it is a life-long battle. Christians no less than non-Christians suffer from it; the fact that one has sought and found the source of all of light does not necessarily mean that one is open to all of the light that the Truth-giver wishes to give. There is need to understand one's continuing degree of blindness, even while one is rejoicing in the degree to which one has come to see. Of course, remorse for one's sin is never meant as an end

in itself but as a means to celebratory victory and joy and personal dignity in Christ.

2. Do not be discouraged when honest openness and seeking produce no clear understanding. Uncertainty is not a barrier to truth; rather it is part of the process toward it. Even when one has searched the Scriptures, prayed intently, consulted wise and Godly friends, sought to empty oneself of prior prejudices and to employ the best of one's reasoning skills, still sometimes doubt remains as to the best possible course of thought or action. This is part of the existential condition in which God has made us. The one who is Love and Truth said, "Seek and ye shall find;" somehow His statement must be lovingly true, even if the seeking is sometimes difficult and prolonged.

3. In the pursuit of truth, it is rarely wise to abandon a position—and the community which may be associated with it—which is functionally and psychologically viable but involving intellectual difficulties, unless and until one finds an alternative perspective that on balance is clearly better. There is no such thing as a world view with no accompanying intellectual difficulties.

4. Truth is wherever you find it. Just as one can find falsity in anyone, so also one can learn from any person and any situation. Even evil is in part truth or it would not be so attractive. Avoid tying your world view too closely to any single human system; look for truth everywhere.

5. Truth-seeking facilitates intellectual fellowship and witness with non-Christians. If both you and your non-Christian friend are, at least to a meaningful degree, focused on seeking truth, you have much in common. If the friend sees you looking for whatever truth exists in his system of thought, then he will more likely be open

51

to seriously consider your presentation of the central Christian message. If she sees you as less focused on telling her what truth is than in convincing her to ask God for herself, then she is more likely to be willing to hear the truth. Indeed, for all of us no search for truth is complete without asking God to reveal, whether on a specific issue or in an open-ended manner, what understanding He wishes us to receive.

6. Truth-seeking facilitates intellectual fellowship with other Christians. What more lovely scene can there be among humans than that of a group of believers frankly acknowledging and celebrating the gifts of thoughtful discourse, mutual learning, transparency, humility, and openness (see Psalm 133). Whether among Christians or between a Christian and a non-Christian, dogmatism repels whereas honesty and charity compel.

7. Lies and the human insistence on believing them are the ultimate explanation of the human malaise. We seek to convince others and ourselves that we are more noble and whole than we actually are. I have seen people who are brilliant at hiding themselves from seeing truth that they don't want to see; it is amazing to hear the logical constructs that can come out of their mouths. By contrast, we tend to view others in lower esteem than is realistic. "Putting down" others helps to elevate us, we think, in the scale of values. And oh, how valuable to us is that "scale of values" that we (or society) artificially construct! This competition for psychological supremacy leads to many of the ills of society; "I win only as you lose" is the thinking, and then when you "lose," you strike back.

Another form of lying works another form of havoc. Some neurotics tend to underestimate their abilities and dignity with respect to others and to believe themselves responsible when they are not. Their misperceptions are more likely to harm themselves than others. Oftentimes their intellectual "dis-ease" leads to physical illness or troublesome symptoms.

Unfortunately society encourages our individual predisposition toward unreality. Much of business is based upon a form of advertising more designed to deceive than inform; and much of politics is based upon a distortion of the character, proposals, and programs of other people. Even such fields as education, psychotherapy, and religion which purportedly are designed to help people overcome the lies they believe, all too often promote a specific school of thought rather than a genuine intellectual openness.

The truth, however, is always healing. The ultimate truth is that God loves each of us supremely and wants to give us His grace as we are willing to receive it. We shrink from truth because it is often very painful; but if it is painful initially, it then leads to pleasure— indeed, to the only ultimate pleasure.

QUESTIONS FOR REFLECTION AND DISCUSSION:

1. Is human closed-mindedness more a result of fear or of willfulness?

2. Is it ever wise to avoid the truth, either for oneself or to keep it from others? If so, when and why?

SUGGESTIONS FOR FURTHER READING:

1. Mortimer J. Adler, "Truth," ch. 94 in *The Great Ideas*

2. Anthony deMello, *The Way to Love*

3. David Gill, *The Opening of the Christian Mind*

4. Douglas V. Henry, "Intellectual Integrity in the Christian Scholar's Life," *Christian Scholar's Review* Fall, 2003, pp. 55-74

5. Arthur Holmes, *All Truth Is God's Truth*

6. Richard Hughes, *How Christian Faith Can Sustain the Life of the Mind*

7. C. S. Lewis, "Man or Rabbit?" in *God in the Dock* (ed. Walter Hooper)

8. George MacDonald, *The Curate's Awakening* (ed. Michael R. Phillips)

9. Parker J. Palmer, *To Know As We Are Known: Education as Spiritual Journey*

10. John Stuart Mill, "Of the Liberty of Thought and Discussion," ch. 2 in *On Liberty*

11. A.W. Tozer, *The Pursuit of God*

9. WINDOWS TO HEAVEN

Truly to hear, you must get near.

—African Proverb

It takes leisure to mature. People in a hurry...are preserved in a state of perpetual puerility.

—Eric Hoffer

The limits of thought are not so much set from outside, by the full-ness or poverty of experiences that meet the mind, as from within, by the power of conception, the wealth of the formulative notions with which the mind meets experiences.

—Susanne Langer

Many are grateful to that veteran missionary, E. Stanley Jones, for his frequent references to his own daily practice of simply asking, "Lord, what do you have to say to me?" and then waiting silently until he hears. Here is a practice in which any person can engage....

—D. Elton Trueblood

A man who loves God necessarily loves silence also, because he fears to lose his sense of discernment. He fears the noise that takes the sharp edge off every experience of reality. He avoids the unending movement that blows all beings together into a crowd of undistinguishable things.

—Thomas Merton

To know anything at all of God's will we have to participate, in some manner, in the vision of the prophets: men who were always alive to the divine light concealed in the opacity of things and events, and who sometimes saw glimpses of the light when other men saw nothing but ordinary happenings.

—*Thomas Merton*

The world is God's epistle to mankind—his thoughts are flashing upon us from every direction.

—*Plato*

The beauty of the world is Christ's tender smile for us coming through matter. The love of this beauty...is like a sacrament.

—*Simeon Weil*

To me the meanest flower that blows can give thoughts that do often lie too deep for tears.

—*William Wordsworth*

[Music] takes us out of the actual and whispers to us dim secrets that startle our wonder as to who we are, and for what, whence, and whereto.

—*Emerson*

Music is well said to be the speech of angels; in fact, nothing among the utterances allowed to man is felt to be so divine. It brings us near to the Infinite.

—*Thomas Carlyle*

...prayer is simply a reverent, conscious openness to God full of the desire to grow in goodness and overcome evil.
—*Unknown Author of <u>The Cloud of Unknowing</u>*

56

Prayer is not an old woman's idle amusement. Properly understood and applied, it is the most potent instrument of action.
—*Mohandas Gandhi*

For God may speak in one way, or in another, …. In a dream, in a vision of the night, when deep sleep falls upon man, while slumbering on their beds, then He opens the ears of men, and seals their instruction.
—*Job 33:14a, 15-16*

We may be turning our backs on God when we do not listen to our dreams. I believe that this dreamer within is none other than the Holy Spirit who God gives as our inner guide, friend, comforter.
—*Morton Kelsey*

For the soul who seriously wants to hear God, how does one catch even the slightest whisper from Him? For the soul who wants to see God, how does one perceive Him even through the tiniest openings in the heavenly wall? God may not reveal Himself from His heavenly throne as much as we would like; however, our faith is that in His love He communicates to us no less than we need if we will but intensely listen and observe.

> Be sensitive.
> Be desirous of hearing.
> Listen carefully.
> Turn up the volume of God's speaker;
> Turn down the volume of the world's noises.

Listening and obeying are interrelated components of the same heart's desire. Note the response of the youthful Samuel during his night-time vision in the Temple: "Speak, [Lord], for Your servant hears" (I Samuel 3:1b-10).

Asking—especially asking with fervency and expectancy—heightens our ability to hear Him (see Matthew 7:9-11). Never underestimate the power of prayer. As Elton Trueblood notes, "it is not irrational to suppose that God's cosmic purpose includes such a self-limitation of His power that some events do not occur apart from the prayers of finite men."

Similarly, not asking and not expecting to see and hear greatly reduces our ability to perceive His presence and voice (e.g. Matthew 13:13-16). One day I went to class knowing that two girls would not be there; I had excused them from attending the first few sessions of the Honors Reading Seminar as they had previously taken this repeatable class, and the first few days involved a discussion of the bibliographical options on the lengthy reading list. One of the girls came to class anyway, but I was unaware. My quick head count of students showed one more person in class than the anticipated maximum number for that day. I tried to resolve the dilemma—perhaps another student had enrolled. But another quick perusal of the class showed no new student. Finally it occurred to me that Cathy, one of the excused students, was in class after all; not having expected her, I had looked over her. What we expect not to see, we tend not to see even when it is there; during His public ministry, Jesus seemed to want it that way. God gives us enough knowledge of Himself to seek Him further, but He hides himself sufficiently that we can choose to ignore Him if we desire.

God can speak to us through anything. Some of His ways of communicating are directed to us all. These universally-intended forms of revelation include 1) nature and, in a way, even our representations of nature in music, art, poetry, and other forms of creative expression (beauty); 2) the moral law within us (i.e., goodness); 3) the Biblical record (i.e., truth); and 4) the Incarnation (i.e., love). If a person can believe in the divinity of Jesus, it is a major advantage in narrowing the sense of distance between God and humans. Christians believe that Jesus, the Incarnate One, is our clearest window to God.

Other ways in which God communicates with us — and the ones which are the primary focus of this essay — include forms that while universally available are individual in their manner of revelation. These include 5) circumstances, 6) meditation, and 7) dreams. God's word may come to you in something as routine as the solicited counsel of a close and mature friend, or it may appear in a dramatic and surprising form, such as an angelic visitation or another type of miracle.

God is all-powerful, all-good, and personal. It is in the context of His power and desire for human fellowship that He created the world with its operational laws. At times the Sovereign One suspends His natural laws to serve His beneficent purposes. So-called miracles, of course, are no more miraculous than was His original act of creation.

Some of what we may consider miraculous is only the normal expression of His love for us in ways that we do not normally perceive and only irregularly need. Special acts of grace may even include supernatural appearances and interventions. Joan Webster Anderson has collected stories of people who believe that God communicated His generous love to them through miracles or angelic visitations. Those of us who have been greatly helped by the writings of C. S. Lewis and J. B. Phillips were stunned to read in Phillips' "testimony," *Ring of Truth*, the matter-of-fact statement by this very rational, objective scholar that during a period of great personal difficulty, the recently deceased C. S. Lewis had appeared to him twice within a period of a week to encourage him with relevant, helpful counsel. It is appropriate to employ our critical faculties when hearing such testimonies, but it is inappropriate to close our minds to the thrilling possibility that in many cases God does transcend his normal laws—or at least normal laws as perceived by us—to demonstrate His personal love, especially in times of great hardship.

Less dramatically, but more regularly, God speaks through meditative prayer. In meditation there is greater emphasis on listening to God than in talking to God as in petition, praise, and creedal repetition. For the mystical Christian, in the words of Morton Kelsey, "meeting God and learning what God wants of us become far more important than what we want of God. Yet the amazing thing is that when we pray in this way, we often receive better than we would have dared to ask on our own."

Finally, there is the communication from God through our dreams and visions (Biblical Greek and Hebrew use the two terms interchangeably). I know of few things that so frequently appear in the Bible and early Christianity yet are so little talked about in modern Christianity. Dream scholar Morton Kelsey states that every major church father in the early centuries after Christ believed that dreams were a means of divine revelation.

Modern scholars tell us that if deprived of the type of sleep which produces dreams, a human becomes mentally unbalanced. Apparently God made us to need dreams no less than bodily rest, food, and water. Why would this be? Perhaps the most significant reason is to get our attention. Just as pain and the fear of death make us more likely to seek God, so also dreams force us to hear God. Have you ever known of people who by will power could keep themselves from having dreams? Even when we try to ignore our dreams, at the least they penetrate our subconscious, where they may serve their most basic purpose. Most of us are surprised to hear the researchers tell us that during a typical night we dream five to seven times, with each dream being 15 to 90 minutes in length.

At the heart of Christianity is the idea that God invites each person to communicate directly with Him, as to a loving human father. People exist in a spiritual world no less than in a physical world. In contrast with Sigmund Freud who thought that dreams were merely the reflection of the depth of the individual, Carl Jung emphasized how dreams can reveal deep religious insights. We need not be intimidated by the difficulties involved in interpreting our dreams. Just as Jesus used parables when teaching the masses and the Old Testament prophets often spoke and wrote in symbolic language, with, in each case, the purpose being that of communicating truth not hiding it, so also we best understand dreams, even in their somewhat hidden-language form, as a serious effort by God in His love to tell us what is good and important for us to know.

So how do we best understand our dreams? The following are some of the principles of interpretation suggested by those experienced in the religious understanding of dreams:

1) Note that the most significant dreams are often the most vivid ones, the most repetitious ones, and the ones which occur just prior to awakening.

2) Write down the most meaningful dreams, recording your memories of them immediately upon waking when recall is the most complete.

3) Discuss these dreams with a good insightful friend who knows you well.

4) Note that the meaning of dreams is highly personal. Almost always when we dream of someone else, it represents a part of ourselves.

5) Continually work at wanting to know the truth about yourself on the assumption that the truth is healing ("the truth shall set you free"). When a dream is very unpleasant, it may be pointing to something in our lives that we do not want to see.

Although there are common patterns to God's communication with His human creatures, He speaks in different ways to different people. It is tempting for some to assume that what works for them should be the medium for everyone else. Similarly, some seek to follow another's mode of experience. The means as well as the content are personal. Also, introverts and extroverts vary in how easily and naturally they meditate. But all need some degree of balance between the internal and the external sides of life. Meditation is for everyone.

> When God speaks to you
> The most important thing is not what He says
> But that He is saying it—
> That he is saying it to you.

> What this really means is that He is there
> That something exists beyond this vale of tears
> That He cares enough about you to talk with you
> That you are safe within His arms
> That He loves you dearly
> That all is right after all
> That you don't have to go it alone.

QUESTIONS FOR REFLECTION AND DISCUSSION:

1. Are there special (personal and unusual) ways that God has spoken or does speak to you and that you would be willing to share with others?

2. Do you focus on seeking to hear God through dreams? Why or why not?

SUGGESTIONS FOR FURTHER READING:

1. Mortimer J. Adler, "Angels," ch. 1 in *The Great Ideas*

2. Joan Webster Anderson, *Where Angels Walk*

3. John Webster Anderson, *Where Miracles Happen*

4. Harry Emerson Fosdick, *The Meaning of Prayer*

5. Morton Kelsey, *God, Dreams, and Revelation*

6. Morton Kelsey, *The Other Side of Silence*

7. C. S. Lewis, *Letters to Malcolm: Chiefly on Prayer*

8. John Sanford, *Dreams: God's Forgotten Language*

9. John Sanford, *The Kingdom Within*

10. THE HOLY SPIRIT

The Spirit stands for the universal presence of God. The Spirit stands for the fact that it is neither possible to lose God in trouble nor to escape God in sin.

—William Barclay

The word "Comforter" as applied to the Holy Spirit needs to be translated by some vigorous term. Literally, it means "with strength." Jesus promised His followers that "the Strengthener" would be with them forever. The promise is no lullaby for the faint-hearted. It is a blood transfusion for courageous living.

—E. Paul Hovey

…the Holy Spirit through Christian history…has been at the heart of Christian experience and Christian proclamation whenever they have been vital and dynamic. But the Holy Spirit has always been troublesome, disturbing because it has seemed to be unruly, radical, unpredictable.

—Henry P. Van Dusen

Knowing the Spirit is experiential, and the topic is oriented toward transformation more than information.

—Clark Pinnock

The mind of man is more intuitive than logical, and comprehends more than it can coordinate.

—Vauven Argues

Being a Christian is more like having your soul possessed by a spirit than having your mind clothed with new beliefs.

—Peter Kreeft

We must not be content to be cleansed from sin; we must be filled with the Spirit.

—John Fletcher

...the Helper, the Holy Spirit, ...will teach you all things...

—John 14:26

To become a mature Christian is nothing other than to become more and more deeply a sharer and partaker in the Holy Spirit.

—William Barclay

...the fruit of the Spirit is love, joy, peace, longsuffering, kindness, goodness, faithfulness, gentleness, self-control.

—Galatians 5:22-23b

The idea of the Holy Spirit is one of the most difficult Christian concepts to understand and explain. Of the members of the triune God (the Trinity is another very elusive topic), the Spirit is the most mysterious. Compared to the Father and the Son, the Spirit is the least revealed in the Bible and the most difficult to visualize. Where He is described in the Bible, the language often involves extensive imagery (e.g. Luke's description of the pivotal event of the Coming of the Spirit at Pentecost, Acts 2:2-3). Despite the abstruse nature of the Spirit, despite the extra-rational nature of his workings, and despite the fact that the gifts He bestows and the counsel He provides are mostly personal and specific rather than communal and general, it is still possible—and vitally necessary—to identify a general theology of the Holy Spirit.

In the Christian concept of the divine, there is God the Father, God the Son, and God the Holy Spirit—three ways of being in one eternal God. The Spirit signifies the continuous presence of God in His world in general and with each of His created humans in particular, empowering them to do His will as they walk in harmony with Him. The God in the heavens who created all that is, is also the God who for thirty-three years came in the flesh (as God incarnate or Jesus) to reveal Himself and lovingly redeem us to Himself, and is also the God whose Spirit abides with us forever.

The continuous presence of God with each human being to give us all that we need is the quintessential meaning of the Holy Spirit. The omnipresent God fully inhabits His creation (in the words of Hildebert of Lavardin, "over all things, under all things; outside all; within but not enclosed; without but not excluded; above but not raised up; below but not depressed; wholly above but not presiding; wholly beneath, sustaining; wholly within, filling.") Ironically this limitless God who can be and is everywhere nevertheless chooses to enter the private space of human affection only by the invitation of those who want Him and His abiding presence. How amazing that a mortal soul can and would choose to live in isolation from the goodness of the Spirit of God! Methodist founder John Wesley understood and taught much about the Holy Spirit, but as he lay dying in London in 1791, he discovered anew the primacy of the indwelling Spirit. His last words, stated and repeated, were, "The best of all is God is with us!"

The Holy Spirit also represents the Divine strength for victorious living. The Old Testament describes the Spirit of God as active in Creation and also as providing special ability to select people in extraordinary circumstances (e.g. Judges 3:10, 11:29; 14:6; I Samuel 16:13; Isaiah 61:1; Micah 3:8). The prophet Joel (Joel 2:28) foresaw a fuller revelation of the Holy Spirit at a later time. Then something changes in the New Testament: perhaps the people drew more completely upon the always available power of the Spirit; perhaps God released the power of the Spirit in an unprecedented manner; perhaps both of these things happened. This new era commences with the Incarnation. Jesus told His disciples that following His departure from the earth, the Spirit would succeed Him as the Divine helper in their midst (John 14:16-17, 26). The Spirit would provide power (i.e., supernatural courage, boldness, physical energy, confidence, skill in speech-making and debate, insight and audience receptivity) for the world-wide spread of the Gospel (Acts 1:8). He would also provide power for daily living for all believers. This power included knowledge for decision-making (e.g. Acts 15); an enhanced understanding in general (see John 14:17, 26, and 16:13, and note John's favorite name for the Holy Spirit, namely the Spirit of Truth); and freedom from the many forms of bondage and fear (II Corinthians 3:17 and II Timothy 1:7). The potency of the indwelling but invisible Spirit is best seen by its work of transformation in the character of the believers (Galatians 5:22-23; Acts 13:52, Colossians 1:8, and Ephesians 4:3-4).

Until the twentieth century, the person and function of the Holy Spirit had long been underemphasized in Western Christianity. The medieval church stressed institutional authority, and the Protestant Reformation focused on the mental and doctrinal aspects of Christianity. It is true, however, that there have always been certain minority groups (e.g. mystics, Quakers, Pietists, and Methodists) that have emphasized the communion of the Spirit with the individual believer. The Pentecostal movement beginning in the early 1900s and the more widespread Charismatic movement which emerged in the 1960s have contributed much to remedy this historical underemphasis, while introducing some new problems. Of course, fellowship with the Holy Spirit is not a doctrine for a few select groups, but is and always has been intended as a personal reality for all peoples. Just as peace-making is not just for the Anabaptists, social justice not only for the Afro-Americans, and rational exegesis not merely for the Calvinists, so also a fully-developed emphasis upon the Divine Spirit is necessary if churches are to preach the whole counsel of God and individual Christians are to experience all of God's graces.

The wise and mature Christian seeks to understand and experience God through all possible means, including active and rational ones such as careful analysis of Biblical revelation, and the passive and experiential ones such as "waiting for the Spirit" or being "filled with the Spirit." Many people fear the Spirit's activity because of the highly subjective experiences of many who emphasize living under the control of the Holy Spirit. Others fear to listen for the Holy Spirit lest they confuse His voice with the other voices that speak to us. These concerns are appropriate. The Bible admonishes us to "test the spirits, whether they are of God" (I John 4:1). Misunderstanding and abuse are always possible but are much less likely when one is sincerely seeking the mind of God rather than seeking to use the power of God for one's selfish purposes. God is not in the business of trickery or deceiving earnest seekers ("...you will seek Me and find Me when you search for Me with all your heart." —Jeremiah 29:13)

Perhaps the most important corrective to 1) disinclination toward participating in the work of the Holy Spirit on one hand or 2) inclination toward participating in bizarre excess in the name of the Spirit on the other hand is to focus on the unity of the Trinity. In the helpful phrasing of Henry Van Dusen: "The Spirit is the Holy Spirit, that is the Spirit of God, which is the Spirit of Christ." Any interpretation of the nature, work, being, and guidance of the Holy Spirit must be consistent with our best understanding of the nature, work, being, and guidance of the Father and the Son. Jesus said, "If you have seen me you have seen the Father." He could as easily have said, "If you have heard me, you have heard the way in which the Holy Spirit will speak to you." One's understanding of the Spirit is unlikely to be more mature than one's understanding of the Father and the Son.

Our relationship with the united Trinity is the key to the development of unity among human believers. The Holy Spirit is the direct communications link between the intra-Trinity communion and created humans individually and collectively. The Spirit transmits to us the love, comfort, joy, peace, wisdom, and power of God as we are willing to receive them. The Trinity communes in love and the Holy Spirit is the overflow valve to us, our means to enter into the Divine dance of joy. Consequently, what is more natural for us humans who have entered into this Divine joy than to be joined together in Spirit-led harmonious union with one another even while here below!

This unity among believers, of course, is the ideal, a goal only partially realizable in this fallen world. Ironically, the great split between Eastern and Western Christianity in 1054 developed from a disagreement over the nature of the Holy Spirit—the very One who invites unity (I Corinthians 12:13, Ephesians 4:3-4)! More recently, the Spirit-focused Charismatic Movement has been at the same time both one of the greatest sources of trans-denominational spiritual unity in modern church history and also a source of significant division, especially within conservative Protestantism. Still there remains the goal of complete union with the Trinity and with fellow believers. Jesus prayed for such union in His passionate prayer (John 17:20-23) the night before His crucifixion: "I...pray...for those who will believe...that they all may be one...as We are one: I in them and you in Me...."

> We are one in the bond of love,
> We are one in the bond of love;
> We have joined our spirit with the Spirit of God,
> We are one in the bond of love.
>
> —Otis Skillings

QUESTIONS FOR REFLECTION AND DISCUSSION:

1. Why do you think that the Holy Spirit has been so minimally emphasized throughout much of church history?

2. Are you comfortable worshiping in a Charismatic church? Why or why not? If not, what can you learn with profit from the Charismatic community? Similarly, what can the Charismatic community learn from the more rationally-oriented Christians?

3. How do you most easily hear the Holy Spirit speaking to you?

4. Why does emphasis upon the Holy Spirit sometimes lead to excess and disunion?

SUGGESTIONS FOR FURTHER READING:

1. William Barclay, *The Promise of the Spirit*

2. Gary M. Burge, *The Anointed Community: The Holy Spirit in the Johannine Tradition*

3. David Edwin Harrell, Jr., *All Things Are Possible: The Healing and Charismatic Revivals in Modern America*

4. Jurgen Moltmann, *The Spirit of Life: A Universal Affirmation*

5. J. I. Packer, *Keep in Step with the Spirit*

6. Clark H. Pinnock, *Flame of Love: A Theology of the Holy Spirit*

7. J. Oswald Sanders, *The Holy Spirit and His Gifts*

8. John R. W. Stott, *The Baptism and Fullness of the Holy Spirit*

9. Henry P. Van Dusen, *Spirit, Son and Father*

11. THE INTERPRETATION OF SCRIPTURE

Men do not reject the Bible because it contradicts itself but because it contradicts them.

— *Anonymous*

The Bible is the one Book to which any thoughtful man may go with any honest question of life or destiny and find the answer of God by honest searching.

— *John Ruskin*

Most people are bothered by those passages in Scripture which they cannot understand; but as for me, I always noticed that the passages in Scripture which trouble me the most are those which I do understand.

— *Mark Twain*

Take all of this book upon reason that you can, and the balance on faith, and you will live and die a happier man.

— *Abraham Lincoln*

Both read the Bible day and night,
But thou read'st black where I read white.

— *William Blake*

If a man fasten his attention on a single aspect of truth and apply himself to that alone for a long time, the truth becomes distorted and not itself but falsehood!

— *Emerson*

No word or words of man can ever for all time confine the meaning of the Bible, for the Bible is a living book and, therefore, an ever-enlarging book.

— *James G. K. McClure*

The devil can cite Scripture for his purpose,
An evil soul producing holy witness
Is like a villain with a smiling cheek,
A goodly apple rotten at the heart:
O, what a goodly outside falsehood hath!

— *William Shakespeare*

Foul shame and scorn be on ye all
Who turn the good to evil,
And steal the Bible from the Lord
And give it to the Devil.

— *John Greenleaf Whittier*

How one interprets the Bible depends at the outset upon how one views the Bible. In general, Christians have believed the Bible to be the revealed word of God, the written record of what God wanted to say to the human race. They see it not only as an historical record but also as a source of ultimate spiritual meaning for every person. They also view Jesus as the word of God, the ultimate revelation of God's nature, including especially His love. Thus they view the Bible as the written word of God about the incarnate Word of God.

Each Christian, when reading the Bible seriously, is asking, "What does this book say to me, about me, and for me? How do I apply this book to my personal situation?" What follows now is a series of principles that I have found helpful in seeking to understand both the Bible as a whole and also specific passages; perhaps you, the reader, may find some of them helpful, also.

1. Seek to understand the major themes of the Bible. These are best identified inductively while reading through the Bible section by section and making changes in your thinking based upon what you understand to be the accumulating textual evidence. This requires careful individual effort. It does not mean than an individual should not listen carefully to the conclusions of a larger entity (family, church, denomination, creedal conference), but that one recognizes that one's ultimate source for authority is the Holy Spirit of God speaking both through the written work and directly to one's heart.

2. Interpret specific sections in the light of these major themes.

3. Interpret a specific section according to its *naturally intended* meaning. When the text says that Jesus sat on a young donkey, the scribe is recording an eyewitness account and it is natural to interpret the passage in a literal, physical manner. When Jesus says, "I am the door," He is speaking symbolically and expects to be heard in that way. In a sense, symbolic interpretation is also literal interpretation; it certainly is real and loses none of its intended power.

4. The Bible seeks to present truth. Sometimes this involves rational statements of physical fact, but Jesus understood that often truth is best received indirectly. There is much that we do not want to accept, and a direct statement is likely to lead to direct rejection; but indirectly presented truth often has a better chance of penetrating through our automatic defense system to our inner consciousness. Thus Jesus told many parables, and frequently He answered questions not as asked but with the answer that the inquirer most needed to hear.

5. Interpret a passage within its immediate context rather than in isolation from it. Who is the immediately intended audience for the commentary? What is the overall truth that the writer or speaker wants them to hear? What are the related truths in preceding and succeeding passages, and how are those related to the present passage?

6. Work to increasingly become a humble truth-seeker. Do not search the Bible merely to find a passage to prove your point ("proof-texting"). Cannot this be using God's name in vain no less than is swearing? When Billy Graham precedes a statement with "The Bible says, ..." he usually is referring to a broad, clear, major concept, but many times when Christians use "The Bible says," introduction, they would be more accurate and more humble to say "This is what I understand the Bible to say," to which, hopefully, they would then add, "but I would enthusiastically welcome any assistance in gaining a better or more complete understanding of the intended message from God."

7. Recognize how sensitive, meditative Bible reading can provide not only general truth that is for you and everyone else but also specific truth that is for you alone. The seeking heart that longs for guidance from God on the myriad of daily circumstances can hear from God through anything; it should not surprise us that for this personal, divine-human communion one of the primary mediums is the Bible ("faith comes by hearing, and hearing by the word of God." Romans 10:17).

8. In seeking to apply the teachings of the Bible to your life, work hard to distinguish its broad universal principles (which are for all) from its specific applications of these broad principles (which are for an immediate audience). Much harm in many places in every era has come from confusing the latter with the former. Examples

of clear, timeless, and universal spiritual themes include the following:

a. The primacy of God's love (e.g. John 3:16, Romans 8:38-39)
b. God's revelation through nature (e.g. Psalm 19:1)
c. Human sinfulness (e.g. Isaiah 53:6)
d. The incarnation (e.g. John 1)
e. Divine grace (e.g. Luke 15:11-31)
f. God's guidance (e.g. Psalm 32:8)
g. God's presence and protection (e.g. Isaiah 43:2)
h. The way to pray (e.g. Matthew 6:8-13)
i. The power of love among humans (e.g. I John 3:11)
j. The triumphal power of the Resurrection (e.g. I Corinthians 15)

But what about the following? Do they present universal principles for all or examples of how those universal principles were applied to the unique conditions of specific situations?

a. Foot-washing (John 13:14-15)
b. Economic communism (Acts 2:44-46)
c. Women speaking in church (I Corinthians 14:34-35)
d. Men's hair length (I Corinthians 11:14)
e. Greeting with a holy kiss (Romans 16:16)
f. Dress styles for women (I Peter 3:3; I Timothy 2:9)
g. Slavery and servanthood (Ephesians 6:5-6; Philemon)
h. The obedience of wives (Ephesians 5:22-23)
i. Drinking wine (I Timothy 5:23; John 2:1-11)
j. Singleness vs. marriage (I Corinthians 7:7-9)
k. The use of force (Matthew 5:38-39)
l. Law suits (I Corinthians 6:1, 7; Matthew 5:40)

Note that Jesus's mode of teaching specialized in presenting timeless, universal ideas from specific situations while Paul, in many cases, sought to apply Jesus's principles to specific situations in specific churches.

In any given situation today the person or people involved must ask 1) what is the universal principle(s) most applicable here; 2) what can we learn from more or less similar, specific situations discussed in the Bible; and 3) how with the aid of the Holy Spirit can we best apply the general Biblical principle(s) to our present circumstances? For example, as a husband, I am to love my wife. One way of accomplishing that may be that tonight we go out for supper. But if she develops a severe headache, the loving thing may be to agree graciously to stay home. Or, if we lived in a different environment where restaurants in general are tainted with evil, it may be that the loving thing would be to not consider restaurants as a part of our social milieu at all. The underlying principle (loving one's spouse) remains constant, but we must seek to use our God-given wisdom to know how to best apply it in each case.

Churches tend to be excessively active in establishing rules and making proclamations which define how everyone in the congregation(s) should apply the universal Christian principles. We need to remind ourselves of how closely this practice corresponds with that of the Jewish religious establishment against which Jesus so strongly reacted. A major nineteenth-century dispute in the religious tradition in which I was raised involved the question of how to apply the Biblical call for the baptism of believers: should it be by water in water (immersion in a river), or by water in the house of worship ("pouring" or "sprinkling")? Few seemed to favor having each member make the choice for himself or herself. No wonder they split and continue to do so. And this was a group that had earlier dissented against allowing the authority of the state to establish religious policy! The temptation to exercise power over others is in us all. Churches, church groups, and preachers would do well to focus on 1) proclaiming the major Biblical truths and 2) instructing their members in the best methods of applying these truths for themselves in their everyday circumstances.

QUESTIONS FOR REFLECTION AND DISCUSSION:

1. How do you best hear God speaking to you through scripture reading?

2. What do you see as the most common error(s) of interpretation which people make when reading the Bible?

SUGGESTIONS FOR FURTHER READING:

1. F. F. Bruce, *History of the Bible in English*

2. Gordan Fee and Douglas Stuart, *How to Read the Bible for all It's Worth*

3. Walter C. Kaiser, Jr., et. al., *Hard Sayings of the Bible*

4. Stephen Neill and Tom Wright, *The Interpretation of the New Testament: 1861-1986*

5. Mark Noll, *Between Faith and Criticism: Evangelicals, Scholarship, and the Bible in America*

6. Bernard Ramm, *Protestant Biblical Interpretation*

7. Willard Swartley, *Slavery, Sabbath, War, Women*

12. THE LOVE OF GOD

The love of God is...the supreme reality.... It is the answer to the great question: What most fundamentally is?

—Peter Kreeft

The supreme happiness of life is the conviction that we are loved.

—Victor Hugo

I know not where His islands left
Their fronded palms in air;
I only know I cannot drift
Beyond His love and care.

—John Greenleaf Whittier

I am convinced that many of my emotional problems would melt as snow in the sun if I could let the truth of God's motherly non-comparing love permeate my heart.

—Henri Nouwen

The love of God is greater far
Than tongue or pen can ever tell,
It goes beyond the highest star
And reaches to the lowest hell;
The guilty pair bowed down with care,
God gave His Son to win;
His erring child He reconciled
And pardoned from his sin.

When years of time shall pass away
And earthly thrones and kingdoms fall,
When men, who here refuse to pray,
On rocks and hills and mountains call,
God's love so sure shall still endure,
All measureless and strong:
Redeeming grace to Adam's race—
The saints' and angels' song.

Could we with ink the ocean fill
And were the skies of parchment made,
Were ev'ry stalk on earth a quill
And ev'ry man a scribe by trade,
To write the love of God above,
Would drain the ocean dry,
Nor could the scroll contain the whole
Tho stretched from sky to sky.

O love of God, how rich and pure!
How measureless and strong!
It shall forevermore endure—
The saints' and angels' song.

—Frederick M. Lehman

This is the most important chapter in the book because it is about the most important subject in the world, namely, the most essential characteristic of the One who made us. There is a lovely apocryphal story that the other disciples criticized the Apostle John, complaining in this manner: "Can't you talk about anything besides the love of God?" to which John replied, "There isn't anything else to talk about." The story is powerful not because it is historical truth (it may not have happened) nor because it is logical truth (it is not literally true), but because it is heart truth (it resonates to the core of one's being), and the recipient responds with exuberance: "That's it! I have found the ultimate truth, and it is good!" In other words, for the seeking soul, to receive the love of God personally, experientially in the soul, so completely surpasses all other realities that it is as if they do not exist. John has been called the beloved disciple almost certainly not because Christ loved him more than the other apostles nor because God loved him more than any other human, but rather because he somehow was able to receive and appreciate the love of God more than have most people. God loves it as we increasingly remove the barriers which prevent us from receiving more and more of His love. How many of the problems of the world would be solved if people would realize how much God loves them and then receive that love!

The most significant way to remove the barriers to receiving the love of God is to discard the blinders which keep us from seeing His love. We have perceptual problems because we succumb to the distortions of Satan whose primary role in the world is that of the great deceiver of humans. For non-Christians, the primary barrier to receiving this love is a willfulness that says: "I want what I want rather that what God has to give me." For Christians the primary barriers are the related beliefs that 1) I have to earn God's love (works), and 2) I have to fear God's judgment more than trust in His love.

I never cease to be amazed at the degree to which Christians and non-Christians alike believe in a works-based salvation. During the decade that I served as a minister, I found it common among unchurched people to respond to an invitation to visit or attend the fellowship by proclaiming: " I am as good a person as many of the church members." Of course, in many cases, their observation was correct, but it missed the central point. Oh that we Christians might better reflect the image of redeemed sinners rather than that of good people, of one group of beggars telling another group of beggars where to find bread, of joyous invitees in the ultimate church supper who wish to share our bountiful table with all who are hungry!

Yet we Christians who understand the theory of grace often practice a works-salvation lifestyle more than we realize. We labor at a feverish rather than a relaxed pace, exhausting ourselves in effort in our careers, communities, and churches. Why? We must really believe that we are not yet good enough for God. How refreshing it is then to be reminded, in the words of Brennan Manning, that

> God's love is based on nothing, and the fact that it is based on nothing makes us secure. Were it based on anything we do, and that "anything" were to collapse, then God's love would crumble as well. But with the God of Jesus no such thing can possibly happen. People who realize this can love freely and to the full. Remember Atlas, who carries the whole world? We have Christian Atlases, who mistakenly carry the burden of trying to deserve God's love. Even the mere watching of this lifestyle is depressing. I'd love to say to Atlas: "Put that globe down and dance on it. That's the way God made it." And to these weary Christian Atlases: "Lay down your load and build your life on God's love." We don't have to earn this love; neither do we have to support it. It is a free gift. Jesus calls out: "Come to Me all you Atlases who are weary and find life burdensome, and I will refresh you."

As with works, so also with fear: both the non-Christian and Christian allow it to keep them from the love of God. The nearly universal fear of death is essentially a fear of God. We pursue a myriad variety of diversions to keep from thinking about both. This is understandable for the non-Christian who believes that God is primarily a malicious, even sadistic power who enjoys threatening and damning His creatures (Note the observation of Franz Kafka that "Our world is merely a practical joke of God."). But God's love is more basic to his nature than is

God's power. Understanding the power of God attracts our attention; understanding the love of God compels our affection. Power begets fear; love begets love. The fear of the Lord is the beginning of wisdom; receiving, returning, and reflecting the love of God is the culmination of wisdom and the ultimate purpose of existence. God is not HALF love and HALF judgment. He is ALL love. His judgment, like all of His other characteristics, derives from His love. His judgment is designed to draw us to Himself. If I were going as a missionary to a superstitious, pagan society, the first concept of God that I would want to introduce is that God is good— "It is okay, you can calm down, the good God is for you; in other words, God is love."

So why do Christians who have received the redeeming love of God through Christ still remain inordinately fearful, "stuck in the fear gear," unable to fully experience the joy of their salvation? One reason is that even though the great deceiver has lost them to God, he delights in keeping them in doubt of that fact. Another reason is that the major commitment of the Christian churches toward mass evangelism necessarily places much emphasis upon fear to bring non-Christians to Christian conversion even while often failing to give equal attention to assuring the already converted. Guilt is a necessary way-station, but it is an awful place for a permanent residence. Thirdly, in reaction to their perception that Liberal Protestantism places too little emphasis upon the judgment of God, Conservative Protestantism often places too much emphasis there—especially for the Christian community, thereby unwittingly contributing to the emotional duress of their most sensitive members.

Christians continue to experience both excessive guilt and a need to prove themselves through works, in large part because both guilt and a strong work ethic are in themselves very good things. What a terrible place this fallen world would be if there was no sense of guilt. But guilt, like strong medication, is usually best prescribed and distributed on an individual basis as needed, rather than through indiscriminately-applied mass inoculation. A serious commitment to work is an important part of our Christian calling as faithful stewards of the kingdom. We enter the Kingdom gates freely and then delight in the work that is given to us to pursue within and for the Kingdom.

The Christian idea of the Incarnation focuses largely upon the teaching and redemptive nature of our Savior, but also very important and often overlooked is the fact that Jesus also came to this world to improve our understanding of what God is like. "He that hath seen me hath seen the Father," Jesus proclaimed. "I and the Father are one." Still, countless people, including professing Christians, see God primarily as an angry Old Testament God of destruction and punishment or in somewhat less harsh terms as the high and mighty whistle-blower who keeps us from having fun. (See "The Resident Policeman" in J.B. Phillips' classic, *Your God is Too Small*.)

Oh that we all might increasingly understand in theory and appropriate in fact the overwhelming love which the Holy Trinity individually and collectively have as their primary posture toward us humans. Such is the basis for all reality and all sanity!

QUESTIONS FOR REFLECTION AND DISCUSSION:

1. How can we get more of the love of God to "come through" to us?

2. Do people tend to associate the love of God more with the Father or the Son? Why?

SUGGESTIONS FOR FURTHER READING:

1. The Gospel and Letters of John

2. Peter Kreeft, *The God Who Loves You*

3. Henri Nouwen, *The Return of the Prodigal Son*

4. Brennan Manning, *The Lion and the Lamb*

5. Mortimer J. Adler, "Love," ch. 50 in *The Great Ideas*

13. CONVERSION

...seek, and you will find....

—Matthew 7:7

...repent, turn to God, and do works befitting repentance.

—Acts 26:20b

...unless you are converted and become as little children, you will by no means enter the kingdom of heaven. Therefore whoever humbles himself...

—Matthew 18:3b-4a

...believe on the Lord Jesus Christ, and you will be saved....

—Acts 16:31

...as many as received Him, to them He gave the right to become children of God, even to those who believe in His name...

—John 1:12

The idea that "belief" is a set of intellectual conceptions apart from action is false. The word "belief" comes from 'by-lief' or 'by-life'—the thing you live by. Your beliefs, then, are the things you believe in sufficiently to act upon, to live by. The unity of theory and practice is a fact. Your theory is your practice, the only theory you have.

—E. Stanley Jones

Faith does not mean assent to some <u>thing</u>; it means the acceptance of a personal invitation with a "yes" which changes the direction of our lives. It means an altered heart. Is there not sometimes a lovelessness, a pettiness, yes, a bitterness in some of the disputes

between Christians which reveals what an over stress on doctrine
to the neglect of conversion can do to men.

—Richard Emrich

Trust and obey, for there's no other way.

—James Sammis

You shall have no other gods before Me.

—Exodus 20:3

God is indeed a jealous God
He cannot bear to see
That we had rather not with Him
But with each other play.

—Emily Dickinson

Martin Luther's experience of salvation as justification has skewed
the Christian understanding somewhat toward legal terms. Justification...captures a truth—the truth of God's unmerited favor—but it
cannot be the model of salvation as a whole. Being saved is more
like falling in love with God.

—Clark Pinnock

The time when I was converted was when religion became no longer
a mere duty, but a pleasure.

—John L. Lincoln

Until love, which is the truth toward God, is able to cast out
fear, it is well that fear should hold; it is a bond, however poor,
between...[God and the developing human] that must be broken,

but a bond that...[should] be broken only by the tightening of an infinitely closer bond.

—*George MacDonald*

Conversion is but the first step in the divine life. As long as we live we should more and more be turning from all that is evil, and to all that is good.

—*Tryon Edwards*

Conversion and the goal of loving our neighbor are separated by a vast distance that can only gradually be closed with considerable effort and help. Our conversion is not the terminus but merely the first stage in the Christian life. ...it sets before us the task of coming to terms with our deep inadequacies so that we may love our neighbor better and come to love God with all our heart, mind, soul, and strength.

—*Diogenes Allen*

...God...alone can know how wide are the steps which the soul has to take before it can approach to a community with Him, to the dwelling of the perfect, or to the intercourse and friendship of higher natures.

—*Johann Wolfgang Van Goethe*

Seeking, repenting, humbling oneself, receiving, believing, accepting, changing, trusting, acknowledging the Lordship of the Incarnate One, obeying, loving the Sovereign One, bearing the marks (i.e. the fruit) of a Christian, following as a disciple, pursuing spiritual development. Somehow all of the above ingredients in their variant expressions are involved in Christian conversion; therefore the process of entering the Christian kingdom can appear complex.

But in practice, the idea of conversion is simple. To convert is to turn to God with an unequivocal proclamation of "yes." To be converted is to want God more than anything—or everything—else; one wants God so much that it is as if one had no other wants and nothing else mattered. Really seeking leads to really finding (Matthew 7:7-8). Of course, the Christian idea of conversion is that those who come to God do so through Christ.

If turning is the central idea in conversion, the central element in turning is the transformation less of the intellect or even the belief system than of the will. A Christian convert is a person who wills to will God's will. While salvation is free with regard to money, the convert does in a sense pay for it by surrendering his or her claim to willfulness. Obedience becomes the new imperative and fellowship (both with the Trinity and other believers) the new privilege. Implicit in the idea that conversion is turning to God is the idea of choice; the concept that one should turn to God means that one can choose to not turn to God.

God's love and our fear operate at the beginning of the conversion process. A human naturally longs for something greater than oneself; this compelling power is the love of God directed toward the individual. The human invariably responds by believing in something, whether God or not. Thus belief in the ultimate One is a vital part in conversion. Fear is a necessary even if in someways a negative response to God's love. If fear is the beginning of wisdom, it is also the beginning of conversion; if one does not experience it acutely, one must at least hold a clear perception of who the Almighty is and what rejecting Him and His grace means.

Conversion, therefore, has both negative and positive components. It is both a turning from something and a moving toward something. It is both an emptying and a filling. It both encompasses a repentance from sin and faith toward Christ. Throughout much of church history and especially in the last three centuries there has existed a false dichotomy between a sudden or "crisis conversion" experience and a gradual turning to God in Christ or "Christian nurture." The result has been much unnecessary disunity and division in the body of Christ. What the disputants have often called theological differences are often more a narrowness of experience or perspective or, worse yet, an insistence—reflecting the less noble aspects of human nature—that the way that I and my group have done things is the way that others must do them also. What is important is not how one comes to conversion but that one has come. Undoubtedly the ideal way to achieve Christian commitment is to grow up in a loving, supportive Christian family where it gradually becomes very natural at an early age to enthusiastically and personally embrace the Christian faith that the parents have long discussed and modeled. Others, however, will lack the opportunity of the aforementioned environment or will not respond positively to it. For some of them the best hope of conversion may lie in the dramatic, emotional confrontation of a public assembly such as a revival meeting.

These two contrasting approaches to conversion are best viewed as complementary methods of evangelism. They are allies not rivals—and certainly not enemies—as Christians use these and other means in the cause of working with God in the building of the eternal Kingdom.

At some point in the discussion of conversion, it is important to distinguish between initial conversion and continuing conversion (or spiritual growth). George MacDonald's classic line that "God is easy to please but hard to satisfy" suggests a major distinction between the two. God delights greatly in an original commitment to move toward Him and to walk with Him; typically this original action per se is what most people associate with the word "conversion," and indeed it is an entrance into the Kingdom of God. But it is a receiving of saving grace, not the achievement of perfection nor even, except rarely, of spiritual maturity. Thus conversion into the Kingdom is merely the first step while continuing conversion from fear and egotism toward Christian perfection (Matthew 5:4; 8) is the ultimate goal. As when God came in the Incarnation, He transcended the Old Testament law, so also when He comes in Christian conversion, He supersedes the old rules that have governed one's life and replaces them with the fellowship of His loving, guiding presence. Spirit replaces Law, Love replaces Fear, and Freedom replaces Bondage. Thus the growing Christian can sing with the writer, Charles Gabriel:

> I'm pressing on the upward way,
> New heights I'm gaining every day.

QUESTIONS FOR REFLECTION AND DISCUSSION:

1. What is your definition of (initial) Christian conversion, using words that encompass all that is essential and nothing that is not essential?

2. Is it necessary or even good to experience acute fear as a part of the conversion process?

SUGGESTIONS FOR FURTHER READING:

1. Diogenes Allen, "Conversion," in *Spiritual Theology*

2. J. H. Gerstner, *Steps to Salvation*

3. The Gospel of John

4. Soren Kierkegaard, *Purity of Heart is to Will One Thing*

5. George MacDonald, *The Curate's Awakening* (ed. by Michael R. Phillips)

6. E. Routley, *The Gift of Conversion*

7. Dietrich Wiederkehr, *Belief in Redemption: Concepts of Salvation from the New Testament to the Present Time*

14. JOYOUS CELEBRATION

A merry heart does good, like medicine.

—Proverbs 17:22

Gladness of the heart is the life of man, and the joyfulness of a man prolongeth his days.

—Ecclesiasticus 30:22

The word "joy" is too great and grand to be confused with the superficial things we call happiness. It was joy and peace which Jesus said he left men in his will.

—Kirby Page

...true Christian joy is more akin to assurance than anything.... Don't seek assurance. Seek God and the assurance will follow.

—Arnold Prater

Joy answers the human need for elated feeling and meaning in our lives, a need which is often filled in modern society by secularized parodies of religion, such as addiction and compulsiveness.

—Verena Kast

Joy is inclined toward transcendence, transcendence of present relationships and of the world's resistance.

—Verena Kast

Where charity radiates its joy, there we have a feast.

—John Chrysostom

In contrast to the serious business of everyday life, the festive oc-
casion seems to be something marginal and secondary. But when
we relate it to the fundamental values of our existence, it shows up
as such a central experience that it seems to sum up everything.

—*Frederik Debuyst*

Come we that love the Lord,
And let our joys be known;
Join in a song with sweet accord,
And thus surround the throne.

The sorrows of the mind
Be banished from this place;
Religion never was designed
To make our pleasures less.

—*Isaac Watts*

If I have faltered more or less
In my great task of happiness;
If I have moved among my race
If beams from happy human eyes
Have moved me not; if morning skies,
Books, and my food, and summer rain
Knocked on my sullen heart in vain
Lord, Thy most pointed pleasure take
And stab my spirit broad awake....

—*Robert Louis Stevenson*

Certainty, certainty, heartfelt, joy, peace. God of Jesus Christ....
The world forgotten, and everything except God.... Joy, joy, joy,
tears of joy.

—*Blaise Pascal*
(a written response to a mystical experience)

My life flows on in endless song;
Above earth's lamentation
I hear the real though far off hymn
That hails a new creation.
Through all the tumult and the strife,
I hear that music ringing;
It sounds an echo in my soul;
How can I keep from singing.

—Shaker Hymn

If the all-good and all-powerful Creator of the universe loves each of us personally and perfectly and invites us into union with Him in a glory which we can experience partially already in this imperfect world and completely and forever in the next one, then why does the Christian community not respond more consistently than it does with ecstatic joy? Of course, in the long Judeo-Christian history there have always been some individuals and groups who have lived in such a state of happiness. While the Old Testament Hebrews associated joy primarily with earthly circumstances, some of the prophetic writings and wisdom literature anticipate the eschatological joy with its return to the bliss of the Garden of Eden. The New Testament writings emphasize how the Incarnation and its meaning are the basis for ultimate earthly expression of joy. The characteristic response of the early Christians to the proclamation that God has come to humankind to offer them victory over their fallen state and participation with Him in the eternal banquet is one of indescribable joy. Since the Renaissance, however, with its emphasis upon the joys of this world, there has been a reduction in the focus upon eternal joy. Of course, the ideal response is to be neither farsighted nor nearsighted but "all-sighted" as we rejoice in God's gifts in the past, present, and future alike. In general it has been the mystics and others who especially sense their neediness (including those groups and individuals outside the socio-economic and denominational

99

mainstream) that have tended to be more joyful—especially in the joys of the next world. Thus the spread of the Pentecostal experience of ecstasy to the main-line denominations is one of the most surprising and noteworthy experiences of the twentieth century.

In general language, people use joy interchangeably with other closely-related words such as happiness and gladness. Happiness is the general word to describe the moods of elation. Joy means a high degree of happiness and, with the words bliss and ecstasy, can even suggest the highest degree of happiness. Perfect or ultimate joy or bliss is union with God, especially in the next life, although we can have temporary incidents of it on earth and even a more general, less intense, more consistent state of bliss—or preliminary bliss—now. The dark side of joy is the deep satisfaction that one can experience in the pleasure of observing the misfortunes of others—especially one's enemies—or even in inflicting pain upon them. Strangely some even describe, if not as joy at least as happiness, the stoical ability to steel oneself from all pain.

Thus there is earthly joy, both positive and negative, related to earthly things, and there is heavenly joy resulting from one's mutually desired relationship with that which is ultimate, namely God. It is largely this later type of joy that the Bible refers to in the over 350 times that it mentions the words joy or rejoice. Such joy transcends pain or pleasure; when God expresses to you His delight in you, it is as if nothing else matters. Truly this is fullness of joy!

If joy is a major reflection of the indwelling of God, there are many other closely related marks of the person who is sincerely united with God. These common "sisters of joy" include the following:
1) Thanksgiving
   Giving thanks is usually the most immediate and visible reaction to the sudden experience of the fullness of joy. One cannot contain

the gladness within, one's "cup runneth over," one "jumps for joy," one cannot keep from singing or even screaming, one runs to tell somebody—anybody—about the pearl of great price that one has found or seen. On a more permanent but more subdued basis, the joy continues as a steady state of confidence and gladness.

2) Readiness to Enjoy Beauty

When a person has experienced the ultimate form of beauty, it is natural to respond with delight to other compelling forms of beauty such as grand music, masterful works of art, spectacular scenes of nature, and human forms of genuine love.

3) The Ability to Play

A too strong commitment to—or compulsion toward—work destroys joy. Children—the people most recently come from God—naturally delight in play. Then as we "mature," most of us lose much of the capacity to delight in genuine play as we become absorbed, often with little pleasure, in the demands of earning a living. Just as we experience the greatest fulfillment when we choose to unite/fellowship/play with our Master, so also the purest earthly play comes when we choose to engage in that which delights us in uplifting ways. I suspect that heaven will include large components of both delightful play and playful work.

4) A Developed Capacity for Sanctified Humor

A person lacking in joy either finds it difficult to laugh or else needs to laugh to feel good. A joyous person laughs naturally because of an internal gladness, ease, and openness. Thus there are various types of merriment. Humor like all of God's gifts can be misused. One can use it to call attention to oneself, to belittle other people or groups of people, or as a diversion or escape mechanism to avoid facing and dealing with basic reality or even an unpleasant aspect of oneself. But humor per se must be a basic good because of its universal appeal. Humor is healing. It is relaxing, reduces tension, helps to put things in perspective, provides balance, and helps us not to take ourselves too seriously. It even can be humbling, especially as we are able to laugh at ourselves. Humor can provide insight and present truth that we might otherwise miss or reject.

5) Self-forgetfulness

Self-forgetfulness is both a result and a cause of joy. When God brings joy to us, we feel acceptance and self-confidence and are thus freed to increasingly focus on God and others. By contrast, often when we are in a state of depression (the frequent cause of which is excessive focus on self when experiencing a sense of discouragement), the antidote is to shift the focus to something else (i.e., "jump out of your skin") by giving to or at least talking with someone else (see the poem "How to Be Happy" in the chapter on Giving). Physical isolation facilitates continuing in the same negative mental rut. The first impression to the children's chorus "If You Want Joy You Must Jump for It" may be that the song has the idea backwards, for do we not first experience joy and then jump as when an athlete after a long, hard-fought effort in a highly-prized contest and despite much fatigue jumps high into the air in celebration. But the song title suggests another valid—and important—principle, namely that we can turn sorrow into joy by initiating the effort to do and meditate on those things which are the basis of ultimate delight.

6) An Intense Desire to Share One's Happiness

Joy screams for expression. When we are intensely joyful we seek to celebrate and bond with like-minded others and at least to share with not-yet-like-minded others. God made us as social beings; though we may come to His grace personally and alone, it is unnatural not to wish strongly to participate in the community of believers in Him. When we do not, almost invariably we are less joyful. Thus we have churches for communal worship, but even more so for communal celebration as we enjoy God together. Note how much the components of a compelling church service reflect the joyous spirit: a) thankful music and testimonies, b) the Eucharist or communion which celebrates by remembrance the primary basis for our joy, and c) the sermon which while it may or even must, at least at times, contain negative elements, does not give primary emphasis to them so as to reflect the uplifting spirit of the New Testament church. Such a joyous church does not ignore the real problems and sorrows of the world. In fact it faces them directly, but then celebrates because it has found the means to victory over them. Genuine celebration by nature is a voluntary response to a personal experience; it cannot be compulsory, begrudgingly given, or perfunctory. Thus the unnaturalness of the traditional state-church system that has operated in the West through much of the Christian era.

In worshiping together weekly, the Christian communion is saying "amen" to God's original acts of creation. The Christian feasts are joyous remembrances of the special events of the Incarnation. Brother Lawrence, in his *The Practice of the Presence of God*, encourages us to celebrate the routine. Paul admonishes us to "Rejoice in the Lord always...." (Philippians 4:4a). And why not, for as the wise interpreter of the overall Biblical record noted, "I've read the end of the Book and we win."

QUESTIONS FOR REFLECTION AND DISCUSSION:

1. The Bible says and we know empirically that "a merry heart does good, like medicine." What are the implications of this for the development of one's philosophy of life, personal theology, life style, and mental preoccupation?

2. Why do we tend to associate self-preoccupation with unhappiness, and self-forgetfulness with happiness?

3. Why are we concerned about the person who has difficulty laughing, playing, taking time to "smell the roses," being thankful (as opposed

to grumbling) and sharing joy? Any why is our concern magnified to the degree that that person holds a public position of power?

SUGGESTIONS FOR FURTHER READING:

1. Mortimer Adler, "Happiness," in *The Great Ideas*

2. The Beatitudes (Matthew 5:3-12)

3. The Book of Philippians

4. Leo Durand, *The Psychology of Happiness*

5. Robert K. Johnston, *The Christian at Play*

6. Verena Kast, *Joy, Inspiration, and Hope*

7. C. S. Lewis, "The Weight of Glory" in *The Weight of Glory and Other Essays*

8. Brother Lawrence, *The Practice of the Presence of God*

9. John Piper, *Desiring God: Meditations of a Christian Hedonist*

15. THE WILL OF GOD

The true laws of God are the laws of our own well-being.

—Samuel Butler

Do you think God cares to have me do His will? Is it anything to Him? I am sure of it. Why did He make you else? But it is not for the sake of being obeyed that He cares for it, but for the sake of serving you and making you blessed with His blessedness. He does not care about Himself, but about you.

—George McDonald

There are no disappointments to those whose wills are buried in the will of God.

— F.W. Faber

In His will is our peace.

—Dante

I have had prayers answered—most strangely so sometimes—but I think our heavenly Father's loving kindness has been even more evident in what He has refused me.

—Lewis Carroll

The best way to see divine light is to put out thy own candle.

—Thomas Fuller

One is not anxious, not restless for what the result will be. One gives oneself and one's capacity to God; then things will be as they will be. ...when worry about the result falls away, a quantity of energy is liberated which earlier was invested in fear. ...stress means that one will do the thing oneself, instead of placing it in

God's hands. ...we can let go of ourselves and our ambitions...[;]
we can relax and take it easy.

—Wilfrid Stinissen

There is nothing quite so suffocating of liberty as an overwrought
conscience in a "humble servant of God" who arriving in high
office, confuses his will for that of Providence.

—Bill Moyers

...the intentional will of God can be defeated by the will of man
for the time being.

—Leslie Weatherhead

Every knee shall bow to Me, and every tongue shall confess to
God.

—Romans 14:11

Finding the will of God is an unusually special concern for serious
Christians of the late adolescent and early adult period. And well it
should be, for this stage of life compels many major decisions. Until
this period, one could simply follow the path established for him or
her by family and other societal institutions. Then, suddenly, the youth
must start making major decisions for himself or herself, with many
of them involving major lifelong consequences. Should I pursue post-
high school education? If so, where? What should be my major area
of study? What career should I choose? Where should I live? Should
I marry? If so, when and to whom? It all can be overwhelming. The
powerful feeling of need for help beyond one's own resources is a
blessing, of course, because it makes it easy to seek the guidance of
the Creator.

What does it mean to seek the will of God? First and foremost, it means that the will of God is worth seeking. It represents a belief that God is wise and benevolent and personally caring. He knows what is best for me and wants to give it to me. If one does not believe this, then it is understandable that one will seek to avoid the designs of God upon oneself as one would seek to avoid the control of a powerful enemy, a benevolent but unenlightened friend, or even an impersonal or indifferent force. The Christian ideal is not that of resignation to the will of God as if, alas, it was an unhappy but necessary chore to complete; rather it means an eager cooperation in, yea even a joyous embrace of, the divine plan, for it recognizes that in receiving God's will, one is receiving God and all of the love and supreme good that is inherent in this union.

Many people find it difficult to embrace fully a sweeping and glowing concept of the will of God such as described in the previous paragraph. They will note that the will of God can be a fearful and troublesome thing, that some of what God calls us not to experience are things that are good in and of themselves, and also that, at times, events and circumstances that people ascribe to the will of God involve blatant evil. These are valid concerns. Certainly some of what God calls us to experience is very, very difficult. Like the basic training experience of a military recruit, those demanding plans are meant to strengthen and develop us into fit soldiers in the cause of the Kingdom; but, unlike the military training, they are always designed for our own good as well as that of the Kingdom. While God's will for us is sometimes difficult, it is always possible. As stated in an ancient message, "if God sends us on stony paths, He will provide strong shoes."

Perhaps the greatest intellectual problem for a sensitive Christian is the question of why a loving God would allow pain and evil to exist in His world (e.g. why the premature death of a child or young mother, major birth defects, widespread disease, plagues and famine, severe mental illness, the havoc wrought by sadistic dictators, seemingly endless warfare, random acts of violence, and the so-called "acts of God" such as tornadoes, hurricanes, and earthquakes?). Some, seeking to find comfort from the trauma of such events, describe them as the will of God. Others strongly object that what we call tragedy can be so easily dismissed as the will of God. One of the latter is Leslie Weatherhead who, in seeking to understand the hand of Providence during Germany's bombing of his native London in World War II, called for a distinction between 1) the intentional will of God, 2) the circumstantial will of God, and 3) the ultimate will of God. Much of what is discussed in this essay corresponds with Weatherhead's "intentional will of God" (the original plan of God for a situation). The "circumstantial will of God" is God's revised plan after sinful human choice has rejected the original plan. "The ultimate will of God" will not be denied by the sins resulting from human freedom. It represents the ideal that good ultimately will win out as the final victory of the Kingdom of God. The will of God, then, does temporarily allow for the existence of evil because it allows for human freedom. That is very different, of course, from attributing evil occurrences to the will of God. Hardship, however, as distinct from evil, may well be a part of God's original and continuing plan for each of us.

How then does the seeking soul find the will of God? The starting point is to be sure that one really wants it. Peter Kreeft has stated, "All problems of discerning God's will are ultimately problems of willing God's will. Once the will, the king of the soul, is subject to the King of Kings, then all the king's men in the soul—including the intellect—will follow; and the intellect will discern the will of the King of Kings." While Kreeft may overstate how easy it is for the willing soul to always know the will of God, it is true that anxiety or indecisiveness may be a sign that what one is seeking is not God's will. On the other hand, such uncertainty may merely mean that one needs great help as God is calling the person to something that is very difficult for him or her, or it may mean that God sees the struggle to find His will as something that is good for the person. Scott Peck has expressed the conviction that when God's will is unclear, the honestly seeking soul will be guided by the Holy Spirit to do the right thing even if at the time one does not fully know that such is the case.

In addition to wanting the will of God, the second basic means of knowing the will of God is to know God well. One day in class I was expounding on the importance of the will of God (we may have been discussing the statement by Anne Boleyn to Henry VIII in *Anne of a Thousand Days* about how it is easy for a person—including the king—to confuse God's will with "doing what one pleases") and how knowing and doing it were the most important things. Jim Nicoloudakis, a bolder-than-normal class member and one of the few Greek Orthodox students to attend our college, corrected me, noting that knowing God was a higher good than knowing God's will. He was right of course (what a delight it is to learn from the students!). Knowing God's will flows from knowing God. The more one walks with God, reads His Word, listens to His Spirit, learns and acquires His nature, the more one thinks like God, generally and specifically.

Other important ways of discerning God's will include listening to the counsel of godly friends, learning through carefully chosen books and other media, examining one's own God-given abilities (Methodist Bishop Richard Raines defined God's will as "the intersection of your abilities and the world's needs"), and carefully reflecting upon opportunities that come your way (the so-called "open doors").

After learning the will of God, we must seek to do it, even if we may never do it perfectly in this life. Doing the will of God, then, is a progressive journey. Obedience and understanding are mutually reinforcing; the one enhances the development of the other. "The path of the just is like the shining sun, that shines ever brighter unto the perfect day" (Proverbs

4:18). God is delighted with our desire to follow Him, pleased with our faithfulness, patient with our failures, and even expectant of our perseverance toward His ultimate vision for us. We, His imperfect followers, should be ever encouraged, ever joyous, but never satisfied.

Dante's classic line, "In His will is our peace" is a statement not just of our call but also of the limits of this call. Following His call is liberating. We are not subject to the tyranny of human expectations, whether our own or those of others. We commit ourselves to our Maker and then everything is up to Him. We become His responsibility. Nothing has to be. No specific human result is necessary, whether involving requests of one's employee, choices of one's children, or calls or opportunities of one's profession. Only seek God and to know Him and enjoy Him and to do His bidding. One need not and should not try to do more. Then there is nothing to prove, nothing to lose, and nothing to fear!

In conclusion, meditate on the following powerful, 250-year-old Methodist call for discipleship, which appears in that denominations's New Year's Eve Covenant Service pledge and prayer.

THE COVENANT PLEDGE

And now, beloved, let us bind ourselves with willing bonds to our covenant God, and take the yoke of Christ upon us.

This taking of His yoke upon us means that we are heartily content that He appoint us our place and work, and that He alone be our reward.

Christ has many services to be done; some are easy, others are difficult; some bring honor, others bring reproach; some are suitable to our natural inclinations, and temporal interests, others are contrary to both. In some we may please Christ and please ourselves; in others we cannot please Christ except by denying ourselves. Yet the power to do all these things is assuredly given us in Christ, who strengthens us.

Therefore let us make the covenant of God our own. Let us engage our heart to the Lord, and resolve in His strength never to go back.

Being thus prepared let us now, in sincere dependence on His grace and trusting in His promises, yield ourselves anew to Him.

THE COVENANT PRAYER

I am no longer my own, but Thine. Put me to what Thou wilt, rank me with whom Thou wilt; put me to doing, put me to suffering; let me be employed for Thee or laid aside for Thee, exalted for Thee or brought low for Thee; let me be full, let me be empty; let me have all things, let me have nothing; I freely and heartily yield all things to Thy pleasure and disposal.

And now, O glorious and blessed God, Father, Son and Holy Spirit, Thou art mine and I am Thine. So be it. And the covenant which I have made on earth let it be ratified in heaven. Amen.

QUESTIONS FOR REFLECTION AND DISCUSSION:

1. If, when you really want it, the will of God is not always easy to determine, is it in like manner easy to mistake?

2. In seeking to determine the will of God, how much should one

depend upon the counsel of the Christian fellowship or selected members of it, and how much upon one's personal, direct communion with God?

SUGGESTIONS FOR FURTHER READING:

1. Dietrich Bonhoeffer, *The Cost of Discipleship*

2. Vernard Eller, *The Simple Life*

3. Soren Kierkegaard, *Purity of Heart is to Will One Thing*

4. Leslie Weatherhead, *The Will of God*

16. THE LIFE EVERLASTING

If a man dies, shall he live again?

—Job 14:14a

...if the death of the body means the end of self-consciousness, then the evident purpose [of life] is being defeated. If a person who has learned and suffered for fifty years is suddenly cut off, with no continuation individually, from what he has learned about living, and with no further opportunity to love, the absurdity is really too great to be believed.

—Elton Trueblood

Every natural longing has its natural satisfaction. If we thirst, God has created liquids to gratify thirst. If we are susceptible of attachment, there are beings to gratify that love. If we thirst for life and love eternal, it is likely that there are an eternal life and an eternal love to satisfy the craving.

—Frederick William Robertson

But now Christ is risen from the dead, and has become the firstfruits of those who have fallen asleep.

—I Corinthians 15:20

Jesus said to her, "I am the resurrection and the life. He who believes in Me, though he may die, he shall live. And whoever lives and believes in Me shall never die. Do you believe this? Let not your heart be troubled; you believe in God, believe also in Me. In my Father's house are many mansions; if it were not so, I would have told you. I go to prepare a place for you. And if I go and prepare

*a place for you, I will come again and receive you to Myself; that
where I am, there you may be also.*

—John 11:25-26, 14:1-3

*If God hath made this world so fair
Where sin and death abound,
How beautiful beyond compare
Will paradise be found.*

—James Montgomery

*Heaven is not to be looked upon only as the reward, but as the
natural effect, of a religious life.*

—Joseph Addison

*It is heaven upon earth to have a man's mind move in charity, rest
in providence, and turn upon the poles of truth.*

—Sir Francis Bacon

*Hell is not so much the prison of the damned as their chosen do-
micile.*

—Paul Johnson

*The idea of human freedom is basic to my understanding of hell.
I think of hell as the culmination of a person's own freely chosen
life-plan. Hell isn't what God does to people; it is what people do
to themselves.*

—Richard Mouw

*People are free in this world to live for themselves alone if they
want to and let the rest go hang, and they are free to live out the*

dismal consequences as long as they can stand it. The doctrine of Hell proclaims that they retain this same freedom in whatever world comes next.

—Peter Kreeft

The earlier essay on death focused on the idea of mortality; this chapter considers the subject of immortality. Central to the teaching of the Christian religion is the idea that God made each individual for an eternal existence. Christians cannot prove irrefutably that humans live forever, but they exercise faith based upon evidence that such is the case. This belief is not so much faith in the idea of everlasting life as it is faith in the One who they believe came from heaven to live and die and conquer death for them, thus providing the way for their never-ending existence.

Apart from the life and testimony of Jesus, perhaps the best case for the reality of life after death is the "argument from desire" developed but not originated by C. S. Lewis. One synopsis of this argument is that by Frederick William Robertson at the beginning of this chapter; another summary is the following one by Lewis disciple, Peter Kreeft, as it appears in his masterful study of the innate human desire for heaven, *Heaven: The Heart's Deepest Longing*:

> The major premise of the argument is that every natural or innate desire in us bespeaks a corresponding real object that can satisfy the desire.
> The minor premise is that there exists in us a desire which nothing in time, nothing on earth, no creature, can satisfy.
> The conclusion is that there exists something outside of time, earth, and creatures which can satisfy this desire.
> This something is what people call God and heaven.

Almost invariably those who do not trust in God to satisfy their inherent longing, either recognize their void but despair of being able to fill it or else seek to avoid thinking about the painful reality of their existence. The former are more intellectually honest and courageous than are the latter; yet they often live a painful and lonely existence, as for example the atheistic existentialists like Friedrich Nietzsche and Jean-Paul Sartre. The latter group are much more numerous, more frequently appear happy at least on the surface, and usually survive by focusing upon temporal interests, whether noble or mundane (Pascal calls them diversions).

Assuming that there is a heaven for which we were created and a means through Christ by which we may go there, still many questions remain:

1. What is heaven like? What do we do there?
2. Can one go there immediately after death or is there an intermediate state?
3. Does that intermediate state involve a place called Purgatory?
4. Upon arrival in heaven do we achieve some sort of instant perfection or do we continue to progress there?
5. Does everyone go to heaven? Can everyone go to heaven? Will very many go to heaven?
6. Does God offer a "final choice" to everyone at death?
7. If God does not offer a "final choice" to everyone at death, can the unevangelized go to heaven? How about the honestly seeking people of other religions? Babies? People who might exist on other planets?
8. Can one move from hell to heaven — and vice-versa?
9. What is hell like? Does it involve physical pain, mental pain, or both?
10. Does hell ever end?

These are among the most important questions that humans can ask, but God has chosen to reveal very limited knowledge about the issues which they raise. We do well to seek to learn all that has been revealed and even to engage in "informed speculation" on the rest but always to distinguish carefully between these two related but different quests. Here are a few suggested principles to follow when seeking to answer the above questions.

1. Reflect carefully on the fact that people as informed and as sincere as you in seeking to understand the Biblical teaching on the above questions will reach different conclusions from those which appear right to you.

2. Reflect on your own sense of assuredness of your own standing before God. Here as elsewhere temperament may influence theology. Are those unduly confident of their position with God more likely to emphasize God's judgment on others, and are those unduly anxious souls in their greater perceived need of reassurance more likely to emphasize God's love for all, including, of course, themselves?

3. Most importantly, study the Scriptures, especially the words of the Incarnate One, with a focus on what they teach about God in general. Then deduce from the overall pattern as to how dominant and decisive in His posture toward us, His human creatures, is each of the following: judgment, justice, retribution, and vengeance; and mercy, grace, longsuffering, and love. Do these two sets of traits conflict with or somehow complement one another? Then let your overall conclusion on the nature of God help you to interpret the issues where Christians reach such different conclusions.

4. A critical issue in "rightly dividing the word of truth" (i.e., Biblical interpretation) is to correctly distinguish between the Bible's use of *literal* (i.e., factual) language and its use of *symbolic* language. The latter is often but not always used in the eschatological discourses of Jesus, John, and the Old Testament prophets. Symbolic language is rarely intended to hide the truth, but rather to reveal it

in a more vivid, dramatic way that is more likely to be heard. Its truth is usually less in its details than in its overall major point or points. Jesus often spoke the language of poetry more than the language of mathematics. We, his modern followers, in many ways the rational/literalist sons and daughters of the Enlightenment, often interpret his words with the precision of mathematical detail. Of course the ultimate goal in each case is to understand best the intention of the speaker or writer.

The above concern with Biblical ambiguity does not mean that there does not exist a core belief system to provide the basis for the Christian hope. Most Christians would affirm the following summary statement:

> Humans were created by God for more than just this life. Just as Christ rose from the dead, so also there exists a general resurrection of the dead. There is a heaven for those who receive God's offer of it, and there is a hell for those who do not receive God's invitation. Those in heaven likely continue to learn, grow and engage in meaningful work and play. Above all, heaven means fulfillment, enhanced fellowship with our Maker and our fellow created beings, and joy unspeakable.

Beyond a consensus credo such as this, I think it unwise to argue dogmatically or proselytize vigorously on the secondary eschatological issues but wise to share graciously and openly our opinions in the ongoing effort to learn from one another. Here, for what they are worth, are some of my current thoughts on these issues on which Christians hold different views (and even on the subject of the existence of differences per se).

1. I think it is a positive sign that recent Christian literature increasingly includes books that in a single volume include a range of perspectives on a specific secondary subject including eschatological issues. Note, for example, John Sanders, ed. *What About*

Those Who Have Never Heard?: Three Views on the Destiny of the Unevangelized; William Crockett, ed., *Four Views on Hell*; and Dennis Okholm and Timothy Phillips, ed., *Four Views on Salvation in a Pluralistic World*.

2. Protestants gasp at the Catholic tendency to rely upon Church tradition as well as Biblical authority in developing its doctrine on issues such as purgatory (the temporary state of those dead who are marked for heaven but are not yet sufficiently ready for it). Nevertheless, most Protestant Christians will declare that spiritual growth is a major purpose of our earthly pilgrimage and will probably concur with the idea that this development continues in heaven even if the next life does not have a separately defined temporary holding area and/or status.

3. One might best define Hell as a next-life state or abode of those who want not God—or do not want God enough to sacrifice their "idols." The strongest candidates for Hell are not those who are weak in the flesh (they may be facing the right direction even if they are viewing from the ditch) or even those wicked in deed, but rather those strong in spirit (in contrast to "poor in spirit"—see Matthew 5:3) who might be in the center of the road by most human standards of goodness but are facing and moving in the wrong direction (i.e., away from God).

Is there any hope for the citizens of Hell? The poet Dante thought not, envisioning an inscription over the gates to perdition, "Abandon all hope ye who enter here." The imaginative writer, Frederick Buechner, disagrees with Dante, arguing: "Dante...must have seen wrong. If there is suffering life in Hell, there must also be hope in Hell, because where there is life there is also the Lord and giver of life, and where there is suffering He is there too because the suffering of the ones He loves is also His suffering. 'He descended into hell,' the Creed says, and 'If I make my bed in Sheol, thou art there,' the Psalmist [states] (139:8). It seems there is no depth to which he will not sink. Maybe not even Old

Scratch will be able to hold out against him forever."

I hope that Buechner is correct. I worry about those who hope that Dante is correct. Of course, one may compassionately hope that Dante's vision is inaccurate, but believe that it is accurate. Annihilation is another possibility, but that, like the Dantean view, suggests that God gives up on part of His creation.

4. Universalism is the belief that sooner or later all humans will be saved. The more radical forms of universalism appear to conflict with the Biblical emphasis upon free will and righteousness with God arbitrarily sending all to heaven even if kicking and screaming in objection and arrogantly willful in evil defiance. More representative is the belief that God, the great timeless One, will wait patiently and lovingly as long as it takes for the last lost creatures to surrender their self-defeating willfulness and be reconciled to Him. I find this latter scenario to be the most appealing option for the ultimate destiny of the human race, but my major problem with it is that I do not find an explicit basis for it in the Bible. It is true that one can infer such a view from certain scriptural passages (e.g. Psalm 86:9, Isaiah 45:22-24, Jeremiah 31:34, Lamentations 3:31-33, Joel 2:28, Habakkuk 2:14, Matthew 18: 12-14, Luke 2:10, 3:6, John 12:32, Romans 5:18, 11:26, Philippians 2:10, I Peter 3:18-19, 4:6, Revelation 5:13), but at the same time one would need to satisfactorily explain the passages which seem to suggest an unending punishment for part of the human race. Also of significance is the debate among those who know Greek as to whether the words *aion*, *aionios*, and *kolasis*, when used in connection with suffering and punishment, are best translated into English as "everlasting" or "for the age" (i.e., temporary). In other words, were the Reformation era scholars influenced by a medieval theological mind-set when translating those words into English?

5. Is it possible that human freedom never ends, that we have unending choice in heaven and hell, that "heaven is eternal, hell is eternal,

and freedom is eternal?" Many would find the openness of such a scenario unsettling, even as temporal freedom in many ways is disturbing as it reduces our sense of security and allows for great evil. Why would anyone choose to leave Heaven? Why did Satan thus choose? Even if the scenario of this paragraph were true, and people could change their basic orientation in the next life, how many would? Not too many, if this life is indicative of the next one. Here with the passage of time people tend to change less and less from their early developed patterns. For example, how many people choose to become Christians after age 25 or 30? There is a difference, of course, between reduced likelihood of change and incapability of achieving it. Perhaps, though, there will be a greater revelation of divine love with a resultant greater tendency on the part of humans to embrace it.

6. In analyzing the specific issues of this chapter including those on which Christians differ, I must start—and end—with the general premise that "God is love." His love is at the center of His essence. While the manifestation of this love toward us is highly demanding, it is also ultimate caring. Inherent in that love is a desire for the best for each of us. As such, He supremely values our freedom and our development. He wants us to freely choose to grow more and more like Him with the natural result being closer and closer fellowship with Him. All else follows from this purpose. Is it not wonderful that for the ultimate resolution of the issues of this chapter, we can trust in the beneficent wisdom of God rather than the modest musings of us finite and flawed mortals?

QUESTIONS FOR REFLECTION AND DISCUSSION:

1. Which ideas about life after death do you see as certain—or certain as a basis for faith—and which do you see as probable, possible, or doubtful? What is the basis for your choices?

2. Can this life and the next one be linked more naturally than they commonly are, both in our emotional experience and in our thinking/theory/theology? How?

SUGGESTIONS FOR FURTHER READING:

1. John Baillie, *And the Life Everlasting*

2. William Crockett, ed., *Four Views on Hell*

3. Peter Kreeft, *Heaven: The Heart's Deepest Longing*

4. C. S. Lewis, *The Great Divorce*

5. Michael Phillips, ed., *Universal Reconciliation: A Brief Selection of Pertinent Quotations*

6. John Sanders, *No Other Name: An Investigation into the Destiny of the Unevangelized*

7. Wilbur Smith, *The Biblical Doctrine of Heaven*

8. Alfred E. Taylor, *The Christian Hope of Immortality*

9. Charles Williams, *Descent Into Hell*

NEIGHBORLINESS

17. LOVING YOUR NEIGHBOR

Have we not all one Father? Has not one God created us?

—Malachi 2:10

To focus foremost on loving self is to love God and others inadequately; such love tends towards exclusivity.
To focus foremost on loving others is unnatural; such love is usually a projection of the love of self or a substitution for the love of God.
To focus foremost on loving God leads to the love of self and others also; such love is naturally inclusive.

—Anonymous

That man who lives for self alone
Lives for the meanest mortal known.

—Joaquin Miller

We cannot do evil to others without doing it to ourselves.

—Joseph Desmahis

There is more pleasure in being shocked by the sin of one's neighbor or one's neighbor's wife than in eating cream buns.

—Robert Lynd

There is a very real danger of our drifting into an attitude of contempt for humanity.... The following thoughts may keep us from such a temptation.... Nothing that we despise in the other man is entirely absent from ourselves.... We must learn to regard people less in the light of what they do or omit to do and more in the light of what they suffer. The only profitable relationship to others—and especially to our weaker brethren—is one of love, and that means the will to hold fellowship with them. God Himself did not despise humanity but became man for man's sake.

—Dietrich Bonhoeffer

The meaning of good and bad, of better and worse, is simply helping or hurting.

—Emerson

Act toward the other in a way most likely to lead to a response of goodness.

—Quaker Saying

When people care for you and cry for you, they can straighten out your soul.

—Langston Hughes

I love you, and because I love you, I would sooner have you hate me for telling you the truth than adore me for telling you lies.

—Pietro Aretino

God does not give...joy to us for ourselves alone, and if only we could possess Him for ourselves alone we would not possess Him at all. (Any joy that does not overflow from our souls and help other men to rejoice in God does not come to us from God.)

—Thomas Merton

O Brother Man, fold to thy heart thy brother;
Where pity dwells, the peace of God is there;
To worship rightly is to love each other,
Each smile a hymn, each kindly deed a prayer.

—John Greenleaf Whittier

When Jesus was asked to identify the greatest commandment, he included in His response what Christians have subsequently recognized as the central principle for interpersonal relationships, namely, "You shall love your neighbor as yourself." When He offered His disciples a model prayer, its continuous use of the plural pronoun form (e.g. "Our Father," "Give us," "forgive us," "do not lead us," and "deliver us") suggests that the mind-set of the praying Christian should be much more than merely that of a person engaged in a private relationship with God. The Christian faith is social no less than it is personal, and any effort to move toward Christian maturity that does not fully recognize this idea is severely deficient. While concern for one's "personal relationship with Christ" is critical, it is also, in and of itself, incomplete.

A person who seeks to increasingly "love one's neighbor" does well to recognize how much the world does not operate this way. More typical than the "you and me together" philosophy is the "me versus you" pattern which Thomas Merton describes in bald form:

> I have what you have not. I am what you are not. I have taken what you have failed to take and I have seized what you could never get. Therefore you suffer and I am happy, you are despised and I am praised, you die and I live; you are nothing and I am something because you are nothing. And thus I spend my life admiring the distance between you and me; at times this even helps me to forget the other men who have what I have not and who have taken what I was too slow to take and who have seized what was beyond my reach, who are praised as I cannot be praised and who live on my death....

While most Christians will not see the preceding paragraph as describing themselves, if they are honest, they may find unsettling the following demanding test suggested—in slightly different form—by C. S. Lewis: Imagine that you hear that your enemy did something evil, had something bad happen to him, or simply failed at something. Then a little later you hear that the first report was not true. What is your reaction to the second, or corrective, account? Is it: "Thank goodness, the misfortune really did not happen!" or is it a sense of disappointment that you can no longer believe the initial report with its confirmation of your assessment of the person's evil character or just reward? The ultimate question to ask in determining whether you love a person (or the extent to which you love him or her) is this: "Do I (or how much do I) want the best for this person?"

The easiest, most natural, and perhaps only way to increase your love for others is to increase your love for yourself; and the only genuine way to increasingly love yourself is to increasingly realize how much God loves you and then to increasingly allow that love to come through to you. If you hesitate to do this for yourself, do it for the sake of others, for there exists a close correlation between your ability to see yourself loved, to love yourself, and to love others. Indeed one might say that the statement, "Love thy neighbor as thyself" suggests description as well as prescription: People tend to love others in proportion to their self-respect. Those who do not feel loved are likely to concentrate their attention on themselves to fill the aching void in their souls; people who genuinely feel loved are more easily able to concentrate their energies on loving others.

A second basic way to increase one's love for one's neighbors is to clearly distinguish between liking them and loving them. To like is to feel whereas to love is to do. If one does not possess affection toward a person, then acts in loving ways toward him or her, the positive feeling likely will follow. Love is a choice. Love actively seeks the best for the other.

What if the other is very unlikable? Then start with the conviction that no situation is irredeemable. Difficult circumstances often provide the greatest opportunities for growth. The Christian must always be willing to initiate the healing process. A student once came to me seeking to identify debating points against the "Christian cult" to which her father belonged. Her father, who was a leader in a congregation of the movement, had deserted their family and she was understandably angry. I advised her that we could discuss theology together and she then could do the same thing with her father, but what she most needed to do was to show love and forgiveness to him. Otherwise she never would be communicating what—for her own soul at least—was the primary issue. Love is always the best apologia.

Our primary social mandate then is to love in deed those closest to us (see John 10:25-37), but this love is not unrelated to a spiritual love for all peoples in all places. Modern Americans have greater opportunity to express a truly universal love than have most peoples in other places or times. Ours is a world-wide immigrant nation like perhaps no country in history; most of us can identify with another fatherland from where our ancestors emigrated, and most of us have many friends whose families came from many other countries. Since the early twentieth century, America, succeeding England, has been the primary missionary-sending and missionary-funding country in the world, and many of us grew up regularly hearing mission field adventure stories in church. Our current senior generation served on multiple continents in World War Two, our middle generation increasingly works in multi-national corporations, and our current young people travel, study, and serve abroad like never before—and when they return, they run to their computers and surf the World Wide Web.

Of course, increased familiarity with the peoples of the world can breed contempt rather than compassion. But it also can allow one's empathy to be more focused and intense. Either way it produces greater responsibility to exercise greater love in spirit and deed for the growing number of the world's peoples with whom we can personally relate.

QUESTIONS FOR REFLECTION AND DISCUSSION:

1. Do you accept as valid the statement, "To like is to feel whereas to love is to do"? Is there anyone whom you find it very difficult to love? If so, is there anything that you can do about that situation?

2. Do you love yourself as much as God does? Do you love yourself as much as God wants you to love yourself? How much does God want you to love yourself?

SUGGESTIONS FOR FURTHER READING:

1. Martin Buber, *I and Thou*

2. M. C. D'Arcy, *The Mind and Heart of Love*

3. Anthony de Mello, *The Way to Love*

4. Henry Drummond, *The Greatest Thing in the World*

5. Eric Fromm, *The Art of Loving*

6. Soren Kierkegaard, *Works of Love*

7. C. S. Lewis, *The Four Loves*

8. Gilbert Meilaender, *Friendship*

9. Anders Nygren, *Agape and Eros*

10. Alan Paton, *Cry the Beloved Country*

11. Ronald Sider, *Just Generosity: A New Vision for Overcoming Poverty in America*

12. D. D. Williams, *The Spirit and the Forms of Love*

18. THE SACREDNESS OF LIFE

So God created man in His own image; in the image of God He created him; male and female He created them.

—Genesis 1:27

To love a thing means wanting it to live.

—Confucius

Can anything be more ridiculous than that a man should have the right to kill me because he lives on the other side of the water, and because his ruler has a quarrel with mine, though I have none with him?

—Pascal

Nothing can be meaner than the anxiety to live on, to live on anyhow and in any shape.

—George Santayana

No passage in all of literature matches the Genesis 1:27 verse above in stating with ultimate authority the inherent dignity of all humanity. If God says that each of us is of inestimable value, then we must view one another in this light. It is not a matter of our generosity; it is an issue of our recognizing—and acting upon—this reality. All deserve our respect: ourselves as well as others; the weak, the poor, and the ill-refined no less than the powerful, the popular, and the pretty; even the sadistic, the self-centered, and the mentally and sexually confused as much as the healthy, the charitable, and the wholesome. This inherent dignity stems not from one's record of accomplishments but from one's existence as a human creation of God. To withhold respect from other persons because of their flaws is to confuse respect with admiration.

Indeed, it is because of our ultimate respect for one another that we endeavor to help one another become more God-like. The only place to start in this redemptive process is with the affirmation and reaffirmation of the dignity of each person we seek to help.

When there is discussion of the sacredness of life, in the modern Christian community, the specific issues usually focus on subjects involving the life and death of the body — abortion, pacifism, capital punishment, and suicide. The body is one important part of personhood to be sure, but our focus must concern one's total welfare, including actions which damage the mind and spirit no less than the body. Above all, to seek to love one's neighbor as oneself is to seek to love and want the best for him or her in the manner that God, the Great dignity-giver, does. Only to the extent to which we have this perspective are we fully prepared to discuss personal points of view and public policies on issues of life and death.

The public policy of allowing the practice of routine and wholesale abortion upon demand is a great evil. The best way to change this is the same way that it was changed during the early centuries of Christianity, namely, to change the hearts and minds of people. As Western civilization became increasingly Christian in the period after 300 A.D., it increasingly adopted the traditional Christian interpretation on the rights of a fetus. A second way to achieve reform is to increasingly focus on political efforts that are readily achievable, even if involving minor compromises. For example, in the United States a small minority of the population supports a total ban on abortions while another minority opposes all restrictions. A large majority, however, both view the casual use of abortion as the birth control method of last resort to be a moral evil and also believe strongly that in unusually sensitive cases such as rape, incest, probable deformity of the fetus, and serious health threat to the mother, that the decision can best be made by the individual(s) involved in consultation with family members, clergy, and doctors. Legislation reflecting such a consensus would make illegal the great majority of current abortions. Then, after the enactment of such legislation, those who hold a more purist position could continue their campaign to try to achieve a new consensus.

It is my belief that intuitively (at least on a subconscious level), nearly all people, including especially nearly all women, view abortion as the taking of life. Those who argue most vehemently for the right to have abortions, I suspect, are often arguing as much to suppress their own guilt as to argue against the opposition. I think that the debate will move to a healthier level when we recognize this more broadly and more openly and then discuss when, if ever, the exceptional action of taking a life is justified. Surely the abortion debate should be more nearly like the ones involving pacifism and capital punishment rather than over when life begins.

Many of the early Christians were opposed to war no less than to abortion. After the conversion of Constantine, Christians acquired political power and less frequently held pacifist views. The case for a Christian-based pacifism includes the following considerations: 1) the strongest Biblical arguments for pacifism come from Jesus, the God-man (e.g. Matthew 5:9, 38-40, 43-44; Matthew 26:50-52); and 2) if the opposing soldier is not a Christian, how can I be both committed to sharing the Gospel with him and shooting a bullet at him when, if the latter is well-aimed, it would end his earthly opportunities to receive the Savior?

The limitations of the case for Christian pacifism include the following: 1) God in the Old Testament, at least, is described as commanding violence (e.g. I Chronicles 5:22, Deuteronomy 9:3 and 20:16-17, I Samuel 15:2-3); 2) Christ never commanded anyone to leave the military, and every Biblical citation of a Roman centurion describes him with honor (e.g. Matthew 8:13-15 and 27:54; Acts 10:22, 23:23, 24:23, 26:23 and 27:43); 3) at times the evil brought by war appears to amount to less than the evil that would continue without its intervention; and 4) in a sinful, fallen world can we have organized, orderly society without the means (including a domestic police force) of enforcing such a structure?

If the Bible as a whole does not present a mandate for unconditional pacifism, nevertheless it (and particularly the Prince of Peace) does urge the way of non-violence to a greater extent than is recognized by most Christians and practiced by most modern states. The peace-maker witness is too central to the heart of the Christian message to be abdicated entirely to the traditional peace churches.*

How can one reconcile this longing for peace while living as a member of organized society in this evil world? One should focus primarily on bringing healing to the world as one is able. Yet at times the use of force is necessary. One should defend himself and his family from personal attack, and few would question the desirability of having a local police force to give protection to the community or a national army to guard the country's borders against invasion. On occasions it may even be necessary for the army to be engaged abroad or for internal revolutionary force to be organized within the country; but use should be made of these forces only in the most dire circumstances. When there exists an extremely aggressive or oppressive situation such as the mass killing of innocent people or the mass subjection of people to systems of slavery that destroy their human dignity, when all efforts to resolve the situation peacefully have been tried and found futile, and when armed intervention to end indignities has a reasonably good chance of succeeding militarily and resulting in a better situation than existed before the intervention, then perhaps the use of the national army abroad or of an internal revolutionary force at home is warranted. When the use of force is necessary, it should be engaged in remorsefully. The officer who teaches his troops to hate the enemy may be producing, in some ways, more effective infantrymen, but he is also producing degraded human beings. Almost equally inhumane is the practice of the people on the home front who hold gala parades and other forms of tribalism to "celebrate" the bloodshed engaged in by their men.

Some day we shall learn of war no more. Until that time the followers of Christ in their appointed role of peacemaker in the world should use their best efforts to see that humanity increasingly uses the resources of God's world to make plowshares rather than swords, and to construct pruning hooks rather than spears.

If one follows the spirit of Jesus in the New Testament (e.g. Matthew 5 and 18 and Luke 10) it is difficult to justify capital punishment as a merely punitive measure. Surely all punishment at its core must involve redemptive intentions for the individual. Perhaps one could argue that for the hardened criminal, the chance to reflect upon impending death could force the type of soul reflection that might not come otherwise. Perhaps in rare cases, the evils of a high profile prisoner like a major political leader are so great both in past record and future potential (especially if freed) that one might argue that execution would be a warranted preemptive action. In most cases of capital punishment, however, I fear that the societal motivation is in significant part revenge or lack of forgiveness. For those for whom such is the case, it would be good to reflect upon the words of Brennan Manning: "What man can serve as the executioner of his brother when God refused to execute those guilty of the death of His Son...[but rather made] out of that murder the cause of His murderers' redemption? After that acquittal, there is no crime on earth, no form of aggression that can justify man's deliberately taking the life of another man."

Suicide involves questions on the sustaining of life under miserable conditions. In taking one's life there is often an inadequate recognition of the fact that spiritual growth rather than freedom from discomfort is the ultimate purpose of life. Countless people have attested to how pain, struggle and tragedy can be, and often are, highly productive of a maturation that otherwise would not have been realized. Still one must be slow to judge those who have chosen to end a painful experience. Mental and physical pain can become extremely heavy burdens, and people vary in their levels of toleration. Particularly disturbing is the not infrequently held belief that a person who commits suicide cannot go to heaven. Such a view overestimates the degree of evil involved with self-destruction in comparison to other late-in-life sins, and it underestimates the grace and love of God. By contrast with initiating a premature ending to life, the artificial prolonging of life in the face of terminal illness often involves a lack of faith in the idea of a better life to come and that death, at least in this fallen world, is a natural process as part of the life cycle.

* Some of this material on war and peace first appeared in my essay "The American Revolution, the 1960s, and the Use of Violence," *Fides et Historia*, Fall, 1971, pp. 36-44.

QUESTIONS FOR REFLECTION AND DISCUSSION:

1. What do you think of the view—called by some "consistent pro-life"—that says that a Christian should oppose the taking of life in any form, including by abortion, war, and capital punishment?

2. Reread the beginning-of-the-chapter quotation on war by Blaise Pascal. It is pointed; is it fair?

SUGGESTIONS FOR FURTHER READING:

1. Roland Bainton, *Christian Attitudes Toward War and Peace*

2. D. Gareth Jones, *Brave New People: Ethical Issues at the Commencement of Life*

3. C. Everett Koop and Timothy Johnson, *Let's Talk: Abortion, Euthanasia, AIDS, Health Care*

4. Frederica Matthewes-Green, *Real Choices*

5. Paul Ramsay, *Ethics at the Edges of Life*

6. Ronald J. Sider, *Completely Pro Life*

7. Lewis Smedes, *Choices: Making Right Decisions in a Complex World*

8. John Howard Yoder, *The Politics of Jesus*

19. THE MISSIONARY IMPERATIVE

The heavens declare the glory of God; and the firmament shows His handiwork. ...There is no speech nor language where their voice is not heard. Their line has gone out through all the earth, and their words to the end of the world.

—Psalm 19:1,3, 4a

Things are...[so structured] with moral law.... [that] Every cause in Nature is nothing but a disguised missionary.

—Ralph Waldo Emerson

That was the true Light which gives light to every man who comes into the world.

—John 1:9

...He did not leave Himself without witness.... Since the creation of the world His invisible attributes are clearly seen, ...even His eternal power and Godhead....

—Acts 14:17, Romans 1:20

Go into all the world and preach the gospel to every creature.

—Mark 16:15

...this gospel of the Kingdom will be preached in all the world as a witness to all the nations and then the end will come.

—Matthew 24:14

...you...have redeemed...to God...out of every tribe and tongue and people and nation....

—Revelation 5:9

The foreign missionary undertaking is the expression of the essential nature of the Christian faith.

—Robert E. Speer

The reason some folks don't believe in missions is that the brand of religion they have isn't worth propagating.

—Anonymous

Without compassion, witness in all its varied forms is ineffective, flaccid, and at times obnoxious.

—Roger Barrett

Constraint is the negation of all spiritual life. We can help others by telling them of our experiences and convictions. But let us have the honesty to tell them of our failures and doubts as well. Above all, we must beware of the natural inclination which makes us think that others must come to faith by the same road as ourselves. If we exert any sort of pressure upon them, we shall inevitably harm them. Pressure of that kind will either force their decision, in which case we shall be usurping God's place; or else it will arouse their resistance, and we shall become for them an obstacle to faith.

—Paul Tournier

Good apologists are not teachers but pointers to the Teacher. Unless they can get their listeners to listen to God, it will do no good at all to get their listeners to listen to them; and if they do get them to listen to God, it will soon be unnecessary to get them to listen to them any more....

—Peter Kreeft

When we want to correct someone usefully and show him he is wrong, we must see from what point of view he is approaching the matter, for it is usually right from that point of view, and we must admit this, but show him the point of view from which it is wrong. This will please him because he will see that he was not wrong but merely failed to see every aspect of the question.

—Blaise Pascal

The root of most atheism is not argument but attitude, not intellection but feeling, not the love of truth but the fear of truth. Any evangelistic or apologetic effort that ignores this psychological fact is naive and doomed to ineffectiveness, except with the small minority who are utterly honest and objective. (They are a small minority among believers too.)

—Peter Kreeft

What the church calls Christian mission is our participation in God's continuous, revelatory love call to all of humankind. It is an inherent part of being a Christian. As emissaries of the God who is love, created in His image, we seek to reflect His spirit as well as communicate the content of His special revelation in whatever geographic region or regions God calls us to live during our earthly sojourn.

We must always remember that mission is God's work in which we are invited to participate, not our work in which we ask God's assistance. Mission began before us and, in at least some forms (e.g. Psalm 19 and John 1:9) always has reached everywhere. The enterprise of proclaiming the good news of God's love transcends all human efforts. Sometimes enthusiastic mission promoters sound as if the Divine is dependent upon us mortals (e.g. "God has no hands but our hands and no feet but our feet") as opposed to choosing to work through us; such excessive claims may aid in the acquisition of resources for a human organization, but as theology, the concept of God is too small. God's work will get done; each of us can choose whether to participate in God's preordained victorious cause.

What follows now are some suggested principles for us human associates in mission:

1. Note carefully the method of mission advanced by arguably the first modern missionary, William Carey of England and India. His plan is still widely followed, and includes the following components: 1) the widespread preaching of the Gospel by every effective means, 2) the translation and distribution of the Bible into the language of the people, 3) the establishment of churches, 4) a thorough study of the culture and thought of the people, 5) the establishment of schools and colleges to train an indigenous ministry, and 6) the providing of medical, humanitarian, and developmental assistance.

2. Continuously work at developing the capacity to love everyone in general and each person with whom you work in particular. For effective witness, what you are and what you feel about the other person is often more important than are the exact words that you speak. We tend to believe good people, Aristotle noted, more readily than others. A regular business traveler to Russia told me that the Russian people listen cautiously as well as eagerly to the flood of American missionary visitors who have entered the former Soviet Union since 1990. After years of being uncertain about the credibility of what they heard from their political authorities, they are eager to hear other views, but in listening they observe carefully the totality of the communication process, seeking answers to such questions as: Does the speaker really believe what he is saying? Does she really care for me? How genuine is this person? Is this attempt at conversion merely another form of imperialism?

    Lifestyle evangelism is reflected in things like William Carey's concern to learn the culture of his host country, Hudson Taylor's choice to embody the culture of his host country, and the widespread practice of incorporating medicine, agriculture, education, relief, and development into the overall missionary program. Ideally, the totality of the missionary cares for the totality of the needs of the people.

3. Dissociate the Gospel from the culture of the missionary and/or the sponsoring group. Not to do this is to dilute if not obscure the Gospel. If the missionaries mix the Gospel with their culture, the indigenous people may do this also, even if in different ways. Alas, some discriminating people may reject the Gospel because, appropriately enough, they cannot accept the cultural preference of the messenger. The pure gospel, of course, is universal and unifying.

4. Witness, like a medical prescription, is best dispensed on a personal basis. Start with the person's situation and thinking, not with your formula. Study the witnessing methods of Jesus. He who "saw what was in their hearts" regularly communicated the message most needed to a given person or persons. To do this He often answered a different question than the one that was asked. Frequently he encouraged the discouraged and brought troubling words to the complacent. Of course Jesus had telepathic powers that we do not possess, but with the gifts that He has given us we can do much to imitate His methods. This emphasis on personal evangelism, of course, does not preclude efforts of mass evangelism any more than the practice of personal medicine precludes campaigns of mass inoculation and programs of broad-based health instruction. Nevertheless, in the final analysis, critical spiritual decisions are always made individually.

5. When witnessing to a person, commend all that you can about the person and his beliefs. Inevitably the person is partly right, holds some legitimate reactions to life's circumstances, and can give you some new insights. Acknowledge all of this specifically. Then you

have created an environment where the person is more likely to listen to your communication of additional truths.

6. Learn the greatest interests of the person. Even when these do not attract you, the idea that they appeal to the person makes them significant to you because the person who values them is important to you. Find a way to use these interests as a bridge to introduce your friend to the ideas and *the Person* most worthy of the interest of us all.

Admittedly mission is in part salesmanship. But it should not be manipulation. It is more like offering a present than advertising or selling a product. For if you have found the thing of greatest value, and if you love your neighbors as yourself, what is more natural than to want to freely and unconditionally share it with them!

QUESTIONS FOR REFLECTION AND DISCUSSION:

1. What mistakes—including common ones—have you observed in efforts of Christian evangelism/mission?

2. By contrast, what are the most exemplary evangelistic methods and/or character traits of specific missionaries that you have observed?

SUGGESTIONS FOR FURTHER READING:

1. David Barrett, ed., *World Christian Encyclopedia*

2. R. Pierce Beaver, *American Missions in Bicentennial Perspective*

3. Sherwood Eddy, *Pathfinders of the World Mission*

4. James and Marti Hefley, *By Their Blood: Christian Martyrs of the 20th Century*

5. William R. Hutchinson, *Errand to the World: American Protestant Thought and Foreign Missions*

6. Patrick Johnstone, *Operation World,* multiple editions

7. E. Stanley Jones, *The Christ of the India Road*

8. J. Herbert Kane, *A Global View of Christian Missions*

9. Kenneth Scott Latourette, *A History of the Expansion of Christianity*, 7 vols.

10. *Mission Handbook: North American Protestant Ministries Overseas*, multiple editions

11. Donald McGavran, *Understanding Church Growth*

12. Stephen Neill et al., *Concise Dictionary of the Christian World Mission*

13. Don Richardson, *Eternity in Their Hearts*

145

14. Ruth Tucker, *From Jerusalem to Irian Jaya: A Biographical History of Christian Missions*

15. Ralph D. Winter and Steven C. Hawthorne, eds., *Perspectives on the Christian World Movement*

20. DEALING WITH CONTROVERSIAL ISSUES

To disagree, one doesn't need to be disagreeable.

— *Billy Graham*

I never met a person from whom I could not learn something.

— *Anonymous*

...a common spiritual concern does not mean a common intellectual agreement.

— *Charles Williams*

When two truths seem to directly oppose each other, we must... remember there is a third—God—who reserves to Himself the right to harmonize them.

— *Anne Swetchine*

Everyone wishes to have truth on his side, but it is not everyone that sincerely wishes to be on the side of truth.

— *Richard Whately*

Minds that have nothing to confer
Find little to perceive.

— *William Wordsworth*

It is in disputes as in armies, where the weaker side sets up false lights, and makes a great noise, to make the enemy believe them more numerous and strong than they really are.

— *Jonathan Swift*

How do you love your neighbor as yourself in the midst of controversy, even deeply felt controversy, and all the more so when it involves religious doctrine? Although controversy exists in part because we are flawed and finite, much controversy is natural and the inevitable consequence of the fact that God has created us humans with the capacity of independent thinking, moral valuing, and intense caring. Problems develop when, in exercising these processes, we grant less freedom to one another than God has granted to each of us.

Here are some general principles to consider when engaged in controversy with others:

1. Value truth more than your pride. Desire to know the truth more than you do the ability, in retrospect, to perceive yourself having been altogether right coming into the debate.

2. Always be open to new light. Even while holding firm to the base that has given stability to your life, actively embrace new truth and incorporate it into your belief system as God reveals it to you.

3. Humbly realize that God distributes His wisdom widely rather than having given it all to you.

4. Hope and pray that the other person or persons in the discussion want to hear God, and that they hear you only to the extent that your voice contributes to that greater recognition.

5. On controversial issues in general, compromise all that you can on secondary considerations, do not compromise at all on genuinely primary ones, and exercise great effort in seeking to understand the difference between the two.

6. Always exercise kindness in the midst of intense debate. Kindness does not preclude a clear recognition of differences; in fact it can contribute to it. A corollary to the old Quaker saying, "Act toward the other in a way most likely to lead to a response of goodness" might be "Reason with the other in a way most likely to lead to receptivity of truth by all concerned." The process (charity) is no less important than the product (truth).

7. Recognize that the providence of God may allow for differing human perspectives on even significant issues.
8. Accept the idea that the reconciliation of human viewpoints is not altogether possible nor necessarily desirable.
9. Learn how to live in an environment of differing perspectives.
10. Celebrate differences as much as possible.

The wise participant in an intense discussion will recognize that often the passion of a given individual stems less from the specific issue at hand than from a longer-standing and more primary and more personal issue (or issues). The latter may involve one or more of the following:
1. Fear that a group decision will displease God (or a God-like figure)
2. Fear that one or one's group will lose power or economic advantage
3. Fear or dislike of change
4. Insufficient respect for and/or understanding of traditions
5. Insufficient respect for the liberties of others
6. A need to overthrow, defeat, or defy a power figure
7. Fear that one's guilt will be revealed (to oneself and/or others)
8. Fear of discovering a truth which would conflict with one's desired belief system and/or lifestyle
9. An inordinate desire to win in all things, including debate
10. Anxiety because the issue at hand reminds one of a major, early-in-life, unresolved and often unrecognized issue, frequently involving one's family, church, or school

The compassionate participant in an intense discussion will seek to give the other person or persons what they most need, whether 1) comprehensive information or insight to clarify thinking on the issue at hand; 2) limited direct advise, gently probing questions, and time to process both; or 3) merely a supportive, listening ear. In each case the purpose is to assist the other(s) toward the resolution of long-standing, underlying issues.

There are several Biblical models for dealing with controversy which are especially useful because of the universal principles which they suggest. Matthew, chapter 18, records Jesus affirming the dignity of all people and emphasizing the importance of gracious actions toward others, especially the young, the lost, the poor, and the offensive. More specifically, in this context Jesus, in verses 15-17, provides a process for dealing with people who have sinned against you, namely engaging direct, immediate dialogue between the two of you, and if this does not achieve reconciliation, then bringing one or more wise friends into the effort of healing. If this procedure is appropriate for you to initiate when the other person has done the sinning, how much more so when 1) you have done the sinning, 2) the fault is shared or not clear, or 3) for whatever reason the relationship is threatened.

Acts 15 provides a classic example for dealing with church-wide controversy on doctrine and policy. Christianity, of course, grew out of Judaism. Early in the spread of Christianity the question surfaced, "Do Gentile converts need to observe the Old Testament Jewish law?" or "Can Gentiles become Christians without becoming Jews?" The issue emerged at Antioch, the early center of Gentile Christianity, and the Antioch church referred the issue to the apostles and elders at Jerusalem for resolution. The resultant Jerusalem Council determined that the Gospel is universal: reconciliation to God through Christ is available to all people in the context of their immediate culture. The universality of the Gospel is a logical development from the earlier Jewish insistence upon monotheism in contrast to belief in tribal religions.

As important as is the specific issue of the universality of the Gospel, the primary focus in this essay is upon the general process of decision-making. In this respect, then, the important factors for the Jerusalem leaders can serve as a model for their heirs in the Christian tradition now; they include the following:

1. The church leaders earnestly sought the mind of the Holy Spirit (see verse 28a).

2. They engaged in debate and discussion in an effort to reach consensus on their best understanding of the Divine mind.

3. They showed sensitivity to the minority group, compromising where they could on secondary issues and wanting not to cause needless offense because of their value upon unity as well as principle.

4. After their formal deliberations and decision-making, they considered their work incomplete until in a careful, personal, and sensitive manner, they reported to and provided measures for the implementation of the decision with the originating group.

The last part of Acts 15 shows that even among people with the same primary purpose, some controversial issues are not totally resolvable, as the missionary team of Paul and Barnabas agreed to work separately because of their differences over having Mark become a third member of their working group. Nevertheless, even when people agree to disagree on a specific issue, they still can agree to 1) desire the mind of God and truth, 2) wish the very best for the other party, and 3) talk and act graciously, loving the other as themselves.

QUESTIONS FOR REFLECTION AND DISCUSSION:

1. Is it ever right not to exercise kindness and respect toward a person with whom you have a disagreement?

2. Is it possible that the providence of God may allow for differing human perspectives on significant issues?

3. To what extent do church groups need to vote to determine a group majority on controversial issues instead of simply living with—and even embracing—the differences?

SUGGESTIONS FOR FURTHER READING:

1. R. D. Bell, *Biblical Models of Handling Conflict*

2. C. M. Cosgrive and D. D. Hatfield, *Church Conflict: The Hidden Systems Behind the Fights*

3. William M. Pinson, Jr., *How to Deal With Controversial Issues*

4. K. Sande, *The Peacemaker: A Biblical Guide to Resolving Conflict*

TOWARD MATURITY

21. SPIRITUAL GROWTH

Our conversion...is not the terminus but merely the first stage of the Christian life. ...our conversion leaves us with much to do; it...sets before us the task of coming to terms with our deep inadequacies so that we may love our neighbor better and come to love God with all our heart, mind, soul, and strength.

—Diogenes Allen

...I know that the divine will, will only be revealed to me at each moment if I exert myself to the utmost....

—Pierre Teilhard deChardin

...the path of the just is like the shining sun, that shines ever brighter unto the perfect day.

—Proverbs 4:18

...but grow in the grace and knowledge of our Lord and Savior Jesus Christ.

—II Peter 3:18a

Growth is the only evidence of life.

—John Henry Newman

Each person is inherently spiritual. The Apostle John talks about "...the true Light which giveth light to every man who comes into the world" (John 1:9). Everyone chooses how to respond to the light within. While few, if any, perfectly receive the light in all areas of their lives, nevertheless there is such a thing as a basic life orientation or commitment. In their life pilgrimage, people walk either toward God or away from

Him; it is as if there are two roads — a high road and a low road — which are parallel but travel in opposite directions (with a divide between which can lead to either road). As the poet, John Oxenham, stated so eloquently: "To every man there openeth a High way and a Low, And every man decideth the Way his Soul shall go."

George MacDonald has said that God is easy to please but hard to satisfy. The "easy to please" part correlates with one's basic life direction, with the essential question being, "in general, do you want God or do you want to be free from Him?" The "hard to satisfy" part suggests the need for continual growth. In essence any step toward God is spiritual growth and any step away from him is spiritual regression.

In one sense the formula for spiritual growth is like the title of the famous gospel hymn, "Trust and Obey, For There's No Other Way." Yet that admonition can sound like a chore, a moralistic duty, even a legalistic command. Preferable, I believe, because of their emphasis upon joyous affection, are expressions like the Psalmist's statement of praise: "I delight to do thy will, O God!", the image of Enoch walking hand-in-hand with God, the word "fellowship," the concept of a passionate love affair, or the spirit of the lovely prayer of Richard of Chichester,

> "Day by day,
> Three things I pray,
> To see Thee more clearly,
> To follow Thee more nearly,
> To love thee more dearly."

One of the most effective ways to develop spiritually, in addition to meaningful, intense, regular prayer and Bible study, is to read and reflect on the great devotional classics. In this respect, note the central idea of one of the shortest of these, Brother Lawrence's *The Practice of the Presence of God*, which reflects the call of Paul to "pray without ceasing." In other words, all of life in all of its activities is to be one continuous act of communion with the Divine. Abraham Lincoln, one of America's most insightful theologians, expressed the importance of this mental focus when he stated: "A man is what he thinks about all day long."

QUESTIONS FOR REFLECTION AND DISCUSSION:

1. Do you really want God? Or not? Do you really want to know and walk with God more and more? Or not? Do you really value the things of the Spirit? Or not?

2. If your answers to the previous questions are in the affirmative, how do you develop your relationship with the Divine?

SUGGESTIONS FOR FURTHER READING:

1. Donald L. Alexander, ed., *Christian Spirituality: Five Views of Sanctification*

2. Diogenes Allen, *Spiritual Theology*

3. E. Stanley Jones, *Abundant Living*

4. Morton Kelsey, *The Other Side of Silence*

5. Thomas a'Kempis, *The Imitation of Christ*

6. William Law, *A Serious Call to a Devout and Holy Life*

7. Brother Lawrence, *The Practice of the Presence of God*

8. Thomas Merton, *No Man is an Island*

9. John Sanford, *The Kingdom Within*

10. A. W. Tozer, *The Knowledge of the Holy*

22. STAGES OF PSYCHO-RELIGIOUS DEVELOPMENT

...the greater part of mankind [has] received even those opinions and ceremonies they would die for, rather from the fashions of their countries and the constant practice of those about them, than from any conviction of their reason.

—John Locke

Inquiry is human; blind obedience brutal. Truth never loses by the one but often suffers by the other.

—William Penn

...that we should no longer be children...but...may grow up in all things into Him who is the head—Christ....

—Ephesians 4:14a,15b

At twenty years of age, the will reigns; at thirty, the wit; and at forty, the judgment.

—Benjamin Franklin

Understanding and love require a wisdom that comes only with age.

—Rollo May

The nurse of full-grown souls is solitude.

—James Russell Lowell

When we rejoice in our fullness, then we can part with our fruits with joy.

—*Rabindranath Tagore*

When one moves from talking about spiritual growth to talking about religious development, it is a change to a different, although overlapping, topic. Spiritual growth involves communing more closely with God whether through a simple, child-like faith or through a wise, discerning faith that usually can come only with experience and maturity. Religious development, on the other hand, is related to what is considered human development in general, and it describes typical (but by no means automatic) stages of religious understanding, insight, and experience. Individuals move or do not move through some or all of these stages at varying rates. Each successive stage usually involves the receipt of greater understanding or light; and somehow, to want to receive more light should equate with a desire to know God better and therefore to love God more nearly with all of one's mind—as called for in Jesus' great commandment (Matthew 22:37-40, Mark 12:29-31, Luke 10:27).

People can do quite different things with the greater understanding they receive. They can use it to be more compassionate (i.e., to love their neighbors as themselves) and to be more spiritual in general. Or they can use their greater understanding and experience to be more cynical, withdrawn, or elitist.

Usually when theorists chart stages of religious development, they do so in a way that interrelates spiritual progress with growth in a combination of experience, knowledge, and the chronological life stages. One should not accept too completely any one paradigm of religious development. There is no one perfect model; even if there were, it would be unwise to seek to easily place people into categories. Few people are altogether in a single stage at any given time. Still, when used carefully, these models can be very helpful in aiding understanding and growth.

Two of the best-known contemporary theorists offering paradigms of what I prefer to call psycho-religious development are James Fowler and M. Scott Peck. Their models are complementary. Fowler developed his model first. The Peck model, which has fewer stages, focuses less upon life age and more upon response and responsibility; it does not include a separate stage of near-absolute sainthood; it clearly identifies the disintegration and destructiveness of sinful willfulness; and it is clearer and crisper in its model types. In the chart summarizing the two models, I have taken the liberty to paraphrase the names of the stages in the Fowler paradigm.

JAMES FOWLER	**SCOTT PECK**
Stages of Faith*	Stages of Spiritual Growth
1. Ages 2-7	1. Chaotic, anti-social (most young children and c. 20% of adults)
2. Grade School	2. Formal, institutional
3. Adolescence (ages 13-18) Conventional and nonanalytical	(most emotionally healthy older children and the majority of churchgoers and Christians)
4. An examined faith	3. Skeptic, individual (often much more spiritually earnest than they seem to be to the more traditional institutional Christians)
5. An intense seeking faith	4. Mystic, communal
6. An activist, incarnational, universally loving faith	(intense seekers of truth through direct communion with God more than through institutional structures; a growing recognition of the mystical realm and the interdependence of the world; includes perhaps 5% of the population)

* The titles of these stages are paraphrased by WCR.

Fowler's stages largely follow a human development model. The imaginative thinking of the pre-school years gradually gives way to the grade school desire to know how things really exist with the latter often determined by the beliefs of the religious community and family. As one moves through childhood into adolescence, there is interaction with a broader range of often conflicting environments, and one asks, "How do I put all of this together? Which of these several external authority sources are valid?" To move to the fourth stage one must begin to develop a sense of authority within oneself (drawing from one's own understanding in communion with God directly). The person establishes 1) a "critical distancing" from one's previously assumed value system and 2) the beginning of a personally developed value system; many people experience the first of these Stage Four changes but not the second, thus defining themselves more by what they do not accept than by what they do believe. The fully-developed Stage Four person struggles intently with the aid of the Holy Spirit and one's God-given mind to follow the counsel of Paul to work out *your own* salvation, whereas a person of Stage Three faith may say, "we believe this" or "my church teaches this." As Stage Four people develop into Stage Five, they acquire an enhanced desire to seek truth wherever it may be found. They have the confidence and self-certainty to do this as they see all truth as God's truth. Stage Six people are few in number and are distinguished from Stage Five people by their ability to come close to fully "loving their neighbor as themselves." They courageously, fearlessly, and selflessly pursue their goals of universal dignity, justice, and brotherhood with little thought to personal safety and security.

Peck's Stage One is a stage of undeveloped spirituality. He calls it antisocial because the adults remaining in it seem to lack the ability to love others. They may appear to be loving but essentially other people exist to facilitate their self-serving goals. A person in this category may acquire much power and prestige, becoming, for example, even an influential preacher or a president. When one makes the transition to Stage Two, it is usually dramatic and even traumatic for adults but quite natural for children, especially those with supportive Christian families. Stage Two is the most common category for church-going older children and adults. Typically they accept—sometimes passionately so—the discipline and definite belief structure of a specific institutional form of religion. But they usually understand the forms of their religion better than its spiritual center. Peck's Stage Three correlates closely with Fowler's Stage Four. Peck emphasizes how this period can often be painful for those—typically late adolescents or early adults—going through it (and their parents) as they rethink for themselves their inherited values. The Stage Two adults in their lives may greatly worry about them, afraid that they are becoming religious skeptics and certain that they "think too much." Often, however, they are merely seeking God for themselves. Advanced Stage Three people are intense truth seekers:

> "If people in Stage III seek truth deeply and widely enough, they find what they are looking for—enough pieces to begin to be able to fit them together but never enough to complete the whole puzzle. In fact, the more pieces they find, the larger and more magnificent the puzzle becomes...[and] they are able to get glimpses of the 'big picture' and to see that it is beautiful indeed—and that it strangely resembles those...[traditional ideas and stories of] their Stage II parents or grandparents" (Peck, p. 192).

Peck's Stage Four people are seekers who have become mystics who regularly, even constantly, commune with God and who have to a large degree come to share His vision of the dignity, beauty, and interrelatedness of all of creation.

The Fowler and Peck paradigms are but two of many useful models of religious growth. What is important for each individual is to develop, at least in experience, that model which leads him or her closer and closer in fellowship and wisdom to the Creator/Father.

QUESTIONS FOR REFLECTION AND DISCUSSION:

1. On the Fowler and Peck (and/or other) scales of psycho-religious development, how do you see yourself? What do you think of how you see yourself?

2. Paradigms such as those of Fowler and Peck are controversial. Why do you think this is so? Can you think of more helpful ways to monitor and encourage growth?

3. Reflect on the John Locke quotation. How have you acquired your primary views and principles?

SUGGESTIONS FOR FURTHER READING:

1. James Fowler, *Stages of Faith: The Psychology of Human Development and the Quest for Meaning*

2. M. Scott Peck, "Patterns of Transformation," Chapter IX in *The Different Drum: Community-Making and Peace*

23. MENTAL HEALTH

The criterion of mental health is not one of individual adjustment to a given social order, but a universal one, valid for all men, of giving a satisfactory answer to the problem of human existence.

—Eric Fromm

Belief in a cruel God makes a cruel man.

—Thomas Paine

That a religion may be true, it must have knowledge of our nature.

—Blaise Pascal

What a curious creature is man! With what a variety of powers and faculties is he! Yet how easily is he disturbed and put out of order!

—James Boswell

Here's an object more of dread
Than aught the grave contains—
A human form with reason fled,
While wretched life remains.

—Abraham Lincoln

A merry heart goes all the day,
Your sad tires in a mile-a.

—William Shakespeare

Whatever games are played with us, we must play no games with ourselves, but deal in our privacy with the last honesty and truth.
—Ralph Waldo Emerson

...some...are more anxious to <u>appear</u> holy before men than to <u>be</u> holy before God and his angels.

—author of <u>Cloud of Unknowing</u>

...a person's own needs and problems seem less threatening when he is busy helping someone else handle theirs!

—James Dobson

The Bible turns the ordinary concept of fear as a negative emotion from which we must be self-helped, into the extra-ordinary notion of fear as the means by which we reach God....

—Robert Hudnut

The study of mental health focuses upon the nature and proper functioning of the human mind and emotions. Mental health theorists and practitioners differ widely both on the degree to which one can define the mentally healthy person and, also, on what that definition should be. Nevertheless, they generally concur that the mentally healthy person should be happy, free, fulfilled, emotionally stable, skilled in decision-making, able to view one's environment with a large measure of reality, and able to relate well with other people. Some would argue that the mentally whole person should also be good or benevolent and able to relate closely with the ultimate purposes in the universe; others would counter that while the latter may be noble goals, they nevertheless are not a part of the domain of mental health. Most would concur that, at the least, sound mental health makes it easier to choose to do good things in the world and also to possess the energy and focus to accomplish them. Christian thinkers would add that a maturing relationship with God through Christ is not only the central ingredient in achieving mental and emotional health but is also the ultimate purpose for human existence; without this recognition, they add, therapy fails to treat the whole person.

The treatment of deficiencies in mental health has changed dramatically in America since the 1950s. As this country has become more affluent, we have devoted sharply increasing time and money resources to the scientific study and treatment of mental disease. Consequently, we know much more about the scientifically measurable aspects of mental illness and offer much better care for the general population. Of major significance is the widely expanding use of psychotropic medication to supplement counseling therapy and other treatments; this has paralleled the growing recognition of the role of neurochemical imbalance as a factor in mental illness.

The recent major focus upon mental health has led some to conclude that our age in history is an extraordinarily anxious one. I doubt this. More likely all ages are more or less anxious, differing primarily on that about which they are anxious. For example, compared to modern times, earlier societies worried more about basic survival concerns and less about status.

Let us return again to the unique Christian idea in the pursuit of mental health, namely the quest to be united in external spiritual fellowship with the Incarnate God who designed and gave us our minds as a part of creating us. "Ye shall know the truth and the truth shall set you free," the Apostle John tells us, even as he points to God who has a synonym for truth as one of the names for His essence ("God is light"). God's second essential name is love ("God is love"). Thus the ultimate reality is that God is ultimate truth and ultimate love; and the foundational basis for healing is that God loves each of us supremely and wants to give us His grace if we are willing to receive it. All other healing truth derives from this reality. Then, from this base, one can best identify specific principles to aid in the search for mental healing. Among these are the following:

1. If God is ultimate truth and love, let nothing keep you from working with all diligence to obtain an accurate-as-possible understanding of God. Love means acceptance. The love of God means complete and ultimate acceptance. The most common type of mental suffering is starvation for emotional acceptance. We all need to feel loved and accepted, certainly by important humans but ultimately by God. Only God, of course, by definition of being God, can provide complete and unconditional acceptance.

2. Be committed to something greater than yourself. Christianity says that such commitment is essential for wholeness because we were created with a need for a relationship with our Maker wherein we walk with Him on the paths He has designed for us. Those who feel that they cannot make such a commitment to Him can at least gain some degree of fulfillment by commitment to something noble beyond themselves (e.g. a family member or members, a humanitarian cause, or other people in general). Although such human commitments can become idolatrous, they need not be, but rather can become an important step away from self-absorption and thus a healing step toward God. As we live for others rather than merely for ourselves, it usually becomes easier to recognize and admit our weaknesses and then deal with them. Self-centeredness tends to produce defensiveness.

3. Recognize that the search for mental wholeness is often painful, especially in the beginning. I know of no way to mental and spiritual growth and development that does not involve tension, frustration, pain, and suffering.

4. The key, therefore, is to embrace the mental suffering, seeing it as a vehicle for personal progress. Recognize that with God and you working together, much good can come from the pain—if you choose to be an actively growing person rather than a passive

sufferer. Solve your emotional problems if you can; use them regardless.

5. Communicate graciously but forthrightly what troubles you to an empathetic, understanding, insightful person. If a specific person is what troubles you, then also discuss the problem with him or her with the purpose of seeking healing and reconciliation. Express your anger or other hurtful emotions so that you can express forgiveness; express forgiveness so that you can find healing.

> I was angry with my friend
> I told my wrath, my wrath did end.
> I was angry with my foe:
> I told it not, my wrath did grow.
>
> — William Blake

6. In assessing yourself or others, avoid the temptation to equate mental illness too easily with moral guilt. Rarely is there a one-to-one correlation between the two. Fortunately modern society understands this better than did previous generations, although it often tends to err in the opposite direction (see Karl Menninger's *Whatever Happened To Sin?*).

7. As a basic and regular habit of life, learn to focus on the real rather than the distortion. One important aspect of mental health is mental clarity. But alas, such clarity is not common. Inaccurate thinking is such a central factor in the fallen human condition! For example, how common is it to believe the distortion that one is generally inferior rather than possessing inherent dignity as a beloved creature of God? This false belief commonly results in 1) psychological distress, 2) an exaggerated desire to receive approval from others or to see oneself as superior to others, and, 3) in its most desperate form, blatant efforts to repress, at least psychologically, entire groups of people whether religious, ethnic, racial, or geographic

groups. This latter malady is based upon the erroneous conviction that "I can only feel good about myself if I see another—or many others—as my inferior." This extreme form of distortion helps to explain the wide appeal of gossip, scandalous stories, continuous criticism of the government, and fellowshipping with people who share your enjoyment of "putting down" other people. A growing confidence in God's love reduces the level of these symptoms as one increasingly focuses on substance rather than image and essence rather than appearance.

8. Recognize that the most fundamental way to heal one's interpersonal relations is to heal one's internal conflicts. A wise man once noted that the idea of loving your neighbor as yourself is descriptive as well as prescriptive. In other words, people tend to love others in a manner similar to how they love—or do not love—themselves. The goal then is to see oneself as God does and to love oneself as much as and in the manner that God does. But it is difficult to love oneself without understanding oneself, and it is difficult to understand oneself without seeing and dealing with one's darker side. To face one's sin honestly is to reduce the compulsion to seek to project it onto others. The more whole one is personally, the more one spreads healing, or wholeness, to others.

9. Do not allow what is wrong with your past to unnecessarily limit your future. If you have been harmed, do not be angry with yourself; rather, be angry at the cause of your hurting. Above all, be forgiving to help bring peace to your remembrance. Certainly do not use the past harm as an excuse to not proceed with your life development. Find faith that sees an ultimate justice that transcends your own experience of injustice. Seek wisdom that allows you to receive and initiate a goodness that can rise out of evil.

10. Reflect on your own anger to learn from it and to be healed from its non-controlled expressions and non-productive effects. When angry, ask yourself, "Am I angry at the other person's flaws because I share them but wish not to recognize that fact; am I angry at another person's standards, whether expressed in word or in action, because they remind me of something in my life that needs to be improved but that I am not ready to change yet; am I angry because I unnecessarily hold the belief that other people should think and act just as I do; and when I become angry at another's negative or even malicious expression toward myself or others, is such anger healthy for me, and is my response the one most likely to lead to a positive change by the wrong-doer?"

11. Help yourself by enjoying and helping others. General isolation from other people prevents both receiving from and giving to them. One of the quickest antidotes to depression is to spend time with friends; even more helpful is to give to others, especially those with acute needs of their own. Too great a focus on oneself is sickening, either causing or prolonging illness.

12. Increasingly learn to distinguish between what you can do to help yourself achieve mental wholeness and what you can do to help another do the same. There are greater limits on the latter. Offer another your care and, when appropriate, your best wisdom; but recognize that to unduly seek to force another to follow your good advise is to insufficiently acknowledge his or her God-given freedom; and to unduly base your happiness upon the other's willingness to accept your principles, good or otherwise, is to carry an impossible burden.

Growth toward greater mental maturity (i.e., toward truth and love) is a lifelong process. Obtain help in moving toward this goal from wherever you can. Sometimes even secular sources can promote Christian ideas of healing without fully knowing it. In many ways, psychology with psychotherapy is one of the most secular fields, yet the Christian faith and applied psychology share many of the most effective general principles for achieving mental health. Both, for example, place much emphasis upon love in intrapersonal and interpersonal relations, ruthless honesty with oneself, and the importance of inner-direction in personal development. Perhaps general psychology is not as far from the Kingdom of God as many think it to be. In most cases, however, Christian counseling clients best thrive when working with a counselor who best understands their most important values.

QUESTIONS FOR REFLECTION AND DISCUSSION:

1. How often is the cause of little problems to be found in the lack of a satisfactory solution to the big issues of life?

2. Why does God allow mental death to precede physical death, sometimes for lengthy periods?

3. Can a person be mentally whole without a positive relationship with his or her Maker?

SUGGESTIONS FOR FURTHER READING:

1. Daniel G. Amen, *Change Your Brain, Change Your Life*

2. Anthony de Mello, *The Way to Love*

3. Archibald D. Hart, *The Anxiety Cure*

4. Robert Hudnut, *Meeting God in the Darkness*

5. Matthew Linn, Sheila Fabricant, and Dennis Linn, *Healing the Eight Stages of Life*

6. Karl Menninger, *Whatever Became of Sin?*

7. M. Scott Peck, *People of the Lie: The Hope for Healing Human Evil*

8. Francis Thompson, *The Hound of Heaven*

9. Paul Tournier, *The Strong and the Weak*

10. Leslie D. Weatherhead, *Prescription for Anxiety*

24. INNER DIRECTION

Helen had supposed she could think because the thoughts of other people had passed through her quite regularly, leaving many a phantom conclusion behind. But this had been their thinking, not hers.

—George MacDonald

Whoso would be a man, must be a nonconformist. He who would gather immortal palms must not be hindered by the name of goodness, but must explore if it be goodness. ...I am ashamed to think how easily we capitulate to badges and names, to large societies and dead institutions.

—Ralph Waldo Emerson

The less structure men have within themselves, the more they will desperately seek to find it outside of themselves.

—John A. Sanford

Many of my daily preoccupations suggest that I belong more to the world than to God. A little criticism makes me angry, and a little rejection makes me depressed. A little praise raises my spirits, and a little success excites me.... All the time and energy I spend in keeping some kind of balance shows that my life is mostly an anxious struggle resulting from the mistaken idea that it is the world that defines me.

—Henri Nouwen

We are not satisfied with the life we have in ourselves and our own being. We want to lead an imaginary life in the eyes of others, and so we try to make an impression. We strive constantly to embellish and preserve our imaginary being, and neglect the real one. And if we are calm or generous, or loyal, we are anxious to have it known so that we can attach these virtues to our other existence....

—*Blaise Pascal*

...the best of us are not so much afraid to offend...[God] as to offend our neighbors, kinsmen, or rulers.

—*Michael Montaigne*

When the people have no tyrant, their own public opinion becomes one.

—*Edward Bulwer-Lytton*

...because you bow your head to God you will hold it erect before men.

—*Richard Emerich*

The thirst [for applause,] if the last infirmity of noble minds, is also the first infirmity of weak ones.

—*John Ruskin*

To walk away from the world of human beings as the prophets and the mystics did is not to walk away from their company but from their formulas.

—*Anthony de Mello*

Common sense suits itself to the ways of the world. Wisdom tries to conform to the ways of Heaven.

—*Joseph Joubert*

We must so desire to know the mind of God and carry out His will that it is as if we do not care what humans think of us. Of course, the best of us do not perfectly understand the will of God, let alone perform it, so, in fact, we do need to solicit and receive the thoughts of others about how we are living. These thoughts, especially from wise and Godly confidants and those closest to us, are indeed an important source of information for self-evaluation. But they must only be sought as means to the end of discovering the good of the Divine for us.

Inner-directedness means union with God. It appropriates in practice the famous line of St. Augustine: "Thou has made us for Thyself, and the heart of man is restless until it finds its rest in Thee." Other-directedness means seeking to fill the God-shaped vacuum in the human soul by means of union with God-substitutes; among the most common of these — varying in their appeal with one's disposition, age, and circumstances — are money, sex, entertainment, power, position, popularity, and acclaim. Often the attraction of these lies less in what they inherently provide than in the status they bestow. We look to these human forms of acceptance to assure us that we are okay, that we are accepted, that we are members of what C. S. Lewis, in his brilliant essay of the same name, calls "the inner ring."

A variant response to this universal need for relatedness is to deny its existence. For example, the secular form of humanism and the secular form of existentialism are both varieties — one positive and one negative — of self-reliance apart from God. Both are excellent half-truths or negative critiques. Both are good as far as they go in seeking to free people from the tyranny of being a fearful slave of the ideas and opinions of others. There is all the difference in the world, however, whether or not one exercises this independence of the opinions of others in order to whole-heartedly seek the mind of God. The secular humanist is headed for grave disappointment, and the secular existentialist acknowledgedly wallows in meaninglessness.

The struggle for the development of inner-directedness is not only an issue of the individual versus the world; at times it can also be an issue of the individual verses the church. Sometimes a person has to say no to the church in order to say yes to God. Some churches encourage or even demand an unhealthy dependency, but even in generally mature churches the individual must determine to listen intently to the leading of the Holy Spirit for specific guidance.

Brennan Manning, in one of the more creative sections of his stimulating *The Lion and the Lamb*, contrasts settler theology and pioneer theology. Settler theology emphasizes receiving, sometimes quite passively, religion through the church. Pioneer theology emphasizes actively and personally walking and talking with God—hopefully with the aid and encouragement of the church—ever seeking, ever exploring, ever learning, ever coming closer to the mind of God.

> Be Thou my Vision, O Lord of my heart;
> Naught be all else to me, save that Thou art—
> Thou my best thought, by day or by night,
> Waking or sleeping, Thy presence my light.
>
> Riches I heed not, nor man's empty praise,
> Thou mine inheritance, now and always;
> Thou and Thou only, first in my heart,
> High King of heaven, my Treasure Thou Art.
>
> —Ancient Irish Hymn

QUESTIONS FOR REFLECTION AND DISCUSSION:

1. What is the optimum degree to care about what other people—or certain other people—care about what you think and do?

2. How much can even churches be manipulative in controlling and enforcing instead of inspiring the most noble aspirations?

SUGGESTIONS FOR FURTHER READING:

1. Vernard Eller, *The Simple Life*

2. Brother Lawrence, *The Practice of the Presence of God*

3. C. S. Lewis, "The Inner Ring" in *The Weight of Glory*

4. Soren Kierkegaard, *Purity of Heart is to Will One Thing*

5. Anthony de Mello, *The Way to Love*

6. John Sanford, *The Kingdom Within*

25. HUMILITY

The ...constant companion [of truth] is Humility.
—Charles Caleb Colton

He bids fair to grow wise who has discovered that he is not so.
—Publilius Syrus

Blessed are the poor in spirit,
For theirs is the Kingdom of Heaven.
Blessed are the meek,
For they shall inherit the earth.
—Matthew 5:3,5

For whoever exalts himself will be abased, and he who humbles
himself will be exalted.
—Luke 14:11

Who builds a church to God and not to fame,
Will never mark the marble with his name.
—Alexander Pope

Should you ask me: What is the first thing in religion? I should
reply: The first, second, and third thing therein is humility.
—St. Augustine

A man who has humility will have acquired in the last reaches of
his beliefs the saving doubt of his own certainty.
—Walter Lippman

No more lessen or dissemble thy merit, than overrate it; for though humility be a virtue, an affected one is not.

—*William Penn*

...perfect humility implies perfect confidence in the power of God, before Whom no other power has any meaning and for Whom there is no such thing as an obstacle. Humility is the surest sign of strength.

—*Thomas Merton*

...unless you are converted and become as little children, you will by no means enter the kingdom of heaven. Therefore whoever humbles himself as...[a] little child is the greatest in the kingdom of heaven.

—*Matthew 18:3b, 4*

He has shown you, O man, what is good; and what doth the Lord require of you but to do justly, to love mercy, and to walk humbly with your God?

—*Micah 6:8*

Many Christian theologians both describe pride as "the great sin" (because, in the words of C.S. Lewis, "it leads to every other vice: it is the complete anti-God state of mind") and humility as the moral opposite of pride. While this does not mean that humility thereby is the greatest virtue, it does suggest that it is at least a necessary one, a precondition to saving faith and spiritual maturity.

Humility is best understood as a realistic view of one's position in the universe. It recognizes that we are not of our own creation, possess nothing that we did not receive, and cannot do one thing nor continue one second on our own resources. Yet it also understands that we humans—all of us—are the culminating act of God's creation, supremely and personally beloved of the Father. Each individual human who possesses this humility perceives clearly both that there is no one in the whole world who is any more important in God's sight than is he or she, and also that there is no one in the whole world who is any less important in God's sight than is he or she. The former realization reduces the tendency toward self-disparagement; the latter one reduces the tendency toward arrogance. Oh, how many of the problems of the world would be reduced to insignificance if we would become fully aware of how highly God values each of us!

In their thinking on pride and humility, Christians and non-Christians alike frequently confuse self-love (i.e. pride) with self-respect and self-disparagement with humility. In each case the differences are profound. Self-love is essentially self-centered to the exclusion of God-centeredness and concern for others. Of one such self-loving person it was said, "Mary's world was bound on the north, south, east, and west by Mary." This type of person interprets all incidents and comments with almost exclusive reference to himself or herself. Self-respect, by contrast, has a larger world view. It sees both oneself and all others as possessing supreme value because that is their endowment from their Creator; it also understands that fulfillment for each is realized only by continuously drawing upon the unlimited Divine resources.

Apparently, many Christians sincerely believe that self-deprecation is the same as humility and thus a great virtue. They constantly talk about how they are not good and everybody is better than they are. If self-deprecation is good, then masochism in general and even ultimately suicide must be very good things. Even worse than a sincere self-deprecation is a faked one. This is often done to protect oneself from criticism (from oneself as well as from others).

Why is the self-deprecation view of humility so widely believed to be true? Some Biblical verses seem to suggest it (e.g. Philippians 2:3b:

"let each esteem others as better than himself;" and I Timothy 1:15b: "sinners, of whom I am chief "). So do the writings of some prominent Christian mystics (e.g. Thomas a' Kempis: "Do not consider yourself to have made any spiritual progress, until you account yourself the least of all men"). These passages are probably best understood as dramatic overstatements for corrective effect. Most people most of the time are hard on others and easy on themselves; these writers call for the opposite approach, emphasizing how it is important to see your own weaknesses (not just your strengths) and the strengths of others (not merely their weaknesses). Also helpful on this subject is the balance provided by Paul in Romans 12 where he says that we should *think of ourselves* (verse 3) with sober judgment but *treat others* (verse 10) with higher priority.

True humility thanks God for life, recognizes the gifts that God has given and not given to oneself, accepts what one has and does not have to work with, dedicates them to God, and then goes about the service of God and humanity as well as one can without calling undo attention to it.

The teaching and example of Jesus—and the record of history—show that for us humans, humility is often strengthened by suffering and enhanced by service. Jesus, the ultimate "suffering servant," humbled Himself through the Incarnation to suffer with and for us (see Isaiah, chapters 40-66 and Philippians 2:5-11). God in his providence gives us humbling circumstances (trials) to sharpen our sense of dependency on Him and nothingness apart from Him that we might more effectively serve Him and others. Countless numbers of people have testified to the development of a humbler spirit through the fire of personal pain. The spirit and action of service not only follow humility; they also lead to humility.

Following the Last Supper in the Upper Room, Jesus, probably in response to the argument among the disciples over their relative status, provided the lowly service of washing their feet. Subsequently he advised them, "If I then, your Lord and Teacher, have washed your feet, you also ought to wash one another's feet." For disciples then and now, the spirit of this ceremony is clear: We are to focus upon meeting the needs of others as if they were our own needs rather than to concentrate on seeking acclaim and power for ourselves.

In summary, the ultimate significance of humility is this: it means to acknowledge and embrace rather than to deny or even defy one's creatureliness with all of the implications that derive from that acceptance of one's identity.

QUESTIONS FOR REFLECTION AND DISCUSSION:

1. What is your best understanding of how a humble person thinks and acts?

2. Is pride the "greatest" sin? Can one so distinguish between categories of sin?

SUGGESTIONS FOR FURTHER READING:

1. Thomas a' Kempis, *The Imitation of Christ*

2. C. S. Lewis, "The Great Sin," Book III, chapter 8 in *Mere Christianity*

3. C. S. Lewis, *The Screwtape Letters*, Chapter 14

4. Andrew Murray, *Humility: The Beauty of Holiness*

26. GIVING

Man discovers his own wealth
when God comes to ask gifts of him.

—Rabindranath Tagore

Life is given to us, we earn it by giving it.

—Rabindranath Tagore

Love is, above all, the gift of oneself.

—Jean Anouilh

A gift, with kind countenance, is a double present.

—Thomas Fuller

Give strength, give thought, give deeds, give wealth
Give love, give tears, and give thyself
Give, give, be always giving
Who gives not is not living
The more you give, the more you live.

—Anonymous

What I kept, I lost
What I spent, I had
What I gave, I have

—Persian Proverb

Presents, I often say, endear absents.

—Charles Lamb

What with your friend you nobly share,
At least you rescue from your heir.

—*Horace*

When you feel like giving up, just keep on giving.

—*Anonymous*

This is what is hardest: to close the open hand because one loves.

—*Nietzsche*

When I was a child, and especially at Christmas, my mother would remind me that it was "more blessed to give than to receive." I thought this was a nice moral maxim designed to make people be less selfish than they otherwise would be. As an adult I began to see that this statement of Jesus was descriptive no less than prescriptive. The total benefits to a person, including character development and self-respect, are greater when giving than when receiving. Of course we all need to do both. In fact, we are capable of giving only after we have received from God and important humans, including our parents or parent-like figures. Getting and giving both become part of a natural cycle. As Billy Graham has said, "God has given us two hands—one to receive with and the other to give with. We are not cisterns made for hoarding; we are channels made for sharing."

Is it possible for the person who has not received much in life to be a giver? Certainly! Although in general a disadvantaged condition makes giving more difficult, in some ways it makes it easier to see and want to help others in similar circumstances. Deprived circumstances early in life can make personal development to be like a baseball player coming to bat as a pinch-hitter with the difficult count of no balls and two strikes: it can give one the motivation to focus with maximum concentration on the remaining opportunity. Regardless of our human background, we all have God's grace and love available, and we all have free will to choose how to respond to our circumstances. At the funeral of First Lady Eleanor Roosevelt, herself a victim of intense loss, rejection, and betrayal—especially as a girl, Presidential candidate Adlai Stevenson, speaking of her unusual sensitivity and effort for the needy, noted, "She chose to light a candle rather than to curse the darkness."

When the Bible calls for giving, it sometimes is referring to financial contributions, but usually the reference is to a general sharing of oneself and one's specific abilities and resources. Some have little money to give (note Peter's comment in Acts 3:6 - "Silver and gold I do not have, but what I do have I give you...."). In our modern affluent society with its government safety net programs (e.g. Social Security and Medicare), other things, including interpersonal caring, are often more important. We all have gifts to share. Too much emphasis is placed on certain gifts (e.g. financial resources, professional ministries, evangelism) to the exclusion of other very significant ones. The most important gifts for you are the ones that God has given to you. The highest calling for you is to be faithful in distributing them.

Where does one begin giving? Start with those situations—however small they may seem—that are in your immediate environment. In other words, "Brighten the corner where you are." How many people have sought to "save the world" but neglected their families in the process? Someday you may be able to give of yourself in some "big" project. In the meantime, do not fail in the small day-by-day situations which really are much larger in their importance than what society generally acknowledges.

The word "giving" is an action synonym for love. Some actions that are called giving are more nearly disposing (see I Corinthians 13:3) or indulging (as when one excessively gives to a child because of a greater concern for one's pleasure than for the child's good). Similarly, at times, receiving is more blessed than giving, as when one wishes to allow another to experience the joy of giving. True giving is not merely a thoughtless impulsive action; it seeks to understand what is best for the other and then provides it.

"If Christianity makes such a difference in one's life," some ask, "why is it that most of us can name many non-Christians who are more giving in nature than many Christians we know?" We err, I think, when we advertise the case for Christianity primarily on the basis of the character of the redeemed rather than on the nature of the redemption process which God gives. About the best that can be argued is that most Christians are more giving people — and hopefully increasingly so as the years pass — than they were before their conversion. Some people, of course, start the Christian life with a much lesser ability to give and love than do others, in part because of factors outside their own choosing (e.g. inborn temperament or family background). We must be charitable and patient with them. As in the parable of the talents, we all probably will be judged on the basis of what we have done with what we have been given rather than on the degree of maturity which we reach at the point of our death. "To whom much has been committed, of him they ask the more" (Luke 12:48b).

The benefits — or promised blessings — that result from being a giving person are many. They include 1) the knowledge that one is living in harmony with the providence of God, 2) enhanced happiness, and 3) an increased capacity to receive. Happiness is usually found indirectly rather than by seeking it directly. Here is one formula — in poetic form — for finding it:

How To Be Happy

Are you almost disgusted with life, little man?
　　I'll tell you a wonderful trick
That will bring you contentment, if anything can,
　　Do something for somebody, quick!

Are you awfully tired with play, little girl?
　　Wearied, discouraged, and sick—
I'll tell you the loveliest game in the world,
　　Do something for somebody, quick!
Though it rains, like the rain of the flood, little man
　　And the clouds are forbidding and thick,
You can make the sun shine in your soul, little man,
　　Do something for somebody, quick!

Though the stars are like brass overhead, little girl,
　　And the walks like a well-heated brick,
And our earthly affairs in a terrible whirl,
　　Do something for somebody, quick!

　　　　　　　　　　　　　　—Unknown Author

Inevitably, the giver is a receiver. One cannot give without receiving in return. There is a good and wise type of self-interest which seeks to get for itself all of those good things which come from giving. Some people call this finding fulfillment in life. St. Francis of Assisi, a man of the Middle Ages and all other ages, understood this concept well and expressed it in his famous prayer:

Lord, make me an instrument of Thy peace. Where there is hatred, let me sow love; where there is injury, pardon; where there is doubt, faith; where there is despair, hope; where there is darkness, light; and where there is sadness, joy.

O, Divine Master, grant that I may not so much seek to be consoled, as to console; to be understood as to understand; to be loved, as to love; for it is in giving, that we receive; it is in pardoning, that we are pardoned; and it is in dying, that we are born to eternal life. Amen.

QUESTIONS FOR REFLECTION AND DISCUSSION:

1. In your current life situation, what do you find to be the most natural and helpful ways to give?

2. How does the concept of giving relate to your choice of a career?

3. Why are some non-Christians more giving in spirit and action than are some Christians?

SUGGESTIONS FOR FURTHER READING:

1. D. J. Hall, *Stewardship of Life in the Kingdom of Death*

2. R. Titmuss, *The Gift Relationship*

3. Paul Tournier, *The Meaning of Gifts*

27. FORGIVING

There is strife between God's ways and human ways; damned by you, we are absolved by God.

—*Tertullian*

Sins cannot be undone, only forgiven.

—*Igor Stravinsky*

What power has love but forgiveness?
In other words,
by its intervention
What has been done
can be undone.
What good is it otherwise?

—*William Carlos Williams*

...be kind to one another, tenderhearted, forgiving one another, just as God in Christ also forgave you.

—*Ephesians 4:32*

Teach me to feel another's woe,
To hide the fault I see;
That mercy I to others show,
That mercy show to me.

—*Alexander Pope*

Love is an act of endless forgiveness, a tender look which becomes a habit.

—*Peter Ustinov*

Endeavor to be patient in bearing with the infirmities of others; for that thyself also hast many failings which must be borne with by others; if thou canst not make thyself such an one as thou wouldest, how canst thou expect to have another in all things to thy liking?
—Thomas a' Kempis

There is a hard law...that when a deep injury is done to us, we never recover until we forgive.

—Alan Paton
(as quoted in Johann Christoph Arnold,
Seventy Times Seven, p. 31)

Forgiveness sees more than evil, toleration sees less.
—Peter Kreeft

Although generally we want forgiveness for ourselves, especially when we know that we have been very bad in our actions, we often are reluctant to give it to others, especially when they have committed—or we believe that they have committed—some great evil toward us or those close to us. Sometimes we become angry when we perceive that others are easily forgiven for being less faithful in a task than we have been (e.g. the elder brother in the Parable of the Prodigal Son, Luke 15:25 ff.), or equally or more greatly rewarded for doing less work than we have done (the day-long laborers in the Parable of the Workers in the Vineyard, Matthew 20:1-16). Often we are pleased when others do not meet—or we think that they do not meet—the terms for divine forgiveness because it gives us a feeling of being especially favored of God (the ultimate extension of the practice of sibling rivalry). Forgiving one's neighbor may be the least popular of the Christian virtues. Jesus gives it a primary emphasis in His teaching because it is both extremely difficult and vitally important.

There is a close correlation in the Scriptures—especially in the Gospels—between God's forgiveness of a person and that person's forgiveness of others. I understand that the Hebrew and Greek languages use the same words for human forgiveness as for divine forgiveness. In the model prayer of our Savior (Matthew 6:9-13), He told us to ask for forgiveness of our sins in the same way that we forgive others of their sins. When He completed that prayer, He immediately repeated —with enhanced emphasis—the forgiveness provision, as if to say that such an attitude toward others was of extraordinary importance.

Forgiving our neighbors is one of the most important applications of another primary principle of our Savior, namely loving our neighbors as ourselves. If we want the best for our neighbors, we want them to receive forgiveness. If we do not want forgiveness for our neighbors, it suggests that we do not want it for ourselves, or at least do not feel that we have received it. It may well be a truism that we love and forgive our neighbors as much as we allow God's love and forgiveness to come through to us. In other words, the principle of loving and forgiving your neighbor as yourself may well be descriptive as well as prescriptive.

So, if forgiving our neighbors of their real and even perceived wrongs against us is so important, how do we develop an increased capacity to forgive? Here are some practical suggestions:

1. Reflect upon how God loves the offending person with a love as passionate and as great as it is for any person who has ever lived.
2. Reflect honestly upon your own flaws and how much you need the forgivingness of others as well as of God.
3. Realize that when others commit a serious wrong against you, this provides an exceptional opportunity for you to bring grace to them—and yourself—by responding in a loving, caring, forgiving, and ultimately redemptive manner. Such is basic Christian peacemaking.

4. Realize that on most of the occasions when others wrong you, your behavior and/or attitude toward them has been less than perfect. If, say, you have been 5% and the other person 95% of the total offense, then your apologizing for the 5% can be very productive. You make it easy and natural for the other person to at least begin to confess. In other words, you may bring grace to the other person as well as to yourself.

5. Meditate honestly on the great harm that you bring to yourself when you refuse to forgive. For many, the desire not to forgive becomes the consuming passion of their lives; they would rather go through the pain of an ugly, costly, damaging divorce, suffer a major illness, or even die (some suicides have revenge as the primary motive) than forgive. Perhaps the most graphic verbal expression of the refusal to love and forgive is the curse that calls upon God to condemn another person. But the curse inherently calls for self-condemnation also; few who utter it, consciously realize this.

6. Fully understand how, as a free moral agent, you possess the power of choice. As we do with sin in general, when we practice unforgiveness, we tend to blame others for our actions. "He made me do it" is the time-worn excuse for returning evil for evil, as if the actions of others determine our actions. Victor Frankl in his classic study of the Nazi Concentration Camp system, *Man's Search for Meaning*, observed that the SS guards could take everything from the prisoners except the ability to choose how they would respond to what was being done to them.

Generally, when God in Christ asks us to work at developing spiritual attitudes and behaviors, it is to become more fully like God in whose image we are created. Peter asked Jesus how often he should forgive a person who had sinned against him, and then offered what he understandably considered a generous answer of "up to seven times." Jesus responded with "...not..up to seven times, but up to seventy times seven," an answer more poetic than mathematical, and generally interpreted to mean infinity. If God wants us to forgive others without limit, can we infer that this is the way that God forgives us? If so, how do we interpret the difficult Biblical discussion of "the unpardonable sin" and the general assumption among Christians that a human cannot receive divine forgiveness after death?

When interpreting a difficult and controversial Biblical passage, a basic principle is to seek to understand the general emphasis of the Bible on the subject. Certainly the Bible as a whole proclaims—at least for this life—the unlimited mercy and forgiveness of God which can be appropriated by anyone who will receive it. Another basic principle of interpretation is to find the meaning of a passage in light of its immediate context. The controversial part of the general passage on the unforgivable sin ("He who blasphemes against the Holy Spirit never has forgiveness," Mark 3:29) is best interpreted in light of the statement of the preceding verse that "all sins will be forgiven the sons of man." The most satisfactory general conclusions is that no specific sin is unforgivable, but that the fundamental sin of rejecting God's offer of mercy cannot be forgiven (as long as an individual continues in that mind set) because of the countervailing freedom of choice given to each individual.

Does the unlimited offer of forgiveness in this lifetime continue beyond time? The first answer is that our finite minds do not know. From Scripture one can reasonably infer an answer either way. The second answer is that it would be the height of folly for an individual to presume that he or she could wait until the next life to seek God (for one thing, it may not be true, and secondly, even if it were true, anyone who thought that there was a real advantage in waiting does not understand the fundamental nature of sin, grace, and God.) The third answer is that it would not be surprising at all if it were true, given what we do know about God's universal love and compassion. Most of the very saintly souls that I know hope that it is true that there are indefinite opportunities for all to seek God's grace, but equally sincere and devout Christians disagree on whether they think that it is possible. For example, C. S. Lewis believes it not to be true, while his mentor, George MacDonald, views God's love as so powerful that not only may souls seek and receive it after death but eventually all will tire of their folly and come to their maker in mercy.

QUESTIONS FOR REFLECTION AND DISCUSSION:

1. Is it possible to forgive someone before he or she commits a specific evil toward you? How much is forgiveness a general attitude toward other people and how much is it a response to a given evil situation?

2. Is forgiving your neighbors for the evil that they commit against you more important for them or for you?

SUGGESTIONS FOR FURTHER READING:

1. John Christoph Arnold, *Why Forgive?*

2. David Augsburger, *Forgiveness*

3. Robert D. Enright and Joanna North, eds., *Exploring Forgiveness*

4. Michael Phillips, *Universal Reconciliation*

5. Lewis Smedes, *Forgive and Forget: Healing the Hurts We Don't Deserve*

6. Simon Wiesenthal, *The Sunflower: On the Possibilities and Limits of Forgiveness*

28. LONG-RANGE THINKING

So teach us to number our days, that we may gain a heart of wisdom.

—Psalm 90:12

Or sells eternity to get a toy.

—William Shakespeare

Eternity for bubbles proves at last a senseless bargain.

—William Cowper

I would rather worry without need than live without heed.

—Beaumarchais

Better be wise by the misfortunes of others than by your own.

—Aesop

The first idea that the child must acquire, in order to be actively disciplined, is that of the difference between good and evil, and the task of the educator lies in seeing that the child does not confound good with immobility, and evil with activity.

—Maria Montessori

Prudence means practical common sense, taking the trouble to think out what you are doing and what is likely to come from it. [God] wants a child's heart, but a grown-up's head.

—C. S. Lewis

Judgment is not upon all occasions required, but discretion always is.

—*Lord Chesterfield*

...common sense has availed many a man more than the seven arts, however liberal they may be.

—*Baltasar Gracian*

One chief source of poverty is the inability to think in the long term.

—*Anonymous*

So much of success or failure in life is determined by how well one establishes well-thought out values, goals, habits, and disciplines from early in life. These include learning from the mistakes of others, making choices on the basis of inner direction rather than peer pressure, developing the ability to see the long-term consequences of abusing one's body and mind, pursuing maximum educational opportunities early in life, establishing early and life-long habits of saving and investing, and living life as preparation for eternity.

Young people do well to regularly talk on a deep level with mature adults, including those who were not mature earlier in life. As an adolescent experiment in a combination of curiosity, witness, and entertainment, I queried adult smokers—in a period when smoking was more socially acceptable than it is now—as to whether they would advise a young person to start smoking. Only one response was even neutral ("Make up your own mind"); the rest advised against beginning the habit. Few things are more important for parents to seek to give their children than a sense of self-worth that makes it easier to resist the counterproductive behaviors that result from the intense peer pressure influences of the teenage years. In the achievement of this dignity there is no substitute for seeing how much one is loved by God both directly and also through one's own parents. Seeing life as a gracious gift, not only to receive but also to share, is a prime incentive to preparation for a life of service and the early acquisition of the training necessary for fulfilling one's calling.

An inadequate sense of self-worth often leads to efforts to feel fulfilled and approved by following the behavioral patterns of sometimes carelessly chosen social groups with the result often being personally destructive behaviors. Lack of self-worth is closely associated with lack of hope in the future. It is difficult to practice delayed gratification or to avoid long-range painful consequences when one has no vision beyond the pleasure of the evening. Many of our institutions of popular culture—especially cinema and television—contribute to this sense of behavioral myopia by portraying the short-term pleasures but not the long-term pains of undisciplined sexual practice and alcohol use. Society has recently become increasingly honest about the pleasure/pain relationship of tobacco use.

Sometimes a person chooses to engage in self-destructive behavior in an effort to alleviate a sense of guilt. The guilt may be real or false, and the effort at self-punishment may be conscious or subconscious. I once worked with a brilliant colleague who, after behaving counter-productively to a degree that he failed to receive a contract renewal offer, then proceeded to relax and make some very valuable contributions to the institution. Unfortunately, sensitive youth can sometimes receive an exaggerated sense of guilt from religious institutions which do not adequately balance their emphasis upon the fear of God with what should be the ultimate recognition of and focus on the grace and love of God. The pioneer American psychiatrist, Carl Menninger, wrote a classic study, *Man Against Himself*, describing the variety of ways—ranging form nail-biting to suicide—that people practice self-destructive behavior.

One of the major factors distinguishing the affluent from the impoverished in society is that the former have the ability and the discipline to save and invest wisely part of their income. Often, the affluent had the opportunity and discipline early in life to acquire enough education to enter a career that provided a level of income that made it not difficult to save. Saving is stewardship. One's attitude toward wealth and what one does with that wealth are prime tests of character. Wise spending, especially that which includes enlightened giving, is often more difficult than is wise saving.

The ultimate way of practicing long-range thinking is to view life not as an end in itself but as preparation for eternity. Eternity, in the larger sense, of course exists now as does its ultimate purpose — never-ending, loving, joyous fellowship with one's Maker. This relationship is the Pearl of Great Price. Valuing it above all else is both the best long-range thinking and the best short-range thinking.

The following homespun verse illustrates well the importance of each society developing structures which make it easy rather than difficult for its youth to make enlightened and constructive choices with positive consequences for both themselves and the larger community.

A Fence or an Ambulance

Twas a dangerous cliff, as they freely confessed,
Though to walk near its crest was so pleasant;
But over its terrible edge there had slipped
A duke and full many a peasant.
So the people said something would have to be done,
But their projects did not all tally;
Some said, "Put a fence around the edge of the cliff,"
Some, "An ambulance down in the valley."

But the cry for the ambulance carried the day,
For it spread through the neighboring city;
A fence may be useful or not, it is true,
But each heart became brimful of pity
For those who slipped over the dangerous cliff;
And the dwellers in highway and alley
Gave pounds or gave pence, not to put up a fence,
But an ambulance down in the valley.

"For the cliff is all right, if you're careful," they said,
"And if, folks even slip and are dropping,
It isn't the slipping that hurts them so much,
As the shock down below when they're stopping."
So day after day, as these mishaps occurred,
Quick forth would these rescuers sally
To pick up the victims who fell off the cliff,
With their ambulance down in the valley.

Then an old sage remarked: "It's a marvel to me
That people give far more attention
To repairing results than to stopping the cause,
When they'd much better aim at prevention.
Let us stop at its source all this mischief," cried he
"Come, neighbors and friends, let us rally;
If the cliff we will fence we might almost dispense
With an ambulance down in the valley."

"Oh, he's a fanatic," the others rejoined,
"Dispense with the ambulance? Never!
He'd dispense with all charities, too, if he could;
No! No! We'll support them forever.
Aren't we picking up folks just as fast as they fall?
And shall this man dictate to us? Shall he?

Why should people of sense stop to put up a fence,
While the ambulance works in the valley?"

But a sensible few, who are practical too,
Will not bear with such nonsense much longer;
They believe that prevention is better than cure,
And their party will soon be the stronger.
Encourage them then, with your purse, voice and pen,
And while other philanthropists dally,
They will scorn all pretense and put up a stout fence
On the cliff that hangs over the valley.

Better guide well the young than reclaim them when old,
For the voice of true wisdom is calling,
"To rescue the fallen is good, but 'tis best
To prevent other people from falling."
Better close up the source of temptation and crime
Than deliver from dungeon or galley;
Better put a strong fence round the top of the cliff
Than an ambulance down in the valley.

— Joseph Malins

QUESTIONS FOR REFLECTION AND DISCUSSION:

1. Long-time Christian college administrator, Milo Rediger, had an oft-repeated talk entitled, "As Now, So Then," which emphasized that we tend to repeat the habits and patterns that we develop in our pre-adult years. Do you have certain habits that you would not like to have in ten or twenty years? Do you not have certain practices that you would like to possess in later years? How soon do you wish to change your life accordingly?

2. Has "eternity" already begun for you?

SUGGESTIONS FOR FURTHER READING:

1. Daniel Goleman, *Emotional Intelligence*

2. Carl Menninger, *Man Against Himself*

3. The Book of Proverbs

29. AGING

Every stage of human life, except the last, is marked out by certain and defined limits: old age alone has no precise and determinate boundary.

—Cicero

For a younger person it is almost a sin—and certainly a danger—to be too much occupied with himself; but for the aging person it is a duty and a necessity to give serious attention to himself. After having lavished its light upon the world, the sun withdraws its rays in order to illumine itself.

—Carl Jung

Age is opportunity no less
Than youth itself, though in another dress,
And as the evening twilight fades away
The sky is filled with stars, invisible by day.

—Henry Wadsworth Longfellow

Old men are always young enough to learn, with profit.

—Aeschylus

Old age deprives the intelligent man only of qualities useless to wisdom.

—Joseph Joubert

The key to success in old age seems to me to be in the abandonment of the will to power. This is more difficult, the more powerful one has been in active life.

—Paul Tournier

For the Christian retirement is liberation for service.

—*Elton Trueblood*

Age in a virtuous person, of either sex, carries in it an authority which makes it preferable to all the pleasures of youth.

—*Richard Steele*

If, as young people, you despise the old, you are preparing your-selves to be despised when you are old.

—*Paul Tournier*

When grace is joined with wrinkles, it is adorable. There is an unspeakable dawn in happy old age.

—*Victor Hugo*

Grow old along with me!
The best is yet to be,
The last of life, for which the first was made:
Our times are in His hand
Who saith "A whole I planned,
Youth shows but half; trust God:
See all nor be afraid!"

—*Robert Browning*

The two great transitions in life are from childhood to adulthood and from adulthood to old age. The senior period is a time for self-development as much and in some ways more than are the earlier periods. Perhaps physical decline is designed to spur deepened spiritual and psychological growth at the end of life. Ideally, age should produce wisdom, increased poise, humble self-confidence, a more realistic self-appraisal, and a reduced level of anxiety.

Everyone ages differently. Many seem to enter old age gradually, some appear to do so suddenly, while most experience elements of both gradualness and suddenness in moving into the last major stage of life. Jolts of sudden transition can come with movement from full-time employment to complete retirement from traditional work, the unexpected death of or late divorce from a spouse, the movement out of the home of the last child, the movement from the home and geographic region of long-time residency, or the experience of a major illness or injury. Most prefer gradual aging and with it the ability to adapt constructively and continuously to the changing circumstances.

Among the principles which characterize the lives of those who experience aging in ways most fruitful for themselves and others are the following:

1. Accept the inevitable but retain choice over the controllable. Children leave home. Physical decline sets in and limits our ability to perform traditional work and other activity. Death comes to us all. To rebel against aging and to deny the reality of approaching death is futile and even counterproductive. To live healthily so as to lengthen life is wise, but to seek artificially to delay aging (e.g. extreme cosmetic surgery) because of a fear to proceed to the next stage of God's timetable is a malady. "For everything there is a season" the wise man tells us. Those who follow his advice enjoy fully the delights of each life phase and then leave it with grace for the adventure of the next one. For the person who thinks "Christianly," the new experiences never end. When in his late 90s, my father advised the students in his retirement-home Bible classes to "think transition, not terminal." And well we all should, for as Paul in I Corinthians 2:9 describes the stage beyond all earthly stages:

> Eye has not seen, nor ear heard,
> Nor have entered into the heart of man
> The things which God has
> Prepared for those who love Him.

Natural stages are one thing; artificial ones are quite another issue. A person should not adopt or abandon a given activity or lifestyle merely because social convention suggests that "this is what people do at your age." Most notably, the greater flexibility which seniors have acquired during the last generation in determining the rate and timing of their movement toward retirement is a notable achievement which will be discussed more fully later in this chapter.

2. Use the increased discretionary time to meditate deeply on the meaning of life and death. More important than what one does in the senior years is what one is becoming. This maturing process, of course, usually begins in the earlier periods, but the greatness of the more leisurely pace of the advanced years is that it provides increased time for reflection. Of course the increasingly imminent reality of death provides greater motivation for serious thinking.

3. Change the mental focus increasingly away from work to leisure, away from getting to giving, and away from controlling to counseling. Throughout the adult period, the average person concentrates largely on career and/or child raising. These roles call for specialization which is good and in some ways even necessary, but they are also restricting. In adulthood, society overemphasizes the importance of work vis-a-vis that of leisure; this partly explains why some people, in reaction, shun all work opportunities in retirement. But the ideal in all periods beyond early childhood is an optimum balance of work and play. Work in retirement often takes new forms; we have greater control over the type and amount of work and sometimes rename it service or volunteerism. Seniors can and

often should spend more time in leisure than they did in adulthood; however, to be ennobling, it should be leisure that recreates the body and spirit, expands the mind, and even helps and encourages other people. Indeed the development of interpersonal relationships with people of all types is one of the most essential activities for seniors. It combats loneliness and depression, two of the greatest problems of old age; it is one of the most natural ways to give to others, especially other seniors and one's own grandchildren and great grandchildren.

The senior years, then, are the richest when one concentrates on giving to others in helpful ways and sharing one's accumulated knowledge and wisdom, especially as sought by the younger generation. Completion of child-rearing and retirement from the traditional work environment should reduce the need to control and order other people. Hopefully one increasingly accepts the natural senior roles of sharer of resources, empathetic listener, dispenser of wisdom, role model, enjoyer of God's world, and enthusiastic anticipator of God's future order.

Let us now return to the specific subject of retirement. While old age is nearly as old as life itself, the retirement from traditional work of a large majority of the senior population is a recent phenomenon, originating only in the twentieth century. During the agricultural era, people worked on their farms to the very end, slowing down in physical labor but compensating with their knowledge and experience. Furthermore, life expectancy was lower, and not many survived to advanced years. But in the late nineteenth century, America grew from the fourth largest to the largest industrial power in the world. Farm boys and Eastern European immigrants alike moved to the large, urban centers to work in the swelling manufacturing enterprises. Unlike the farms, the industries experienced alternating periods of high employment and reduced employment. Beginning with the Great Depression, the solution to the problem of unemployment was to retire with a public pension (Social

Security) the older workers with their declining physical strength and stamina (their wisdom and experience did not count for much on the assembly line). With the growing affluence in the country in general, an increasing number of businesses added a private pension system to the federal subsidy offered their workers. With such financial arrangements, few workers complained as increasingly they were required to retire at a specific age, usually 65. When Social Security began in 1935, the average American died at age 63. But with the continued improvements in health care, life expectancy had increased to 71 in 1970 and 76 near the end of the century; also the birth rate had declined noticeably. Consequently the percentage of the population over 65 had grown from 4% at the beginning of the century to 12% in the early 1990s.

Recognizing their growing political power (in addition to their increased numbers, they voted in high percentages) and learning from the example of the youthful protesters of the 1960s, the elderly organized into political groups like the "Grey Panthers" to lobby for favorable government action. Led by their congressional champion, the elderly Senator Claude Pepper of Florida, in the late twentieth century they pushed through Congress the abolishment of the traditional mandatory retirement age of 65 and the passage of the Individual Retirement Acts which aided the ability of more people to prepare for better and more reliable late-life income than that which depended so much upon the traditional Social Security system.

Even with the fiscal uncertainties of the Social Security system, the status of the senior population is better economically than it is socially and psychologically. The saying "man does not live by bread alone" applies to the aged no less than others. Here are some non-economic ways in which society in general can increase the quality of life for seniors (and subsequently for all of us):

1. Work intentionally to develop a general milieu which increasingly respects and appreciates the seniors. Condescension toward and even contempt for the old is a major problem in western culture. Such perspectives contribute more than is generally recognized to the depression, physical decline, and dementia of the aged. We tend to idolize the young and greatly value innovation, especially technical innovation; by contrast we tend to undervalue the wisdom and knowledge of the seniors and their continuing ability to contribute to society.

2. Develop systems that naturally incorporate the skills of seniors with societal needs. With the increased quantity and quality of life for seniors, they have more to give than ever before. Receiving what they can offer will enrich both them and society in general. Such systems of "part-time" work will help many seniors to find greater fulfillment and balance in their lives. Resourceful seniors find ways to contribute now; many others would become meaningfully involved with the help of a formal system. These part-time careers should match societal needs with retiree skills. For example, our children need more attention; qualified seniors could work as tutors, teachers' aids, and child-care givers. Humanitarian organizations need volunteer workers. The more society is attuned to the totality of human need and to the value of meaningful giving by seniors, the more readily will it be able to identify useful positions of service.

3. Organize educational systems that provide continued physical and mental stimulation. The active use of mind and body is no less critical for the aged than for the young people. Few would argue that the only purpose of education is preparation for full-time work and economic production. How wonderful it would be if society could develop and formally implement a concept of education that has as a primary goal human development *for all*. Currently the seniors are the only major group that is both capable of formal learning and

also not fully occupied by vocation and/or child rearing, for whom society does not provide a widespread comprehensive system of learning.

Here is a proposal that each city, county, or school district provide a regular curriculum for seniors with categories of study such as the following:

1. Exercise classes of various levels
2. Practical life skills classes especially directed to the needs of seniors (e.g. Consumer Economics; Financial Planning; Computer Literacy; Death and Dying; Cooking for Widowers; and Beginning, Maintenance, and Enhanced Driver Training)
3. Vocational Guidance (for those interested in part-time, second careers)
4. Intergenerational Communication
5. Regional Geography for Travelers
6. Hobby Classes
7. General education, "broaden-the-mind" courses such as "The Great Ideas" or "The Great Minds"
8. Philosophy and/or Religion classes that would assist in the quest for the meaning of life

Ideally the seniors themselves would provide much of the instruction.

Aging is not a concern of only the aged. Most of us 1) have aging parents, grandparents, or other close relatives or family friends; 2) believe that we benefit from interacting with, learning from, and loving people of all age groups; and 3) hope to become seniors ourselves sometime and to live those years well because of our prior preparation.

QUESTIONS FOR REFLECTION AND DISCUSSION:

1. Is the following principle equally applicable to the retirement years as to the pre-retirement years: find what for your situation is the optimum balance between meaningful work and meaningful play? Explain.

2. What do you see as the advantages and disadvantages of providing greater educational opportunities for seniors?

SUGGESTIONS FOR FURTHER READING:

1. Ronald Blythe, *The View in Winter: Reflections on Old Age*

2. Nicolas Coni, William Davison, and Stephen Webster, *Aging: The Facts*

3. R. O. Hanson, *Relationships in Old Age*

4. Jay Kesler, *Grandparenting: The Agony and the Ecstasy*

5. Tim Stafford, *As Our Years Increase*

6. Paul Tournier, *Learn to Grow Old*

INSTITUTIONS AND STRUCTURES

30. THE FELLOWSHIP
OF BELIEVERS

*...that you...may have fellowship with us; and truly our fellowship
is with the Father and with His Son Jesus Christ.*

—I John 1:3b

*...where two or three are gathered together in My name, I am in
the midst of them.*

—Matthew 18:20

*The Church is a religious home, a sanctuary for worship, a school
for religious instruction, ...[and] it gathers into relations of mutual
helpfulness people of every age and condition, ... The Church is
the most broadening and catholic organization among men, since
its vision is to the ends of the world whither the gospel is being carried, and since its citizenship is in heaven as well as in the earth.*

—Worth M. Tippy

Jesus foretold the Kingdom and it was the church that came.

—Alfred Loisy

*The greatest sin of the church is that it holds the gospel from itself
and from the world.*

—Emil Brunner

*The tragedy of [the spirit of "churchiness"]...is not difference of
opinion, which will probably be with us till the Day of Judgement,
but the outrageous folly and damnable sin of trying to regard God
as the Party Leader of a particular point of view. No denomination*

has a monopoly of God's grace, and none has an exclusive recipe for producing Christian character.

—J. B. Phillips

What a wonderful world this would be if we creatures sought more to be controlled by God and less to control others. Indeed, this desire to control is at the heart of human depravity, and if Christians in general have a better record in this respect than others, it is only a difference of degree rather than of kind. Indeed through much of church history the institutional church has displayed an embarrassing tendency to influence through intimidation and force rather than through a compelling love and an inviting grace.

—Anonymous

...the unloving fellowship is an heretical fellowship, so far as Christianity is concerned. How strange, in light of the Biblical insistence on love as the principal thing, that we have emphasized it so little in comparison with other elements.

—D. Elton Trueblood

With all its faults, the Church is the best serving institution in the world. It has many critics but no rivals in the work of human redemption.

—E. Stanley Jones

The more a church—whether Catholic, Protestant, or Orthodox—is not only called Christian but behaves in a Christian way, the more will it become open, welcoming, hospitable, truly credible; the more easily will it be to solve...church problems...; and the more will it truly give hope to men and women.

—Hans Kung

Kneeling ne'er spoiled silk stocking: quit thy state
All equal are within the church's gate.

—*George Herbert*

...religion...must limit itself strictly to the plane of supernatural
love which alone is suitable for it. If it did so it would penetrate
everywhere. The Bible says: "Wisdom penetrates everywhere on
account of its perfect purity."

—*Simone Weil*

By this all will know that you are My disciples, if you have love
for one another.

—*John 13:35*

The basis for Christian fellowship is the Incarnation and its meaning! The Christian church dates from Christ. It develops from who He was, what He said, what He did, and what He offers.

The Church of Jesus Christ exists wherever there is the intersection of the divine love and fellowship of the Holy Trinity with the human love and fellowship of a group of believers. The fellowship follows and presupposes human faith but it transcends and expands from mental consent and verbal proclamation of theological constructs to the dynamic and electric reality of ultimate love and joy. It is eternal participation in the divine banquet and the divine dance.

It is important at the outset to distinguish between what Jesus called "the Kingdom of God" and Christendom. The former is the vision, the ideal, the potential, and even the earthly realization in Christianity at its best; the later is the flawed, all too common historic record of the humanly administered organizations of those who have identified themselves as followers of Christ. Much of the criticism against Christendom is justified; however, most of the objections to Christianity are really objections to Christendom. Christendom is an organization based upon power; the Christian ideal is a fellowship based upon a common and mutual love. Of course, in practice the typical local church contains elements of both power and love. The wise church will seek to maximize divine authority and minimize human authority. The wise and humble church leader will not want and certainly will not seek, let alone demand, an unquestioning personal followership. Rather, in the Spirit of John the Baptist, he or she will ask the parishioners to "follow me no more than the extent to which I follow Christ, or better yet just seek to follow Christ as closely as you can."

How then does "following Christ" express itself in a local church? The following are some basic characteristics:

1. The members of the fellowship want to meet together regularly. Is it possible to be a Christian without going to church? Yes, of course, but it is not natural and usually not conducive to mental and spiritual health. God made us as social creatures. Christianity is a social religion as well as a personal one. We rarely function well in prolonged isolation. We want to share and celebrate that which is most important to us. We need to regularly participate in an environment of mutual encouragement.

2. This fellowship is informal and readily available as well as formal and scheduled. If we are to pray without ceasing and meditate upon the Scriptures day and night, then it will be natural for the fellowship and its external witness to be easily accessed when needed. This concept is often understood well by Sunday School classes, small groups, rescue missions, shelter houses, coffee shops, and hot-line systems. Taverns understood well the universal need for social interaction; people patronize them for psychological no less than physical reasons — and they are readily available. Churches would do well to imitate the availability of taverns, perhaps by operating a late afternoon/evening eating and gathering place whether on their premises or elsewhere. The book of Acts frequently describes the

early Christians as "breaking bread together."

3. The fellowship members celebrate in union their common discovery of the One Great Thing, namely the coming to us of the love of God in Christ. This union is so valuable that the members refuse to focus on secondary issues if doing so threatens the joy of their collective oneness with their Maker. The fellowship is creedal but the group is wary of an emphasis upon creed and structures and formal membership in a manner that unnecessarily divides, as has happened so regularly in church history. It recognizes that unity in Christ is both precious and precarious.

4. The fellowship makes it easy for its participants to hear God. It is determined that nothing interfere with this. The messenger must not get in the way of the message. The system must not obscure its reason for being. A focus on secondary issues must not dilute or divert the focus on the central reality.

5. The believers genuinely care for one another. Jesus said that "You will know them [people in general] by their fruits" (Matthew 7:16), and also that the primary way you shall know or recognize Christians is by the love that they have for one another (John 13:35). The church, with the family, is one of the best human institutions for providing growth, encouragement, correction, unconditional acceptance and affirmation. There exists a well-nigh universal need to be legitimatized and even affirmed by one's significant others in that to which one most aspires: the fellowship offers this. The believers accept each other in celebration of their general acceptance with God; they view rejection as a contradiction of their essence. Also, the fellowship doesn't reject the spiritual contributions of any of its members as they come from the gifts and spirit of God; it doesn't accept the idea, for example, that only people of one race or one sex can participate in realizing the most important thoughts or making the most important decisions.

6. This all-encompassing love extends not only inwardly to the group but also externally to the entire world. In its outreach, the group

seeks both to share the good news of God's love in Jesus and also to "give the cup of cold water in Jesus' name." One might argue that the most effective and natural way of witness is for the group to focus with utter seriousness on being a loving fellowship and then inviting visitors to experience how a gratefully redeemed group functions; then once they observe the community dynamics, they then can decide if they wish to join the believing fellowship. While preparing this essay I discovered a marvelous example of "giving the cup of cold water" directly to the external world. My wife (Becky) and I were visiting in a city in Canada where I discovered in the local telephone book a specific Christian denomination that had listings for the following organizations and services: a refugee church for Laotian immigrants, a "middle-man" distribution center for Third-World crafts, a coalition for refugee support, a Third-World aid and development organization, a local thrift shop, and an office for peace and conciliation services.

At its best, the Christian church has been the most widespread significant source for good in the world; often, however, it has fallen far short of its ideals. In one sense the latter is not surprising, for the Church has long been such an influential institution that it is understandable that the powerful—and those seeking to be—have sought to be members and leaders for a variety of wrong reasons. Each of us does well to be fully aware of this negative record even while building and maintaining our branch of the worldwide Christian fellowship by focusing primarily on 1) the person of our Savior and 2) the example of those who have most faithfully followed Him.

QUESTIONS FOR REFLECTION AND DISCUSSION:

1. What are some of the problems which result when a person has difficulty distinguishing "Christendom" from the Kingdom of God?

2. If you were to describe an ideal but workable local church, what would be its central characteristics?

SUGGESTIONS FOR FURTHER READING:

1. Avery Dulles, *Models of the Church*

2. Vernard Eller, *The Outward Bound*

3. Hans Kung, *The Church*

4. Leslie Newbigen, *The Household of God*

5. J. B. Phillips, "God in a Box," pp. 36-39, in *Your God Is Too Small*

31. PURITY AND UNITY
IN THE CHURCH

Whoever...does not abide in the doctrine of Christ does not love God."

—II John 9

teach no other doctrine [than]...the Lord Jesus Christ, our hope..., nor give heed to fables and endless genealogies, which cause disputes rather than godly edification....

—I Timothy 1:3b, 1b, 4

they continued steadfastly in the apostles' doctrine and fellowship....

—Acts 2:42a

...that they all may be one, as You, Father, are in me, and I in You; that they may be one in Us....

—John 17:21

Behold how good and how pleasant it is for brethren to dwell together in unity.

—Psalms 133:1

I plead with you brethren...that there be no divisions among you.

—I Corinthians 1:10

No kingdom has ever suffered as many civil wars as Christ's.

—Montesquieu

If instead of resting in God by faith, we rest simply in the proposition or the formula, it is small wonder that faith leads to anxious hair-splitting arguments, to controversy, to perplexity, and ultimately to hatred and division. ...we must make every effort to believe the right formulas. But we must not be so obsessed with verbal correctness that we never go beyond the words to the ineffable reality which they attempt to convey.

—Thomas Merton

Truth is a river that is always splitting up into arms that reunite. Islanded between the arms the inhabitants argue for a lifetime as to which is the main river.

—Cyril Connolly

It is always possible to bind together a considerable number of people in love, so long as there are other people left over to receive the manifestations of their aggressiveness.

—Sigmund Freud

He drew a circle that shut me out—
Heretic, rebel, a thing to flout.
But Love and I had the wit to win!
We drew a circle that took him in!

—Edwin Markham

Other sheep I have which are not of this fold; ....

—John 10:16a

Throughout church history, Christian groups have experienced inevitable tension between the desire to maintain correct belief and experience on one hand and the desire to achieve unity of spirit and organization on the other hand. Most would agree with the general solution expressed eloquently by seventeenth century Puritan minister and theologian Richard Baxter, who certainly experienced more than his share of religious controversy:

> In necessary things, unity;
> In doubtful things, liberty;
> In all things charity.

The difficulty has existed in applying this formula to specific situations. For example, few groups have agreed on the exact list of beliefs to be called "necessary." There has also been disagreement over the importance of the disagreements. Perhaps the biggest failure has been the failure to employ sufficient charity in dealing with our differences; ironically, of all the aspects of this dilemma, this is the one over which we should have the most control.

How wonderful it would be if church organizations would 1) earnestly seek to include only primary ideas in their formal doctrinal statements, or if they wish to include secondary beliefs, to clearly identify them as such in a separate section; and 2) recognize that to indiscriminately blend secondary ideas — whether in formal doctrinal statements or in ex cathedra religious and political pronouncements — with primary ones is to dilute the importance of the primary beliefs. Elton Trueblood thought it "a mark of maturity to believe fewer doctrines, but to believe them with greater intensity."

Certainly, correct doctrinal belief is foundational. For any organization to exist there has to be some commonality of belief and tradition. But so often Christian groups split over an insistence upon uniformity on secondary issues. Few tasks are more important for a Christian group than to carefully and precisely define what it believes to be central Christian doctrine and to sharply distinguish such points from whatever else it may believe and do. The former should be a precious and vital few that distinguish Christian from non-Christian and provide the basis for unity. If then the group really wishes to add a defining statement on secondary beliefs and practices, it would be well for it to begin with a declaration of the importance of Christian charity on such issues and how the "always-seeking-for-the-truth" fellowship of believers welcomes and even delights in the diversity of thought received by individual believers as the Holy Spirit works through their unique personalities producing a broad range of insights. Then, of course, the members can freely share their thoughts and learn from each other and develop together.

Correct Christian practice must correlate with correct theology. There are certain universal experiences which are meant for all Christians at all times. Jesus neatly summarized them in His statement of the two greatest commandments ("love...God with all your heart...soul... strength, and mind, and your neighbor as yourself " —Luke 10:27). Other well-known, concise statements of the universally intended Christian experience include Paul's call to practice love, joy, peace, longsuffering, kindness, goodness, faithfulness, gentleness, and self-control (Galatians 6:22-23); and the delightful little prayer of the Bishop of Chichester, asking God for assistance to "know thee more clearly, follow thee more nearly, and love thee more dearly."

To achieve the above universally-intended experiences, there are always in all times an infinite host of specific, God-ordained, individual experiences. God leads us Christians along different paths to achieve the same ultimate goal, namely, eternal fellowship with him. The means differ; the end does not. Doctors prescribe different medications or means to achieve the same goal—health, wholeness, healing. So does God.

Sometimes certain well-meaning people are very moved by how God has spoken to them and worked wonderfully in their lives, and then preach a gospel of how all should find God exactly as they did, duplicating their experience. They are like a doctor who prescribes only one medicine. Similarly, other well-meaning but less aggressive people are also moved by the specific ways that God has spoken to them and worked wonderfully in their lives, and then hearing other Christians describe how God has led them through different experiences, become doubtful or rejecting of the validity of the means through which the other persons claim to have encountered the divine fellowship. All need to remember the advice of Gameliel in Acts 5:33-39 to be slow to express judgment.

Still, while it is important to avoid the error of censorious fundamentalism, it is also important to avoid the error of relativistic liberalism. We must seek to be wise as serpents as well as harmless as doves. Whenever a Christian proclaims something that appears novel to you, ask yourself 1) Is the idea or experience in direct contradiction to clear Biblical teaching for Christians, and 2) Is the person genuinely seeking God and giving evidence of that reality by reflecting the Spirit of God (Galatians 5:16ff)? Our infinite and personal God is great in the diversity and personalness of His wondrous works. He brings to each of us that which He knows is best for us.

While some of the disunity within individual churches and among branches of Christendom stems from lack of understanding — both of the differences between primary and secondary beliefs and practices, and also of the diversity of God's grace, unfortunately some of the disunity is a result of basic sinfulness, especially the willful tendency to seek to control and dominate other people. So often, when we think that we are safeguarding true doctrine (perhaps even suggesting that God needs us to protect Him and His cause), we really are saying, "My church or preacher or family or heritage is better than your church or preacher or family or heritage," or worse yet, "I simply want my way," as opposed to "How can we best understand the mind of God?"

What a wonderful world this would be if we creatures sought more to be controlled by God and less to control others. Indeed, this desire to control is at the heart of human depravity, and if Christians in general have a better record than others in this respect, it is a difference of degree rather than of kind. Through much of its history, the institutional Christian church has displayed an embarrassing tendency to influence through intimidation and force rather than through a compelling love and an inviting grace (for one discussion of this record see E. H. Broadbent, *The Pilgrim Church*).

The Modernist-Fundamentalist conflict of the early 1900s influenced the thinking of the Christian church throughout this century, with the Liberals tending to emphasize unity at the expense of purity and the Conservatives doing just the opposite. Perhaps now we are ready to continue the best of both traditions. The barrenness of the Liberal agenda, with its de-emphasis upon the supernatural elements of the Christian faith, came to fruition in the last generation of the century with the decline in influence of the Liberal church and its institutions; meanwhile the Conservatives or Evangelicals increasingly provided the major spiritual impetus in American Protestantism. There are hopeful signs that in the twenty-first century the Evangelicals will not only continue to lead the spiritual renewal movement, but, from their solid base in historical orthodoxy, could also head the ecumenical movement of the future, with the new ecumenicity being not a passion for togetherness in and of itself but rather a unity of truth and love stemming directly from the life, teaching and Resurrection of the Incarnate One. This combination of orthodoxy, evangelicalism, and ecumenicity has long been promoted by such twentieth century voices as E. Stanley Jones, John R. Mott, G.W. Bromiley, Carl Henry and Donald Bloesch, and it has been realized most widely through the Charismatic Movement, which more than any other recent development has brought together in spirit nearly all types of Protestant, Roman Catholic, and Eastern Orthodox believers.

This desired spirit of unity among Christians also must extend as much as possible to all of God's human creatures. The bases for the Christian identifying with all other people include the following Biblical concepts: 1) God created all; 2) God created all in His image; 3) God loves all supremely; 4) Christ died for all individually; 5) all are actual or potential spiritual children of God; and 6) we are admonished to love all people (all of our neighbors) as ourselves. There exists an even greater foundation for fellowship between the Christian and the non-Christian who is sincerely seeking God. The ultimate basis for human fellowship, of course, exists between those who hold in common, as their most prized possession, their relationship with Christ, and who also participate individually and together in the eternal fellowship with the Divine Trinity.

QUESTIONS FOR REFLECTION AND DISCUSSION:

1. What are the risks/dangers when a group emphasizes doctrinal purity over spiritual unity? Similarly, what are the risks/dangers when a group emphasizes love and unity over theological purity?

2. If the Modernist-Fundamentalist conflict defined Christian thinking and polity through much of the twentieth century, what do you think may be the new prominent issues of the twenty-first century?

SUGGESTIONS FOR FURTHER READING:

1. William J. Abraham, *The Coming Great Revival: Recovering the Full Evangelical Tradition*

2. Donald Bloesch, *The Future of Evangelical Christianity: A Call for Unity Amid Diversity*

3. E.H. Broadbent, *The Pilgrim Church*

4. Gary Dorrien, *The Remaking of Evangelical Theology*

5. Carl Henry, *The Uneasy Conscience of Modern Fundamentalism*

6. George MacDonald, *The Lady's Confession* (ed. Michael R. Phillips)

7. J. Gresham Machen, *Christianity and Liberalism*

8. Alister McGrath, *A Passion for Truth: The Intellectual Coherence of Evangelicalism*

9. H. Richard Niebuhr, *The Social Sources of Denominationalism*

10. E. Pickering, *Biblical Separation: The Struggle for a Pure Church*

32. CHRISTIAN MUSIC

Sing aloud to God our strength;
Make a joyful shout to the God of Jacob.

It is good to give thanks to the Lord.
And to sing praises to Your name, O Most High;
To declare Your loving kindness in the morning,
And Your faithfulness every night.

Praise Him with the sound of the trumpet;
Praise Him with the lute and harp!
Praise Him with the timbrel and dance;
Praise Him with stringed instruments and flutes!
Praise Him with loud cymbals;
Praise Him with high sounding cymbals!
Let everything that has breath praise the Lord.

> *—Psalms 81:1, 92:1-2; 150:3-6a;*
> *Selections from the Order of Worship in the*
> *Daily Services of the Old Testament Temple.*

Music, words excluded, should not be judged as inherently right or wrong, but rather should be judged as right or wrong, acceptable or unacceptable, for what it means to those who use it.

> *—Irene Lindeman*

The real ecumenical crisis today is not between Catholics and Protestants but between traditional and experimental forms of church life.

> *—Harvey Cox*

From time immemorial music has been one important means by which humans have worshiped the Divine. In the Christian tradition, the exact forms of this musical worship have shown both continuity and evolution through different eras and cultures, with difficulty and conflict typically accompanying the periods of major change.

During the late twentieth century, few issues in Christianity have caused as much controversy and accommodation as has Christian music. The innovations of this period—led and embraced primarily by people born after 1950—have included guitars and drums, rock beats and loud volume, evangelical youth concerts, amplification, softer praise music for congregational singing, singing "off the wall" (words projected on a large screen) or by rote, and reduced emphasis upon gospel songs, hymns, and anthems.

It is helpful to place the conflict over these innovations in a larger historical context. While to many this late twentieth-century struggle may have appeared unique because few then alive remembered the last such major era of change in worship music (the Gospel Hymns of the Moody-Sankey revival period, c. 1875), nevertheless, it is true that controversy typically has been the norm rather than the exception during such musical revolutions. For example:

1. The European religious authorities violently opposed the idea of congregational singing introduced by the Moravians in the fifteenth century.
2. When Louis Bourgeois, chief musician of Geneva, Switzerland, and composer of the "Doxology," introduced part-singing in church, he was expelled from the city.
3. English and new-world Puritans alike debated with intensity and over many years whether any changes in the traditional practice of psalm singing, including those introduced by Isaac Watts, could be tolerated.

4. The Anglican Church never really accepted hymn-singing as introduced by Charles Wesley and the Methodists until forced to do so by popular pressure in the early nineteenth century.

We are rightfully embarrassed by the narrowness exhibited in such earlier conflicts over musical forms. As has been the case in the contemporary twentieth-century controversy, the primary criticisms of the traditionalists were not against poor theology, oversentimentalism, or excessive subjectivity in the lyrics, but rather against the music or tunes themselves. Music, per se, of course, like language or technology, is morally neutral. Why then the intense conflicts on this issue? Here are three possible reasons:

1. Spiritually serious people are concerned with rightness in religion, including an avoidance of "worldliness." Often throughout history new church music has involved forms which were adopted from previously existing secular music (e.g. folk, dance, popular, and rock). For a member of the "older" generation, it can be very difficult to hear Christian lyrics tied to musical forms that they had always associated with non- or even anti-spiritual thinking. The effect is psychological dissonance. Gradually, they may be assured by observing the spiritual earnestness of the "younger" generation as they use the new music for edification and evangelism.

2. For nearly all people, music provides an important emotional bond to their formative period. The nostalgic effect is reassuring, providing a sense of rootedness. Many adults do not object to the music of the youth as much as to the idea that the new forms are not to be added to the old forms but rather to replace them. The wisest churches find ways to incorporate multiple styles into their worship services and to do so in ways that promote maximum understanding and graciousness.

3. Many young people see music as a means of expressing a growing sense of independence, and when this independence means

the movement toward a personalized seeking of God for oneself, it is not only acceptable but of ultimate importance. Sometimes the introduction of new forms by youth and others is designed to stimulate spiritual renewal as much as a separate identity for the youth. Over time, what had been novel can become formalized and routine and then a new style emerges to break the formality. Ultimately, of course, what is important for us all is the continuous renewal of spirituality whether through new means or old.

In summary, the ideal for a Christian is to experience, understand and even enjoy a broad range of worship music, especially that which is artistically the most exquisite, to readily see and appreciate the genuine spirit of worship which operates through a broad variety of musical styles, and then to employ for oneself primarily those forms which at any given time most readily facilitate communion with the Almighty.

QUESTIONS FOR REFLECTION AND DISCUSSION:

1. Is it good for each new generation to work out personally, with its God-given creativity, the forms by which it can best worship God? If so, what then are the valid bases for critique by the older generation?

2. If a given church serves a full range of age groups with diverse music-style preferences, how can it best both be sensitive to honoring the preferences of the different groups and also encourage the different groups to develop an appreciation for multiple styles?

SUGGESTIONS FOR FURTHER READING:

1. F. Blume, *Protestant Church Music: A History*

2. L. Ellinwood, *The History of American Church Music*

3. K. G. Fellerer, *The History of Catholic Church Music*

4. E. H. Fellowes, *English Cathedral Music from Edward VI to Edward VII*

5. Donald Hustad, *Jubilate! Church Music in the Evangelical Tradition*

6. D. B. Pass, *Music and the Church: A Theology of Church Music*

7. E. Routley, *The Church and Music*

8. Sandra Sizer, *Gospel Hymns and Social Religion*

33. MARRIAGE

To have and to hold from this day forward, for better for worse, for richer for poorer, in sickness and in health, to love, to cherish, and to obey, 'til death us do part.

> —*The Church of England*
> *Book of Common Prayer*

The Christian religion, by confining marriage to pairs, and rendering the relation indissolvable, has by these two things done more toward the peace, happiness, settlement, and civilization of the world, than by any other part in this whole scheme of divine wisdom.

> —*Edmund Burke*

Romantic love is an illusion. Most of us discover this truth at the end of a love affair or else when the sweet emotions of love lead us into marriage and then turn down their flames.

> —*Thomas Moore*

I...chose my wife, as she did her wedding gown, not for a fine glossy surface, but such qualities as would wear well.

> —*Oliver Goldsmith*

An ideal wife is any woman who has an ideal husband.

> —*Booth Tarkington*

Marriage with peace is this world's paradise; with strife, this life's purgatory.

> —*Politeuphuia*

It doesn't much signify whom one marries, for one is sure to find next morning that it was someone else.

—Samuel Rogers

Keep your eyes wide open before marriage, half shut afterwards.

—Benjamin Franklin

Where there's marriage without love, there will be love without marriage.

—Benjamin Franklin

A relationship is as good as its communication is clear.
A marriage is as strong as its communication is honest.
A family is as healthy as its communication is open.

—David Augsburger

To fail to confront [one's spouse] when confrontation is required for the nurture of spiritual growth represents a failure to love equally as does thoughtless criticism or condemnation and other forms of deprivation of caring....

—M. Scott Peck

Why do not words and kiss, and solemn pledge,
And nature that is kind in woman's breast,
And reason that in man is wise and good,
And fear of Him who is a righteous Judge,—
Why do not these prevail for human life,
To keep two hearts together, that began
Their springtime with one love.

—William Wordsworth

It takes patience to appreciate domestic bliss;
Volatile spirits prefer unhappiness.

—George Santayana

Love is something far more than desire for sexual intercourse; it
is the principal means of escape from the loneliness which afflicts
most men and women throughout the greater part of their lives.

—Bertrand Russell

Life has taught us that love does not consist in gazing at each other
but in looking outward together in the same direction.

—Saint-Exupéry

The Christian idea of marriage is the commitment of one man and one woman to the spiritual, psychological, and physical development of both partners individually and in union. The relationship is exclusive or monogamous—" 'til death us do part." It usually involves, especially at the onset, romantic feelings, but it is not dependent upon them, for love at its essence is a commitment rather than a feeling. It is what you do—givingly do—more than what you feel.

Marriage can and is meant to be one of life's most rewarding and fulfilling experiences, but a good marriage does not happen easily or even naturally. It involves a focused will to make the relationship work. This requires time, clear commitment, self-sacrifice, forgiveness, and much prayer. When disagreements come into your marriage, as they do for us all, look at them as occasions for growth both personally and as a couple. Often when a partner hurts the other, it is because he or she is responding to some hurt inside himself or herself. Why not hold hands and each look to the ultimate healer for help in healing each other. Why else do we marry one another if not for this?

In most wedding ceremonies, the rings are the most obvious symbols. The ring is circular, symbolic of an unending state, of eternity, if you will. In this temporal realm called time, this emblem symbolizes the ideal of the security of the marriage relationship, of its " 'til death do us part" promise of love and faithfulness. This pledge of constancy is not always easy to keep, but then Christian marriage possesses a special resource as symbolized by another geometric figure, namely the triangle, in which the husband and wife join together with their Creator in a three-way relationship which marshals all of the best resources of the universe for the development of the maturity of the marriage relationship.

The wedding celebration itself is also a symbol (see Revelation 19), indeed the ultimate, climactic New Testament symbol of God's passionate love for us humans, the crowning act of His creation. In the words of Robert Farrar Capon, "the grandest—and the final—imagery the Bible uses for ...[God's] love is precisely that of lover and beloved, bridegroom and bride. It is the marriage of Christ and the church which is the last act of the long love affair between God and creation." Thus in human marriage also, passion is natural and normal, even if not central, as a part of a loving, giving commitment to the permanent welfare of the union.

To say that the two are one does not mean that one or both lose their identity—that would be absorption rather than unity. Rather it is that each think of the good of the other and of the union as well as the good of oneself in this most focused application of the command of our Savior to love your neighbor as yourself. It is like you for me and I for you: us together. The good of the one is the good of the other.

On the question of decision-making in the family, Christians disagree on whether the Bible emphasizes that the husband should be the head or whether the couple should interact in a more egalitarian manner.

My observation in families that work well is that 1) practice is often more moderate than theory, and 2) the exact model followed is less important than whether each partner is lovingly and sacrificially committed to the welfare of the other.

The premature end of a marriage is always a tragedy. It is, in the words of C. S. Lewis, "something like cutting up a living body." Functionally a marriage ends, whether temporarily or permanently, by abandonment, severe abuse, a break from monogamy, and/or legal separation or divorce. Almost always the underlying cause is a lack of original or continuing commitment. Most divorces are accepted too easily. Reconciliation is usually possible, even if not easily accomplished. Forgiveness, by God's grace, is always possible.

QUESTIONS FOR REFLECTION AND DISCUSSION:

1. If giving, clear and regular communication, loving and caring confrontation, wanting the best for the other, unending love and commitment, and passion describe both an ideal marriage and also the relationship that God seeks with each of us personally, what does this say?

2. What are the ways that society could reorder itself to reduce the incidence of divorce? What are the ways that individual couples can structure their marriage to increase the likelihood of a " 'til death do us part" marriage?

SUGGESTIONS FOR FURTHER READING:

1. Diogenes Allen, *Love: Christian Romance, Marriage, and Friendship*

2. David Augsburger, *Healing and Growth in the Passages of Marriage*

3. D. S. Bailey, *The Man-Woman Relation in Christian Thought*

34. SEXUAL UNION

The Lord God said, "It is not good that man should be alone; I will make him a helper comparable to him." ...Therefore a man shall leave his father and mother and be joined to his wife, and they shall become one flesh. ...Then God saw everything that He had made, and indeed it was very good.

—Genesis 2:18, 24, and 1:31a

God did not wince when Adam, in seeing Eve, was moved to get close to her. Male and female were created sexual to be sexual together.

—Lewis Smedes

Sexuality is the human drive toward intimate communion. Beyond the glandular impulse, the human sexual urge is always toward another person. ...The Bible describes what is true for most people; but...many persons have managed a beautifully whole existence without sexual intercourse.... Virgins can experience personal wholeness by giving themselves to other persons without physical sex. ...They capture the essence without the usual form.

—Lewis Smedes

...where the body of the beloved person is made the sole object of love, or if sexual pleasure <u>only</u> is sought without regard to the communion of a soul and mind, true love does not exist.

—Richard von Krafft-Ebing

> *Like the bee its sting, the promiscuous leave behind them in each encounter something of themselves by which they are made to suffer.*
>
> *—Cyril Connolly*

Sexual union is one of the many good gifts which God gives to his creatures. It is intended to be an integral part of the marriage union, and as such this powerful physical and emotional force not only assures the perpetuation of the human race that God loves so much but also is associated with the nurturing environment of a family unit that supports the caring development of each new generation of humans.

It is essential that parents explicitly teach their children that in Christian theology the physical universe in general and the human body, including sexuality, are inherently good. Many other forces—religious and otherwise—would deny this. Christianity has no dualistic division subordinating body to mind and the physical realm to the spiritual one. It teaches that 1) God created the physical world and then stated "behold it is very good", 2) God the incarnate one came to us in human physical form, and 3) one day our human bodies will be raised into an eternal form.

Sex is a blessing of God that is too good to waste before or outside of marriage; like other gifts of God, it is meant to be enjoyed within the divinely appointed boundaries. I know no good thing in this created universe that does not exist for our pleasure if we pursue it in the way in which God intends.

By the time young people graduate from high school they have developed a broad range of thoughts and experiences concerning human sexuality. Some have been careless and need to develop discipline; some suffer from inordinate fear and false guilt and need to find assurance; some suffer from real guilt and need to find and accept forgiveness; some need to forgive others for inadequate teaching and modeling, or even abuse; all need to seek and find maximum understanding and victory. Some sexually well-intentioned Christian youth confuse natural, God-given attraction to members of the opposite sex (It is a tragedy not to possess this!) with Jesus' statement about committing adultery in one's heart (Matthew 5:28). Rather, as stated well by John Sanford, "To look at a woman lustfully is the desire to have her only for the purpose of pleasurable gratification." For those who experience a continuing and oppressive sense of guilt for offences of the past, the need is to meditate upon and more fully appropriate the grace of God. It is important for us all to recall how much more condemning Jesus was of the sins of the Spirit than of those of the flesh, in part because we are more aware of the latter than the former and thus less likely to cover them.

Homosexuality is one of the most controversial issues in the late twentieth century both among Christians and also in society in general. An important but not common starting point for discussion on this subject is to distinguish between homosexual orientation and homosexual practice. The appropriate response to the former is pity and compassion. What a great burden to bear such an orientation must be--all the more so when added to its inherent disorientation is the pain resulting from the misunderstanding and even false assumptions and accusations of those who often should be very sympathetic helpers. One of the greatest tragedies is that the person of homosexual orientation may end up believing that to possess—for whatever reason—homosexual feelings means that one has little if any choice but to act them out in practice. Rather, the message for the Christian of homosexual orientation is that celibacy is an option. It may not be easy, but the Christian possesses the basis for Divine help in this as in all other areas. Furthermore, it is not as if the homosexual is the only type of person who needs to practice celibacy during at least a part of his or her life.

In conclusion, all persons, whatever their sexual orientation, must exercise discipline in the area of sexuality. Not to do so not only involves disobedience to God but also produces a myriad of social problems: marital and family disruptions, ill-health, strained relationships, unwanted pregnancies, abortions, single-parent families, poorly-raised children, juvenile delinquency, reduced opportunity for personal development and achieving the optimum level of education, and economic disadvantage for the individual and society. There are few areas of life where lack of discretion and control result in such dire consequences. Yet, on a happier note, there are few areas of life where the proper expression produces more human fulfillment.

QUESTIONS FOR REFLECTION AND DISCUSSION:

1. Why do so many people do so many things (either at all or at the wrong time) that are going to cause them so much trouble in so many ways? Isn't the avoidance of pain a greater priority than the experience of immediate, preliminary or counter-productive pleasure?

2. In the public discussion of the issue of homosexuality, why isn't greater attention given to the distinction between orientation and practice?

SUGGESTION FOR FURTHER READING:

1. Johann Christoph Arnold, *A Plea for Purity*

2. Letha Scanzoni, *Why Wait: A Christian View of Premarital Sex*

3. Lewis Smedes, *Mere Morality*

4. Lewis B. Smedes, *Sex for Christians*

35. THE FAMILY

...the most important part of our culture is our particular family.
                                                    —*M. Scott Peck*

Remember always that your work or ministry or position never dare keep you from your family. If you fail them, you fail your greatest responsibility— and you are a failure in life.
                                                    —*Ted Engstrom*

No matter what you've done for yourself or for humanity, if you can't look back on having given love and attention to your own family, what have you really accomplished?
                                                    —*Lee Iacocca*

The most important influence on a child is the character of its parents, rather than this or that single event.

                                                    —*Eric Fromm*

Children need models rather than critics.
                                                    — *Joseph Joubert*

It takes patience to appreciate domestic bliss; volatile spirits prefer unhappiness.
                                                    —*George Santayana*

Train up a child in the way he should go, and when he is old he will not depart from it.
                                                    —*Proverbs 22:6*

Parents lend children their experience and a vicarious memory; children endow their parents with a vicarious immortality.

—*George Santayana*

Blessed be childhood, which brings down something of heaven into the midst of our rough earthliness.

—*Henri Amiel*

Let the little children come to Me, and do not forbid them; for of such is the Kingdom of God.

—*Mark 10:14b*

Children are a poor man's riches.

—*English Proverb*

The father who raises his son to have a profession he once dreamed of, and the mother who uses her daughter as the adult companion her husband is not; the parents who urge their children into accomplishments as status symbols—all these and many more are ways of subordinating a child's authentic self to a parent's needs.

—*Gloria Steinem*

In the little world in which children have their existence, whoever brings them up, there is nothing so finely perceived and so finely felt, as injustice.

—*Charles Dickens*

The life of children, as much as that of intemperate men, is wholly governed by their desires.

—*Aristotle*

There is no end to the violations committed by children on children, quietly talking alone.

—*Elizabeth Bowen*

The family is the basic human institution for providing economic and psychological security and spiritual and intellectual nurture. No form of human organization is older or more universal. The word "family" describes primarily 1) the most immediate and primary nuclear grouping of husband, wife, and any resultant children, and 2) multi-generational groupings of kin, but also 3) extended family units of tribe, clan, ethnic groups, local community, church, denomination, or the transdenominational "family of God." Also, sometimes people talk (in spirit at least) of a nation as family, or of a family of nations (e.g. the United Nations), or of all people as a universal family of brothers and sisters (i.e. a spirit of brotherhood).

Just as God created us with an intense longing for fellowship with Himself (see chapter 2 on "Longing"), so also He created us with needs for dependable, supportive human connections. Men and women experience strong physical and emotional attraction to each other; and we have marriage. Also, people feel a need to experience companionship, security, and encouragement in personal and social development and value formation; and we have nuclear and extended families, as well as the church, the school and other social organizations.

During the past generation, intense debates have raged in America on family-related issues. Traditionalists warn that we are experiencing a sharp "decline in the family" compared with the practice of previous generations, and that we must fight a vigorous battle to retain the historic emphasis upon "family values." Progressives counter that while there is much validity to the concerns of the traditionalists, nevertheless, would-be reformers must be careful neither to generalize excessively about the past nor to confuse the norms of a given era with Biblical standards. In the practice of family, then, how did the record of earlier societies in the Judeo-Christian tradition and in Western Civilization compare with the record of both the early twentieth century and contemporary America? The answer is complex. This following brief historical analyses will focus primarily on 1) overall family organization, 2) the role of the wife and mother, and 3) the status of children.

The contemporary American family suffers from an increasing shortage of fathers due to the rising incidence of divorce (the mothers usually keep the children) and out-of-wedlock births. Further complicating the present family problems is the fact that the Western family has gradually changed from the open lineage family of the Middle Ages (family group-ings that include intergenerational kin and even community members along with specific parents and children) to the nuclear family (parents and children only) groupings of today. Therefore when parental absence occurs, the typical result is a greater crisis than if there were a larger number of adults in the family group to help raise the children.

One of the greatest achievements of Western civilization has been the improvement in the dignity of and opportunities for women. Ironically, it is these very improvements that in certain ways have led to many of the problems in the modern family. Ancient Greece was largely a man's world. Women had very little social life; men could freely express themselves sexually outside of marriage and easily obtain a divorce. The Romans held a high view of marriage until they adopted the Greek practices beginning about 200 B.C. And then Jesus came. Nothing in all of history has done more to improve the standing of and respect for women than has the teaching of Christianity.

One of the greatest stabilizing agents in all of Western civilization has been the primary nurturing role of mothers for their children. To the extent that women and women's movements fully recognize this fact and embrace this role, they are better prepared to continue to seek a fuller level of dignity and opportunity for women. If historically, mothers (and women in general) more than fathers (and men in general) have focused on helping others, then surely the proper agenda of the Women's Liberation Movement should be for women to continue to remind men as well as themselves that all are best served by seeking the good of all. Healthy families no less than healthy societies cannot exist without a deep mutual respect for and commitment to all their members.

Inherent tensions exist—especially for mothers of growing children—between the goals of the women's movement and the needs of the family. The wise woman seeks to find an optimum blend of personal fulfillment for herself with no less concern for the development of her children and other family members. This requires much energy, careful time-management, and, inevitably, self-sacrifice.

The status of children like that of women has improved historically from ancient times to the past century; however, while opportunities for women continue to increase in the twenty-first century, the lot of children has declined during the past half-century. With some exceptions, the social position of children in the ancient classical West was as low or lower than that of women. War-preoccupied Sparta raised its children as cogs in its military machine. Greek and Imperial Roman societies freely practiced child abandonment and infanticide, and the Romans increasingly neglected the children that did survive. As was His attitude toward women, the teachings of Jesus with regard to children was revolutionary, even for the Hebrews with their relatively humane child-raising practices. Jesus described the humility and trusting nature of children as exemplary for all who would enter the Kingdom of God.

Beginning with the Protestant Reformers' growing focus on individual religious conversion, through the movement toward the more affectionate, nuclear family and the growth of the public school movement—and despite the use and abuse of children in the Industrial Revolution—the general trend in Western society until the mid-twentieth century has been toward an increased valuing of, greater attention to, and an enhanced status for children. Then came 1) the movement of families from the farms, where there were plenty of chores for the children and more regular adult supervision, to the urban areas, where children were no longer an economic asset and there were greater temptations to participate in delinquent activities; 2) the increased entry of mothers into the out-of-the-home work force and the resultant growing economic independence of women; and 3) the sharply increasing abortion and divorce rates (children, of course, are victims of divorce no less then are their parents; divorce is a breakup of the entire family). The most tragic consequence of the decline of the family is the decline in the well-being of children.

Finally, let us change from a focus on the family in the past to offer some specific principles for family leaders (e.g. parents) as they seek to nurture the members of the next generation.

1. Child raising is comparable to the help which God offers all of us to mature throughout our lives. In both cases the idea is to love, instruct, discipline, enjoy, and interact in fellowship.

2. Above all else, somehow communicate to the child clearly, strongly, early and often, how exceedingly great and all-pervasive is the unconditional and personal love of God for her or him and for everyone else. This intense love of God is not dependent upon one's skills, grades, physical appeal, or popularity as so often is the case with human acceptance. Nothing is more important for the child to understand than is this intense love.

3. Make it as easy as possible for your children to desire God. This is best done by modeling, as well as one can, the character of God,

helping them to positively associate their human father and mother with the Heavenly Father. Thus, in human as well as divine relationships, unconditional love and care is the essential beginning point.

4. Provide regular religious and moral instruction. The home must be the first and foremost school in value formation. Other institutions are only secondary. When the parents offer such instruction systematically and early, it will be less difficult to introduce, when appropriate, the especially sensitive subjects such as human sexuality (see chapter 34). Such instruction in a loving, supportive environment does much to enable the children to resist the negative aspects of childhood and adolescent peer pressure influences.

5. Make it as easy as possible for your children to find wholesome friends. This will increase the likelihood that the peer pressure influence will reinforce rather than challenge the values taught in the home. The single best way to accomplish this is for the family to participate in a church which provides mature instruction at all levels and a compelling program for children and youth.

6. Recognize the real limits on what well-intentioned parents can do to assure that their children develop well. Whereas some parents do not work hard enough at parenting, others attempt to control too much or feel inappropriate responsibility. All that a parent can do is lovingly show the young one the way and then increasingly get out of the way as the youth gradually assumes enlarged responsibility for his or her own person. Excessive parental control produces either rebellion or —what sometimes is worse in the long run—restricted progress toward maturity. Another negative consequence of too much parental control for too long is that the parent may experience inappropriate guilt for the mistaken choices of the children. The fact is that, even when the parent might wish

it otherwise, children do increasingly become free moral agents; hopefully the parent aids rather than restricts them in the process. One wise formula advocated for child raising is called the "inoculation theory" whereby the child in the safe environment of the family receives both gradually increasing amounts of exposure to secular ideology and also gradually increasing degrees of control over his or her personal affairs.

7. Parents who have never fully resolved their anger at their own parents must work—with forgiveness and a realization of the perfect love of God for them being basic components in the process—to be liberated from the dark clouds of the past that continue to haunt their present. This will enable them to further develop both in their own personal maturation and also in their parenting skills.

No parents do a perfect job of raising their children just as no husband or wife does a perfect job of being a spouse. In all cases love—together with forgiveness—covers a multitude of sins. It is less harmful to err on the side of too much or too little discipline or instruction than on the side of too little love (the children usually know the difference). Many errors of action come because of lack of love. May God help us all!

QUESTIONS FOR REFLECTION AND DISCUSSION:

1. Are children more innocent or more selfish?

2. Do you know anyone who chose his or her vocation based upon
    parental wishes rather than—or even in opposition to—personal
    preference?

3. For the working mother who has children at home, what is the
    optimum balance between being at home and being in the work-
    place?

SUGGESTIONS FOR FURTHER READING:

1. R. Pierce Beaver, *American Protestant Women in World Mission:
    A History of the First Feminist Movement in North America*

2. Don Browning et al., *From Culture Wars to Common Ground:
    Religion and the American Family Debate*

3. Carl Degler, *At Odds: Women and the Family in America From
    the Revolution to the Present*

4. James C. Dobson, *Dare to Discipline*

5. James C. Dobson, *Hide and Seek*

6. E. F. Frazier, *The Negro Family in the United States*

7. Jay Kesler, *Emotionally Healthy Teenagers*

8. Jay Kesler, *Ten Mistakes Parents Make With Teenagers (And How
    to Avoid Them)*

9. Christopher Lasch, *Haven in a Heartless World: The Family Be-
    sieged*

10. Roderick Phillips, *Putting Asunder, A History of Divorce in Western
    Society*

11. John Scanzoni, *Shaping Tomorrow's Family*

12. Letha Scanzoni and Nancy Hardesty, *All We're Meant to Be: Biblical Feminism for Today*

13. John Sommerville, *The Rise and Fall of Childhood*

14. Lawrence Stone, *The Family, Sex, and Marriage in England, 1500-1800*

15. Ruth A Tucker and Walter L. Liefield, *Daughters of the Church: Women and Ministry from New Testament Times to the Present*

36. VOCATION

[God's call for you] is the intersection of your abilities and the world's needs.

—Richard Raines

Far and away the best prize that life offers is the chance to work hard at work worth doing.

—Theodore Roosevelt

We are immortal until our work is done.

—George Whitefield

Life is unbearable unless it has meaning, and the chief way in which it can have meaning is for our little effort to contribute to some larger whole.   *— D. Elton Trueblood*

I must work the works of Him who sent me while it is day; the night cometh when no man can work.

— John 9:4

In the West almost everyone agrees in proclaiming in words, in theory, the supreme value of the human person.... But in reality things are quite different. The general social atmosphere...teaches us the superior importance of work. Really, one might have expected something different...from a religious tradition so solidly founded on the gospel—the primacy of man over work, and not of work over man.

—Paul Tournier

Our minds need relaxation, and give way
Unless we mix with work a little play.

—*Moliere*

The idea of working hard and well is fundamental in the Bible and has remained so throughout most of the Christian tradition. It is a prime way of living our lives in the image of God as creators and contributors to the welfare of the world. All work is holy if it helps people and is pursued in a spirit of service to God. Note that in the creation narrative (Genesis 2), Adam receives a vocation (gardener) immediately after his creation. The general curse that followed the entrance of sin into the world (Genesis 3) did result in labor becoming much more difficult but that does not preclude the idea that work, per se, is an existential blessing rather than a curse.

Unfortunately, in this sinful world many positions of work have involved more abuse than blessing. Invariably such situations involve a violation by those in power of the command to love your neighbor as yourself. Perhaps the most severe example of this is slave bondage in which people are denied the freedom of their person to serve the economic self-interest of others.

In modern capitalistic countries, due to their regulatory legislation, the likelihood of overt, gross misuse of the workers is much less than what existed during the earlier stages of the Industrial Revolution. Still, our Western economic systems, driven largely by the profit motive, emphasize efficiency which leads to tightly controlled production processes, which in turn results in inadequate opportunities for workers to employ their creative abilities. Likely, this lack of creative participation is what was influencing the shift worker who, upon leaving a Detroit assembly plant, casually remarked to me as a young tourist, "Don't ever get a job in a place like this!" Not only professional workers and supervisors, but all workers are created in the image of God and function best when they are empowered to contribute creatively in their work environment rather than expected to exclusively perform mindless and even mind-dulling routines. The goal of our national economists and individual enterprises should be effectiveness (i.e., human development) rather than efficiency (getting the most "out of " the workers); ironically, the extent to which this happens, production no less than human happiness tends to increase. In addition to creating a constructive environment for employees, the center of enterprise should be concerned with producing constructive products for consumers. Some products, of course, are inherently abusive.

The Bible identifies some correlation between hard work and financial and spiritual prosperity. Solomon, in Proverbs, offers many maxims on labor including 19:15, 20:4, 24:30-34, the humorous 26:13-16, and the famous passage—emphasized in American churches each Mother's Day—on the "super-mom" businesswoman, 31:10-31. Paul expresses similar sentiments (e.g. Romans 12:11 and II Thessalonians 3:10). Jesus' famous parable of the talents (Matthew 25:14-30) emphasizes the rewards of employing all of one's God-given resources in faithful stewardship.

Of course, hard work is not always a good thing. Workaholics typically use it to escape facing a problem in another area of their lives and/or to pursue career and financial development even at the expense of neglecting other important things. While workaholics need protection from themselves, all workers need protection from the excessive demands of their work environments. This is the reason for humanitarian, work-related, protective legislation including wages and hours laws, worker health and safety legislation, child-labor laws, and what was perhaps the earliest worker protection law of them all—the fourth commandment. Actually the idea of a day of rest is built into nature. The practice of freedom from regular labor on one day in seven compares to the yearly rotation of seasons and the daily rotation of day and night.

Societies (e.g. France during its Revolution) and individual industries which work their population without a regular day free from the normal routine soon discover adverse effects in health and efficiency. There is a golden balance between work, recreation, rest, and spending time with family and friends. Problems result when one spends too much or too little time in any of these.

John Wesley noted another problem with working hard, namely that it often becomes a factor in loss of spirituality. Religious conversion, he observed, tended to make people work harder, which made them more prosperous, which, in turn, made them more likely to trust in their affluence more and in God less. The solution he proposed was not to work less but to give more: "Work all you can, save all you can, and give all you can." One pundit had Wesley describing in this manner the philosophy of those whom he saw as corrupted by their hard-earned wealth: "Get all you can, save all you can, and sit on the can."

Despite the risks of working hard and in spite of the difficulties in labor introduced by the fall, it continues to be true that work, in itself, is a blessing of God that gives meaning to our lives in a way that nothing else can.

QUESTIONS FOR REFLECTION AND DISCUSSION:

1. Do middle-class Protestants in their orientation toward the "Protestant work ethic" overemphasize work in proportion to other virtues such as the joy of living, the development and practice of social skills, meditation, and play?

2. Can non-creative work be made fulfilling? How?

SUGGESTIONS FOR FURTHER READING:

1. John Bernbaum and Simon Steer, *Why Work? Careers and Employment in Biblical Perspective*

2. Archibald Hart, *The Crazy-Making Workplace*

3. Robert K. Johnston, *The Christian at Play*

4. Harold D. Lehman, *In Praise of Leisure*

5. Calvin Redekop and Urie Bender, *Who Am I? What Am I? — Searching for Meaning in Your Work*

6. Leland Ryken, *Christian Perspectives on Work and Leisure*

7. Dorothy L. Sayers, "Why Work?" in *Creed or Chaos*

8. E. F. Schumacher, *Good Work*

9. Elton Trueblood, "Work," Chapter IV in *The Common Ventures of Life*

10. Graham Tucker, *The Faith-Work Connection: A Practical Application of Christian Values in the Marketplace*

37. COMMUNITY-BUILDING

Where love rules, there is no will to power;
And where power predominates, there love is lacking.
The one is the shadow of the other.

—Carl Jung

In genuine community there are no sides. ...the members...have
learned how to listen to each other and how not to reject each other.
...they respect each...[other's] gifts and accept each...[other's] limi-
tations, ...they celebrate their differences and bind each... [other's]
wounds, [and]...they are committed to a struggling together rather
than against each other.

—M. Scott Peck

That government is the strongest of which every man feels himself
a part.

—Thomas Jefferson

Mankind has become so much one family that we cannot insure
our own prosperity except by insuring that of everyone else. If
you wish to be happy yourself, you must resign yourself to seeing
others also happy.

—Bertrand Russell

What should young people do with their lives today? Many things,
obviously. But the most daring thing is to create stable communi-
ties in which the terrible disease of loneliness can be cured.

—Kurt Vonnegut

Solitude vivifies; isolation kills.

— *Joseph Roux*

Community-building is the acting out organizationally of the second greatest commandment, the call to "love your neighbor as yourself." Community-building is partly about structures and systems but mostly about spirit and empowering people. On the assumption that individuals naturally give attention to themselves, the community ethos encourages the individual members to concentrate upon the development of the other members. Of course, this process automatically means that each member will receive aid as well as give it. Consistent with this emphasis upon giving help, the overall organization never demands primary loyalty or the suppression of personality, but rather serves the purpose of encouraging its individual members to understand and realize the call of God upon their lives.

The spirit of community identified above works most naturally in religious groups and most easily in small groups like the family and departmental work units, but many of its principles can work well in large and secular organizations such as corporations or even states and nations. Among the principles that contribute to the building of a genuine spirit of community in organizations are the following:

1. An effective sense of community is dependent upon a widespread and deeply-held commitment to common values and interests by it members. Whatever the specific nature and purpose of the organization, it must always hold as an underlying correlative cause the ennobling of the lives of its members. This mutual commitment of its members to their organization can be greatly enhanced if the organization has a rich tradition with which to identify. Each family organization, movement and nation needs to have a story. For example, Christianity, the most historically-based of the major

world religions, cites the creation of the world and the coming of God into human history as major parts of its tradition.

2. A community provides acceptance, safety, and a sense of belonging for its members and wishes these for all peoples even if, because of natural limitations, they cannot accommodate all in their organization.

3. Membership in a specific organization is as inclusive as possible, given its nature and function. The constituency of a family is limited by who marries, is born or adopted into it. Membership in a state is limited by geography. Membership in a religion, by contrast, can be worldwide with no limits for anyone who identifies with its articles of faith.

4. In one sense, the leadership of an organization should be as broad as the membership; in another sense leadership must be determined in a very careful manner. In genuine community everyone's ideas are significant, and therefore, in a real sense, everyone is a leader; this ideal works best in smaller groups but is still possible in some ways in larger settings. In large groups and in special-focus, smaller organizations, the leaders for specific tasks must be carefully selected based upon expertise, character, temperament, and ability to encourage and inspire. Such leaders must care greatly for the organization and its individual members. They must consciously and constantly look for ways to give sacrificially of themselves and their resources for the welfare of the group and its cause. They must studiously be committed to fairness, to an awareness of their own limitations, and to the establishment of group morale.

Transition into and out of leadership positions should be easy and natural. The organization and its cause should be larger than its most visible leaders, and the best leaders will work to make this happen.

Then at the right time they can smoothly resume a less demanding role in the organization.

5. All members of the community think of how they can best contribute to the cause of the organization rather than of how to exert power over others. He or she thinks not "what position can I occupy" nor "what authority can I possess" but "what am I most effectively equipped to share of those things which are most needed." There is general recognition of the legitimate dynamic of giving; as Father Stephen Kumalo heard from his confidant, Msimangu, in one of the most moving novels of the twentieth century, Alan Paton's *Cry the Beloved Country*: "...there is only one thing that has power completely, and that is love. Because when a man loves, he seeks no power, and therefore he has power."

6. All members think of providing tangible assistance to others rather than acquiring prestige for themselves. Organizational watchwords are "cooperation," "disinterested benevolence," and "mutual burden-bearing." Also central is mutual counsel to assist individual members to best understand, exercise and share their talents, and to best hear the personal instruction of the voice of God within.

7. The members of the group must be open and honest with one another. The more groups members love one another, the easier this can happen. Such love allows one to trust his or her motives in initiating discussion on sensitive, interpersonal issues, and it compels the effort to communicate to promote development and healing. Merely listening with empathy to others as they bare the troubles of their souls is almost invariably therapeutic. A general environment of openness between individuals does much in the group in general to reduce the human tendency toward pretense.

8. Richly meaningful and mature community is possible only when the group encourages and actively solicits broad-based participation in the ever-ongoing process of community-building (and maintenance). In a fully developed community, the views of all members and groups are inherently important. Essentially this is a description of a community-based as opposed to a hierarchical-based system of decision-making. Of course, except in very small groups, implementation decisions are best made in a hierarchical manner. By contrast, policy and personnel issues of major, long-range and broad-based significance are best determined in a community mode, preferably in a Quaker-like consensus-building discussion manner.

9. The group works hard to develop and implement natural conflict-resolution procedures. It instructs the new members that even as they are deeply committed to the good of the organization, it is perfectly acceptable and normal for them to think differently from one another and to freely express their differences as appropriate. When differences in ideas or actions lead to strained relationships, or when conflicts in interpersonal relations occur, the community expects the members involved to immediately talk about their problems in calm voice, good will, and expectation of harmonious resolution. When necessary, they seek and receive the aid of one or more other community workers. All of the above are formally defined as regular group processes.

When a community is large and involves civic and economic responsibility for all people who live within a defined geographic region (e.g. parish, county, state, nation), special considerations apply. A major test of the humaneness—or Christian-like nature—of a political entity lies in how it deals with the problems of poverty and delinquency internally and of how it views and relates to peoples in other political societies. In a perfectly humane society, everyone would work. The idea is less that everyone must work than that everyone would have the right to work, thereby not only earning their own keep but also acquiring the important satisfaction of contributing to society. (Appropriate provisions, of course, would be made for the very young, the aged, and the infirmed; students and mothers of young children would also not be expected to be otherwise employed.) This would not necessarily involve a collectivist economy, for under a primarily privatized system the government could serve as the employer of last resort. (For further discussion of the idea of "economic dignity for all," see the chapter on Governance.)

As children grew up in such a system, it would not only keep them meaningfully occupied during the potentially troublesome years of late adolescence; it would also greatly help to provide them with a sense of self-worth, the lack of which often contributes to delinquency. When the youth or their elders violate the criminal codes of the society, they would be treated with a "tough love" designed to correct rather than to punish for its own sake, on the understanding that as this is the way God treats us erring creatures, so also it is the way we should treat one another. Of course those who are a serious threat to the well-being of others would need to be restrained.

A nation that operates from a spirit of community-building will not only seek the best for all its members; it will wish the best for all peoples in all nations. A morally sound community will consider the effects that their programs and policies have on other locales and seek the benefit of all involved. Therefore it takes great care to avoid practicing ethnocentric isolationism, narrow nationalism, or aggressive imperialism. In other words, the community-building nation, in seeking to "love its neighbor as itself," operates as did Jesus with a broad definition of the word "neighbor."

QUESTIONS FOR REFLECTION AND DISCUSSION:

1. How can we best create an environment in which people, at least in their primary groups, will find it natural to care for each other if not as much as themselves at least sincerely and to a meaningful degree?

2. Is American Christianity in general, as presently constituted, more communal or more individualistic in nature? How do you react to your answer?

SUGGESTIONS FOR FURTHER READING:

1. Eberhard Arnold and Thomas Merton, *Why We Live in Community*

2. Robert N. Bellah, et al. *Habits of the Heart: Individualism and Commitment in American Life*

3. Paul Benson, *The People Called: The Growth of Community in the Bible*

4. Alfie Kohn, *No Contest: The Case Against Competition*

5. Thomas More, *Utopia*

6. M. Scott Peck, *The Different Drum: Community Making and Peace*

7. Ron Sider, *Rich Christians in an Age of Hunger*

38. GOVERNANCE

During the time that men live without a common power to keep them all in awe, they are in that condition which is called war; and such a war as is of every man against every man.

— *Thomas Hobbes*

Government and co-operation are in all things the laws of life; anarchy and competition the laws of death.

—*John Ruskin*

...what is government itself but the greatest of all reflections on human nature? If men were angels no government would be necessary.... In framing a government which is to be administered by men over men, the great difficulty lies in this: you must first enable the government to control the governed; and in the next place, oblige it to control itself.

— *James Madison*

Social institutions including government structures do not make men worse than they might have been; but rather these institutions, however bad, are better than nothing and have the effect of making humans appear a little more virtuous than they really are.

— *Herbert Butterfield*

The proper function of a government is to make it easy for people to do good and difficult for them to do evil.

—*Jimmy Carter*

Little else is requisite to carry a state to the highest degree of opulence from the lowest barbarism but peace, easy taxes, and a tolerable administration of justice: all the rest being brought about by the natural cause of things.

— Adam Smith

The inherent vice of Capitalism is the unequal sharing of blessings; the inherent vice of Socialism is the equal sharing of miseries.

— Winston Churchill

Normally speaking, it may be said that the forces of a capitalist society, if left unchecked, tend to make the rich richer and the poor poorer and thus increase the gap between them.

— Jawaharal Nehru

Intellectuals tend to be liberal for the simple reason that inequality—if only you will focus on it and think about it—is at first blush abhorrent to most men. The strong burden of proof is against it.

— Paul Samuelson

Capitalism needs and must have the prison to protect itself from the criminals it has created.

— Eugene Debs

Christianity has been from its inception a tireless critic of, and indeed, the opponent of, those forms of economic activity that we have come to denominate "capitalistic." ...there must be some more gracious and humane form of economic and political organization than capitalism.

—Page Smith

The answer to the question, "Am I my brother's keeper?" must always be "No—! I am my brother's brother."

—Paul Klapper

Governments are best classified by considering who are the "some-bodies" they are in fact endeavoring to satisfy.
—Alfred North Whitehead

The greatest happiness of the greatest number is the foundation of morals and legislation.
—Jeremy Bentham

...the world is organized to abolish poverty whenever the people of the world so will.
—Carl Sandburg

The right of a man to live by his work—
What is this right?
And why does it clamor?
And who can hush it
So it will stay hushed?
And why does it speak
And though put down speak again
With strengths out of the earth?

—Carl Sandburg

...the democratic parties of the developed nations have...[used] the state to force capitalism...to control the business cycle and reap-portion income in favor of those whom Jackson called the "humble members of society."
— Arthur Schlesinger

Letters to Young Scholars

In every human soul there is a socialist and an individualist, an authoritarian and a fanatic for liberty....

—*Richard Tawney*

We humans need to organize ourselves into governmental units for three reasons: 1) because we can be bad and this badness needs to be opposed systematically; 2) because there are certain practical tasks that can best be done with the entire community acting together; and 3) because we can be good and thus can do this good on a large scale. A good government provides a basic level of order, security, and structure while assuring its citizenry a basic level of freedom.

In this sinful world, the most fundamental task of government is to help to keep us from harming one another. We do not keep God's law, including the interpersonal provisions of the ten commandments, yet we acknowledge that we should do so. So we employ presidents, legislators, judges, police, and soldiers to assist us in the process. Yet legal officers and institutions are no less corruptible than are the rest of us. They can concentrate on securing their own political security and personal advantages rather than promoting the general welfare (James Russell Lowell observed: "He who is firmly seated in authority soon learns to think security, and not progress, the highest lesson in statecraft"). Also, with the physical power they command, political leaders can impose evil on a large scale, drawing upon the power of the state—including especially military resources—too quickly and for the wrong reasons. Therefore the best governments establish codes and procedures which limit the ability of the government to use its power for evil (see essays #7 on Human Freedom and #39 on "Democracy"). The government must be able to control the people, but the converse is no less vital.

Since the era of the Vietnam War and the Watergate scandal, the American public, encouraged by the American journalists, has been very distrustful and critical of public officials. In many respects this criticism has been appropriate, yet part of such criticism, now as always, represents a projection of our own sinfulness away from ourselves. In modern democratic countries, at least, the politicians in general are probably not less ethical than is the populace as a whole. Abraham Lincoln once responded to the question of why there was so much corruption in politics by stating: "You can't dip clear water from a muddy stream." Politicians thus tend to represent the public in nature as well as perspective.

In addition to preventing evil, a second purpose of government is to provide for certain services which multiple private contractors usually cannot offer well. For example, how many competing private sewer lines, communication cables, transit systems and toll roads should there be cluttering and clogging the space above and beneath the ground in cities and countryside? The practical answer, of course, is a limited number of utilities and systems, some of which may be privately owned but all of which are carefully regulated. When the utility is privately owned, the government usually offers it freedom from competition in exchange for reasonable rates and responsive service for the public.

If protective services and utilities services can best be provided or contracted by the public sector, then the development of agriculture, industry, technology, and wealth can best be achieved by private initiative. Most people work the hardest when they possess large control over the conditions and outcomes of their work. Capitalism is consistent with freedom and individualism. Unfortunately it is less consistent with community and a "love thy neighbor as thyself" ethic. Capitalism produces winners, but it also produces losers and even victims. One of the most important functions of government is to provide the freedom for capitalism to contribute to the growth of the economy while at the same time assuring that all of its citizens can be participants—as both givers and receivers—in the resultant degree of affluence. After the effective critiques of the late nineteenth and early twentieth century reformers, we produced a more humane capitalism by regulating it. What is needed now as we enter the new century is a concept of government that is committed to the economic dignity of all its peoples no less than to their economic freedom; the truly good society seeks to achieve an optimal blend between the two goals.

In many respects we in the United States have introduced programs designed to realize economic dignity for all peoples. Perhaps the most effective of these are Social Security and Medicare for the senior generation as they are available universally and without humiliation; less effective in the latter respect are Medicaid and traditional programs of welfare assistance. Promising but still developing are the newer "workfare" programs. In dire need of reform is our system of free public education, which traditionally has been one of the most effective of the public humanitarian programs. As it has evolved in the second half of the twentieth century, the monolithic public school system has increasingly fallen short of meeting one of the major goals of public policy, namely personal freedom; the best solution to this problem in our pluralistic society would be to offer parents a modest degree of choice among distinct types of schools for educating their children.

The most needed reform in moving toward a government policy of economic dignity for all is a program in which the government would become "the employer of last resort." Built upon the base of regulated capitalism, this public employment program would supplement the capitalist system as necessary in assuring that every family would have a bread-winner. Ideally the government would recruit some of its best thinkers and planners to identify and organize the most needed areas of employment, and determine how best to train what in some respects would be a short-term work force, and how to structure the system to provide the maximum respect for these public workers. Alternatively, perhaps the government could accomplish much of the same goal through grants to not-for-profit private development organizations or by offering large tax incentives for giving to charities that focus on economic development.

The resultant income and sense of dignity on the part of the newly employed should help to meaningfully reduce the myriad of social problems that result from the deprivations, frustrations and anxieties of chronic unemployment. Such a program would be costly, but what cost are we paying now for not having such a system? And, whatever the cost, is it spiritually tolerable not to have some such system if we really believe that we should love our neighbor as ourselves?

A governmental program to achieve economic dignity would not work perfectly. It would be implemented by flawed people, not all of whom would share its idealism. It would seek to help people some of whom would not be hard-working. The program would not create a heaven on earth, but it would represent an increased effort to achieve social justice and make this world a better place. The error of the political liberals is that in their noble idealism they underestimate the toughness of evil and overestimate what the mere passing of laws can do. On the other hand, the error of the political conservatives is that in their awareness of the pervasiveness of evil—and in part because of their own complacency—they fail to even try to make the world as good as it might be.

In the plan for government described in this essay, I have had in mind primarily the infrastructure of the modern affluent industrial nations. Such economically advanced nation states, however, do well to share of their abundance with the less-developed regions of the world. The United States government does this primarily through military aid and involvement; surely it would better contribute to the long-range good of the human race if we devoted a higher percentage of our resources to international relief and development causes. There are those who will remind us that charity begins at home. I once asked a socially-minded Latin-American theologian who was addressing my class, "What can we Americans do to help with the problems of deprivation in the South American continent?" His response was, "You have your own impoverished; help them first."

Modern American Christians are appropriately concerned about applying Biblical principles to the contemporary political scene. One major problem in achieving this application is that our form of government is very different from that of the Ancient Near East. The Biblical writers on government had in mind totalitarian regimes, theocracies, and religious institutional polity rather than secular democratic states. Nevertheless, we can deduce from their writings some universal ideals which transcend time and governmental form. These principles include the following:

1. The citizen should normally obey the government (e.g. Matthew 22:17-21; Romans 13:1-6; I Peter 2:13-14; Acts 4:18-20 and 5:27-29; Revelation 13 and 14; Exodus 1:15-17, 20a; Daniel 3:15-18 and 6:7).

2. Government and religious leaders should behave righteously themselves and should execute just policy; when they fail to do so, the Godly people should exercise their prophetic function in calling them to act in God-fearing and judicious ways (e.g. II Samuel 12:7-13; Jeremiah 21:11-12 and 22:1-5; Ezekiel 45:9-10a; Matthew 23:4, 14; Luke 11:37-54).

The commandment to obey the government is less a call to uncritically follow the whims of whoever happens to be in a seat of power at any given time than a commitment to the ideas of public order and community justice. The exercise of community justice includes not only the maintenance of fair legal codes and processes (e.g. Deuteronomy

16:18-20) but also societal provisions for aiding those least able to help themselves (Exodus 23:11; Leviticus 19:9-10 and 25:5; Deuteronomy 15; Psalm 41; Isaiah 58; Matthew 25:31-46; and II Corinthians 8).

May God grant us wisdom to realize His will through our public polity no less than in our private piety.

QUESTIONS FOR REFLECTION AND DISCUSSION:

1. Reread the Butterfield quotation. Do you agree with it? What would the contemporary political minority known as Libertarians think of it and why?

2. In your own words, what do you see, in order of their importance, as the most important specific purposes of government?

3. What do you see as the strengths and weaknesses of the "government as the employer of last resort" and "every family has a right to a breadwinner" ideas?

SUGGESTIONS FOR FURTHER READING:

1. Mortimer J. Adler, "Government," Chapter 31 and "State," chapter 90 in *The Great Ideas*

2. Stephen Carter, *The Culture of Disbelief: How American Law and Politics Trivialize Religious Devotion*

3. August Cerillo and Murray W. Demyster, *Salt and Light: Evangelical Political Thought in Modern America*

4. Robert Clouse, ed., *Wealth and Poverty: Four Christian Views of Economics*

5. Jacques Ellul, *The Politics of God and the Politics of Man*

6. Mark Hatfield, *Between a Rock and a Hard Place*

7. Paul Marshall, *Thine is the Kingdom: A Biblical Perspective on Government and Politics Today*

8. Richard Mouw, *Politics and the Biblical Drama*

9. H. Reinhold Niebuhr, *Christianity and Culture*

10. Mark Noll, ed., *Religion and American Politics from the Colonial Period to the 1980s*

11. Ronald Sider, *Rich Christians in an Age of Hunger*

12. Arthur Simon, *Christian Faith and Public Policy: No Grounds for Divorce*

13. J. W. Skillen, *International Politics and the Demand for Global Justice*

14. Alan Storkey, *Transforming Economics: A Christian Way to Employment*

15. Glenn Tinder, *The Political Meaning of Christianity*

16. Nicholas Wolterstorff, *Until Justice and Peace Embrace*

17. John Howard Yoder, *The Politics of Jesus*

39. DEMOCRACY

No one form of human government is inherently more godly than another. Any one of a number of systems in and of themselves has been virtuous enough, at least if we consider them in the abstract; however, at the bottom of them all is an inadequacy in human nature itself, which sooner or later corrupts the system and turns a good thing into an abuse.

—Herbert Butterfield

Great men are almost always bad men; power tends to corrupt and absolute power corrupts absolutely....

—Lord John Acton

That a peasant may become a king does not render the kingdom democratic.

—Woodrow Wilson

Man's capacity for justice makes democracy possible, but man's inclination to injustice makes democracy necessary

—Reinhold Niebuhr

The essence of a republican government is not command. It is consent.

—Adlai Stevenson

No one pretends that democracy is perfect or all-wise. Indeed, it has been said that democracy is the worst form of Government except all those other forms that have been tried from time to time.

—Winston Churchill

Democracy substitutes election by the incompetent many for ap-pointment by the corrupt few.

—*George Bernard Shaw*

Democracy...is a charming form of government, full of variety and disorder, and dispensing a sort of equality to equals and unequals alike.

—*Plato*

Nor is the people's judgement always true: the most may err as grossly as the few.

—*John Dryden*

Democracy...is the only form of government that is founded on the dignity of man, not the dignity of some men, of rich men, of educated men or of white men, but of all men.

—*Robert Maynard Hutchins*

The Bible has much to say about government but very little if anything to say directly about democracy. Therefore, those who would seek to defend democracy on the basis of Biblical Christianity must do so by deduction from general principles rather than by induction from specific verses.

In theory, the best system of government would be a theocracy in which God would govern His human creation directly. However, this is not a present option for us.

The second best system would be one which gave large control to the most enlightened, benevolent and saintly individuals among us. One major problem with this system, however, is that these noble people often have little interest in governing. Even if a nation—or any other political entity—would succeed in placing these most benevolent leaders in authority, it would be very difficult to assure an indefinite succession of governors who would rule with the same degree of grace.

Of all the viable governance models, democracy is preferable because it best recognizes the sinfulness of humankind (including especially rulers and potential rulers) on one hand and the essential dignity and freedom of humans on the other hand. At its best, democracy is a public acknowledgment that people are created in the image of God, thus possessing inherent dignity and value. If God made us as free moral agents, then the state should structure its systems to ensure that all individuals possess basic human freedoms. At the same time, man is a deeply sinful creature with pridefulness and the power impulse being at the heart of this sinfulness. Therefore, no individual should be trusted with an undue amount of authority, particularly when the mere acquisition of that power provides increased temptation to self-centeredness and abuse.

Modern democracy developed most immediately from the political liberalism introduced by the seventeenth and eighteenth century revolutions in Europe and America with their emphasis upon a limited monarchy, the sovereignty of the people, the equality of all classes before the law, and religious toleration. If political liberalism emphasized the need for protection from the tyranny of rule by the few, maturing democratic systems recognized the additional need for protection from the tyranny of the many. Therefore, perhaps the most important characteristic of a modern democratic system is its provision for checks and balances whereby any one individual, party, or governmental branch is limited both by its restricted span of responsibility and also because of the existence of systems of accountability to the other governmental divisions and the populace in general. In summary, democracy is the best form of government in our present world because all individuals and forces are tainted with the potential for evil; thus, none of us can be trusted with totalitarian power.

The strength of democracy lies more in what it prevents than in what it creates. Even when pursuing its primary task of preventing evil, it is capable itself of inflicting evil. This is especially likely, as Edmund Burke reminds us, when it moves from being a watchdog force to seeking to create a good society by exerting large amounts of control. Also, the natural effect of democracy's balancing forces, as noted by Thomas Carlyle, James Fenimore Cooper, and Ralph Waldo Emerson in the nineteenth century, is toward mediocrity.

Perhaps modern democratic government best contributes to the societal goal of achieving the greatest good for the greatest number by providing basic political and religious freedoms and by assuring minimal cultural and economic opportunities for all its citizens. From this base of freedom and security, its citizens can be empowered to pursue their own concepts of fulfilled living both individually and through their private agencies.

QUESTIONS FOR REFLECTION AND DISCUSSION:

1. What is your idea of the best possible human government?

2. From your knowledge of history, can you think of specific auto-
    cratic governments which at least for a limited period of time have
    worked better than the average modern democracy? If so, or if not
    so, what do you conclude from this?

SUGGESTIONS FOR FURTHER READING:

1. Edmund Burke, *Reflections on the Revolution in France*

2. Thomas Jefferson, *The Declaration of Independence*

3. Alexander Hamilton, James Madison, and John Jay, *The Federal-
    ist*

4. John Locke, *Two Treatises of Government*

5. Reinhold Niebuhr, *Children of Light and Children of Darkness*

6. Jean Jacques Rousseau, *The Social Contract*

7. Alexis de Tocqueville, *Democracy in America*

40. POPULAR CULTURE

It is not enough to show people how to <u>live</u> better: there is a mandate for any group with enormous powers of communication to show people how to <u>be</u> better.

—*Marya Mannes*

Our minds need relaxation, and give way
Unless we mix with work a little play.

—*Moliére*

The true object of all human life is play. Earth is a task garden; heaven is a playground.

—*C. Wright Mills*

We live in what is, but we find a thousand ways not to face it. Great theater strengthens our faculty to face it.

—*Thornton Wilder*

Television was not intended to make human beings vacuous, but it is an emanation of their vacuity.

—*Malcolm Muggeridge*

In America, it is sport that is the opiate of the masses.

—*Russell Baker*

Greek philosophers considered sport a religious and civic—in a word, moral—undertaking. Sport, they said, is morally serious because mankind's noblest aim is the contemplation of worthy things, such as beauty and courage.

—*George F. Will*

Finally, brethren, whatever things are true, whatever things are noble, whatever things are just, whatever things are pure, whatever things are lovely, whatever things are of good report, if there is any virtue and if there is anything praiseworthy—meditate on these things.

— *Philippians 4:8*

For the mature Christian thinker who is seeking to assess popular culture (e.g. television, radio, the Internet, music, sports), the beginning question is not "how many of these things may I do" but rather "what does it mean to be a Christian in society?" The beginning answer, of course, is the same as the underlying principle for all of life, namely, "you shall love the Lord your God with all your heart, with all your soul, and with all your mind. This is the first and great commandment. And the second is like it: you shall love your neighbor as yourself " (Matthew 22:37-39). Only as one starts from this foundation is he or she prepared to determine the manner and extent to which the forms and tools of popular culture can assist in the realization of one's overall values and commitments. The mediums of popular culture can aid one in seeking to understand both truth in general and also the goals and values of a non-Christian society to whom one is attempting to be salt and light. Furthermore, they can aid in the realization of one's God-given need for recreation and play. In some cases they can be a means of vocation including Christian ministry. Of course, they can also be and often are tools of evil.

Television, perhaps because of its great influence, receives much criticism. One thoughtful critic, Malcolm Muggeridge, although talking about his England, would undoubtedly have said the same things about the United States: "The media in general, and TV in particular..., are the greatest single influence on our society today, exerted at all social, economic, and cultural levels. This influence...is...largely exerted irresponsibly, arbitrarily, and without reference to any moral or intellectual, still less spiritual, guidelines, whatsoever." He concludes: "I think the best thing to do is not to look at television, and to that end, I have... disposed of my set. But that is just my personal opinion." Some of my students have told me that their parents chose to raise them without television in the home. Also, my dear friend and colleague Jay Kesler has, for himself, reached a similar decision with regard to certain cultural forms. I am sure that I share much of their thinking. I, too, avoid some cultural practices, but with television and cinema I choose to practice carefully selective participation. For example, in evaluating films that would be worth the time of my wife and myself, I find that of the new Hollywood productions about 40% are "bad," 40% are "dumb," 15% are fairly good and 5% or less are both enlightening and/or redemptive and also relatively tasteful. It is this latter noble remnant that I seek to find and enjoy.

In addition to the issue of quality there is also the question of quantity. One needs not merely to recreate well but also to recreate for an appropriate length of time. For example, spending excessive amounts of time with the television or the Internet, even when the programming is not objectionable, is usually symptomatic of an inadequately developed sense of calling or stewardship. Also, it often retards the development of socialization skills.

Perhaps an even greater concern is the use of media as a means of escaping from thinking deeply or honestly about personal problems or ultimate meaning. Some cannot tolerate being alone in private quarters without tuning in the media — often at a high volume level. It is difficult to hear the voice of God if the human voice — and especially a shallow and sensual human voice — is continually blaring. We do make choices about what we place in our minds. Lincoln said, "A man is what he thinks about all day long."

One of the major attractions of popular music is that in each generation of youth coming of age, it is a means of facilitating the very real need for differentiation. God made us to develop into individual, free moral agents, and the wisest parents welcome and facilitate the process. The adolescent years begin the transition from the status of dependent youth to that of independent adult. Popular music not only reflects an awakened sense of romance and sexuality, but it also usually reflects a cultural form with which many parents will find it difficult to identify. That, of course, is much of its appeal. It serves as a declaration of independence. Sometimes its expression is noble; more often it is silly or immature; sometimes it is dangerous or even evil. How wonderful it is when youths focus not merely on being different but on being different in a better way. There certainly is always plenty in the previous generation upon which to improve.

Competitive sports are more interesting than important, while exercise is more important than it is interesting. We were created with a need to have a balance between work and play (re-creation) activities, to interact socially with other humans, and to exercise our bodies as well as our minds and spirits. Watching competitive sports can help us to fulfill some of these human needs. Participating in team sports can be a means of teaching cooperation and discipline in developing skill. But competitive athletics is a double-edged sword. For example, while it can teach skill development, (competing primarily with oneself to be as good as one can be), it can also lead one to pursue the false god of beating down other people. Victory in the more meaningful sense is not measured in wins and losses but in the development of one's person. When victory on the scoreboard becomes the ultimate goal rather than a factor in the means to achieving the more important goals (recreation, socialization, skill development, exercise), then sucess in athletics becomes a false god. Unlike competitive athletics, physical exercise should be an important part of the life of everyone, and should be maintained at a level appropriate to one's physical condition throughout life.

In summary, popular culture like the world in general is largely corrupted, but in limited ways it can be redemptive. Different people seeking God's mind come to different conclusions on when to totally abstain and when to selectively participate in the formal and informal structures of society.

QUESTIONS FOR REFLECTION AND DISCUSSION:

1. In developing your philosophy for participation in the cultural activities of the general society, are you more likely/willing to err on the side of being indiscriminate or the side of being joyless? Why?

2. How much latitude do you allow others in determining their manner of involvement in the activities of popular culture? Why?

SUGGESTIONS FOR FURTHER READING:

1. Peter Kreeft, "Diversions," chapter 13 in *Christianity for Modern Pagans: Pascal's Pensees Edited, Outlined and Explained*

2. Tony Ladd and James A. Mathisen, *Muscular Christianity: Evangelical Protestants and the Development of American Sport*

3. Malcolm Muggeridge, *Christ and the Media*

4. H. Richard Niebuhr, *Christ and Culture*

5. Quentin J. Schultze, *Redeeming Television*

SOME BARRIERS
TO BELIEF

41. THE PROBLEM OF EVIL

I suspect that the problem of evil drives more thoughtful people away from religion than [does] any other difficulty.

—*Paul Johnson*

What we most want to ask of our Maker is an unfolding of the divine purpose in putting human beings into conditions in which such numbers of them would be sure to go wrong.
—*Oliver Wendell Holmes, Sr.*

How could I say to Him: "Blessed art Thou, Eternal, Master of the Universe, Who chose us from the races to be tortured day and night, and to see our fathers, our mothers, our brothers, end in the crematory? Praised be Thy Holy Name, Thou who hast chosen us to be butchered on Thine altar?"
—*Elie Wiesel*

It is so soon that I am done for, I wonder what I was begun for.
—*Epitaph for a deceased infant*

The atheist argues: "If there were a God, how could there be injustice?" To which Pascal replies: "If there is injustice, there must be true justice for it to be relative to and a defect of; and this true justice is not found on Earth or in man, therefore it must exist in Heaven and God."

—*Peter Kreeft*

The search for a personal philosophy of life must both allow for the worst tragedies which can take place and also for a way to transcend them.

—Herbert Butterfield

The Lord God is subtle, but malicious He is not.
—Albert Einstein

What attracts men to evil acts is not the evil in them but the good that is there, seen under a false aspect and with a distorted perspective.
—Thomas Merton

It is not so much the sin itself that is evil...but the refusal to acknowledge it that makes it evil.
—M. Scott Peck

It is my intuition that Satan does not use...[demon possession] today because evil spirits are so little believed in by our society. Instead possession today takes the form of neurosis or psychosomatic disease....
—Morton Kelsey

Every evil to which we do not succumb is a benefactor.
—Ralph Waldo Emerson

...you meant evil against me; but God meant it for good....
—Joseph (Genesis 50:20a)

The major barriers to belief include four discussed in this section of the book: evil, pain, intellectualism, and scientifically-influenced doubt. These and other inhibitors of faith tend to fall into one or more of the following categories: 1) lack of a sense of need of God, 2) wrong ideas about God, 3) reactions to the imperfections of the Christian Church, and 4) willfulness. Those especially vulnerable to an underdeveloped awareness of their dependency upon the Almighty (i.e., people in the first category) include young adults with their vigor and newly acquired independence, the strong, the intelligent, the talented, the beautiful, the wealthy, the powerful, and the popular. They often seem unable to see that they have nothing but what has been given to them, and little that cannot be taken from them at any time and which will decline and disappear in a few short years. They need a long-range perspective.

Category two people may well sense a clear need of God but they possess intellectual doubts about the trustworthiness of God. The Divine is not good enough, not wise enough, not powerful enough, or not personal enough in the application of His goodness, wisdom, and power. Thus the problem of evil and the problem of pain. One's conclusions are only as good as the data upon which they are based. Category two people need better data.

Those in category three usually see quite accurately when reacting against the foibles of the organized church. Like historian Herbert Butterfield, they observe, "Sometimes I have felt in reading history that Christianity can be unattractive and almost an intolerable religion in some of its manifestations when not accompanied by humility and charity." Yet, even when one focuses on the countless acts of piety and charity by multitudes of Christians, individually and collectively, it still never is appropriate to deduce the nature of God from any human being or group.

Undoubtedly, many who reject Christianity because of the spirit and actions of Christendom are doing so more as an excuse for their willfulness than as an objective deduction. Like many of us, at least on lesser issues, they offer the best-sounding reason for doing what they want to do. Such willfulness when applied to the ultimate issue — do I want God or do I want my independence? — is the most fatal barrier to faith.

If the most deadly obstacle to faith is willfulness, the most common such obstacle for thoughtful, sensitive, relatively honest people is the problem of evil in the world, especially if one is seeking to believe that God is all powerful and all good. The general theoretical question "Why does God allow evil to exist?" becomes much more intense when someone commits a great evil against oneself or those close to oneself. Even more troublesome intellectually is when that evil is not done by another person against me but rather is done by nature (i.e., God) against me, as, for example, when my home is destroyed and my family is killed in a storm. Then the question moves beyond "Why does God allow evil?" to "Does God, himself, commit evil against me?" These questions appear more difficult than does the subject of the next chapter, "The Problem of Suffering." It seems easier to imagine God allowing suffering for our good than God allowing or participating in evil for our good; the latter seems self-contradictory.

There are many explanations for and reactions to the existence of evil. The Christian Scientists deal with the problem by denying its existence. The concept of evil is illusory; rather all is good. The Pantheists solve the problem by denying that God is uniquely good; evil — even human evil — is a part of God. Those followers of Eastern Religions that believe in reincarnation view evil as Christians view Hell, namely as punishment for past actions. Process theology declares that God is still developing and thus is not all powerful nor capable of preventing all evil. Dualism similarly disassociates God from evil by saying that God has honorable intentions but limited ability to execute them. He, as the good force, competes for control of the world and the world's creatures with a second great and independent power, the force of evil — Satan or a Satan-like being.

The most common Christian explanations for the existence of evil are the importance to the one powerful benevolent God of providing for 1) human freedom and 2) human development. God so much wants us human beings to be able to be completely unfettered in choosing for Him that He provides a clear, opposite alternative for us, namely choosing evil over good. If providing this choice risked our making the mess of the world that we have, then that has been a necessary, even if most unfortunate, side effect. The human development explanation, by contrast, emphasizes that the best way to facilitate spiritual growth is to have a world laboratory where we are prodded to grow by direct and continuous struggle against an evil environment. This facilitates—if we allow it to do so—our making an alliance (or a closer alliance) with the only power in the universe greater than the force of evil. The Book of Job provides the classic case study of this dynamic.

While this essay focuses primarily on the problem of why God allows another being to do evil things to me, an even more existentially significant issue is why I commit evil against myself. The greatest such wrong that an individual does to himself or herself is to lie to oneself in general and to lie about who one is in God's sight in particular. The most fundamental barrier that we can create for ourselves is to refuse to see the evil within us ("the refusal to meet the shadow," in the words of Carl Jung), for what we refuse to see we cannot begin to heal.

Returning to the immediate question of this essay, how can we best find a practical, relatively satisfying resolution to the problem of evil? Personally, I find no workable solution short of a combination of forgiveness, faith in the wisdom of God, and a deep and abiding conviction that good ultimately and completely wins over evil. Forgiveness is redemptive for us, whether God forgiving us or we forgiving others. Not forgiving others their malicious actions toward us involves us in a four-fold evil, namely the original harm to us, our subsequent harm toward our malefactor, our harm toward ourselves in being unforgiving, and our standing with God given Jesus' correlation between forgiving others and being forgiven by God (Matthew 6:14-15). The wise person not only sees clearly the dangers in being unforgiving (Samuel Johnson noted that such an individual "will make haste to forgive because he knows the true value of time, and will not suffer it to pass away in unnecessary pain."), but also recognizes how situations of evil done toward us provide prime opportunities to grow in grace.

The intellectual "problem of the existence of evil" exists for the Christian only because of his or her belief that God is all-powerful and all-good. If one adds "all-wise" to the list of the attributes of God that are relevant to this issue, then the magnitude of the problem is sharply reduced; for then we have a God who is not only omnibenevolent in intention and omnipotent in ability, but also omniscient in understanding what is good and even needful for us. It makes all the difference if one can really believe, in a personal practical way as well as a theoretical manner, the statement of Romans 8:28 that "all things [including evil ones] work together for good" because God knows what is good for me and can deliver it for me.

The acclaim, "I've seen the end of the Book, and we win" can be misused as a chest-beating, even condescending expression of triumphalism or, more appropriately, it can be a deeply held faith statement by those who humbly seek to do good and to identify with the ultimate Good. From the philosophical ideas of Socrates and Plato (a good action is always more advantageous than an evil one), through the humble trust of the martyrs of history, through the latest generation of little children most recently come from God (who universally find happiness and satisfaction in their fairy tales as long as the antagonist loses before their bedtime), the intuitive belief rings strong that good ultimately wins. It may not happen in this life (as the wise farmer expressed, "God doesn't balance His books in October"). There exists no compelling resolution to the problem of evil that does not involve a more judicious form of life after death.

In summary, Biblical Christianity does not so much seek to provide a rational apologia for the Creator God who made a world where so many people could go so wrong as to encourage hope that the ultimate Will of the Redeemer God will not be frustrated by the temporary power of evil.

QUESTIONS FOR REFLECTION AND DISCUSSION:

1. How accepting of the traditional Christian answers to the problem of evil are Christians when extraordinary evil affects them or those close to them?

2. To what extent is the problem of evil (and of pain as well) a problem of understanding the providence and wisdom of God? To what extent is it a lack of willingness to forgive?

SUGGESTIONS FOR FURTHER READING:

1. Augustine of Hippo, *On Free Choice of the Will*

2. Henri Blocher, *Evil and the Cross*

3. Severinus Boethius, *The Consolation of Philosophy*

4. Martin Buber, *Good and Evil*

5. Brian Hebblethwaite, *Evil, Suffering, and Religion*

6. Fred E. Katz, *Ordinary People and Extraordinary Evil*

7. M. Scott Peck, *People of the Lie: The Hope for Healing Human Evil*

8. J. B. Phillips, *Your God Is Too Small*, book one

9. Alvin Plantinga, *God, Freedom, and Evil*

10. Jeffrey Burton Russell, *The Devil: Perceptions of Evil from Antiquity to Primitive Christianity*

11. A. W. Tozer, "Why We Must Think Rightly About God," chapter one in *The Knowledge of the Holy*

12. Elie Weisel, *Night*

42. THE PROBLEM OF PAIN

There is no man in this world without some manner of tribulation
or anguish, though he be king or pope.

—Thomas a Kempis

Nothing begins and nothing ends
That is not paid with moan;
For we are born in other's pain
And perish in our own.

—Francis Thompson

As flies to wanton boys are we to the Gods.
They kill us for their sport.

—William Shakespeare (<u>King Lear</u>)

If you are distressed by anything external, the pain is not due to
the thing itself but to your own estimate of it; and this you have the
power to revoke at any moment.

—Marcus Aurelius

Much of your pain is self-chosen. It is the bitter potion by which
the physician within heals your sick self.

—Kahil Gibran

...pain, which is contrary to pleasure, is not necessarily the contrary
of happiness or of joy.

—Thomas Merton

Adversity is the first path to Truth.

—Byron

He who learns must suffer. And even in our sleep, pain that cannot forget falls drop by drop upon the heart, and in our own despair, against our will, comes wisdom to us by the awful grace of God.

—*Aeschylus*

Adversity is sometimes hard upon a man; but for one man who can stand prosperity, there are a hundred that will stand adversity.

—*Thomas Carlyle*

Affliction teacheth a wicked person...[sometimes] to pray; prosperity never.

—*Ben Johnson*

Think of some of the painful events in your life. For how many of them are you grateful today, because thanks to them you changed and grew?

—*Anthony de Mello*

Perhaps we suffer so inordinately because God loves us so inordinately and is taming us. Perhaps the reason why we are sharing in a suffering we do not understand is because we are the objects of a love we do not understand.

—*Peter Kreeft*

If we need to suffer to become wise, if we need to sacrifice some pleasure to be virtuous, if too much pleasure would make us fools, if an easy life would make us less virtuous—if this were so then suffering would not contradict a good God.

—*Peter Kreeft*

It is the clear lesson of the Old Testament that tragedy is redeemable.

—*Herbert Butterfield*

Those [things] which others term crosses, afflictions, judgements, misfortunes, to me who inquire farther into them than their visible effects, they both appear, and in event have ever proved, the secret and dissembled favors of his affection.

—*Thomas Browne*

Blessed is any weight, however overwhelming, which God has been so good as to fasten with his own hand upon our shoulders.

—*F. W. Faber*

In many respects this chapter is a continuation of the previous one. Both are concerned with why a perfect God would allow such an imperfect world. The previous chapter considered the difficult question of why evil people can and often do commit great harm against innocent people. The current chapter focuses on why so many of the experiences and situations in life cause us to hurt and suffer in body, mind, and spirit, sometimes to a severe degree.

When I was young, I used to think that the ideal life would be trouble-free and capped by a death experience that would be like going to heaven "on a bed of roses." I no longer believe this for I have seen so much growth in faith and spiritual maturity in people because of their positive responses to the experience of difficulty. God must have something better for us than a care-free existence — something that can come only through trial and testing. In terms of providing opportunity for growth for us, maybe there is less difference than we think between the wrongs done to us by evil people and the trials lovingly given to us by a benevolent God, for both can and should lead to spiritual growth (i.e., moving closer to God in fellowship, trust, and obedience). Such maturing may well be the primary purpose of our existence.

Of course, spiritual maturity is not an automatic consequence of trouble. Our response to difficulty is always a multiple choice scenario. We can choose, as Job's wife counselled him during his difficulty, to curse

God; we can withdraw into hopelessness; or we can choose to ask God, "What would you have me hear and become through this?" and then rejoice in the opportunity for growth.

The specific sources of suffering are many and include the following:
1. Personal sin

   While not all suffering stems directly from our personal, sinful choices, some does. In such cases, pain is a mercy to encourage us to corrective action.

2. Sins of our ancestors

   One likely effect of the accumulated acts of sin by our ancestors is a bodily system less capable of environmental resistance and advanced longevity than were the bodies of our original forbears. Also the character flaws and sins, especially of our most immediate ancestors, have provided negative models which we both suffer from and imitate.

3. Collective guilt

   Somehow in one way or another and to one degree or another this sinful inheritance from our own ancestral lines crosses all genealogical lines and represents a universal guilt or fall of all humans and probably even all nature.

4. Vicarious suffering

   Christians readily recognize that God the Father grieves generally as a response to human sinfulness, while the Incarnate One suffered uniquely through the crucifixion atonement. Perhaps part of our growth to become more like the Divine One is to share partially in His sufferings for the human race. This idea may help to explain why some people seem to suffer disproportionately to others and to their own need for growth; maybe they are suffering more to help other people somehow than to facilitate their own development. In such cases suffering becomes less a tragedy than a high calling.

5. Neediness

   Pain beyond an easy tolerance level quickens our awareness—which otherwise might be very much repressed—of our dependency upon God. C. S. Lewis has stated that "God whispers to us in our pleasures, speaks to us in our conscience, but shouts in our pains: it is His megaphone to arouse a deaf world." I shudder to think what we would become if we lived in a world in which all of our needs and reasonable desires were met and we knew that such would always be the case. Would not most of us forget God and the desire for Heaven?

Surely even for Adam and Eve before the Fall, God made a chancy world. Painful mistakes happen apart from sinfulness (e.g. a misdirected hammer landing on one's thumb). But accidents do not happen by accident. God intentionally chose not to make a risk-free world. Human awareness of risk promotes a sense of dependency, and dependency points to the need for trust in something beyond our own resources.

For the Christian the ultimate resolution to the problem of suffering lies less in getting rid of suffering per se than in getting rid of the idea that all suffering is altogether evil and serves no good purpose. Now to seek relief from pain—our own and that of others—is natural, normal, and even good. The Incarnate Divine, Himself, during His public ministry, gave much attention to healing human suffering. But it is also true that He healed a limited few, and there is no evidence that the recipients of His healing power remained pain-free during the remainder of their lives.

If the complete removal of pain from the world is not possible, neither is it desirable, for suffering is an indispensable ingredient in the growth of grace, goodness and wisdom in the human race. Not only does suffering help us in our personal development narrowly defined, but it also helps us to be more empathetic with other sufferers, especially those who suffer in a similar manner. This solidarity even when applied only locally is an important step in moving toward the Creator's universal Divine love. Suffering also promotes creativity; most, perhaps all positive creativity, is born from the refining fire of pain. This emphasis on the great value of pain is not to diminish its dreadfulness and dominance through all of life. As Hans Kung has noted, "Who can deny that human existence—under whatever social and economic system, and even after all reforms and revolutions—is and remains an existence shot through with pain, anxiety, guilt, suffering, sickness, and death and is in this sense a thwarted and unsatisfactory thing?" This suffering life is indeed an awful thing, but in large part it is an awful mercy. It can lead to something glorious. Indeed it must so lead, for it hurts too much not to be able to profit from it somehow.

So often we rail against pain because we have difficulty seeing the long-range beneficent plan of God for us and all of creation. To understand and live from the foundational conviction that pain is a necessary short-term experience on the road to the ultimate glory that will succeed it, takes more than reason and more than experience; it takes a deep and abiding faith that "grows more and more unto the perfect day."

QUESTIONS FOR REFLECTION AND DISCUSSION:

1. What things are as effective as pain in leading humans to trust in God?

2. Did pain exist before the entrance of sin into the world?

SUGGESTIONS FOR FURTHER READING:

1. Gustavo Gutierrez, *On Job: God-Talk and the Suffering of the Innocent*

2. Douglass John Hall, *God and Human Suffering*

3. Hermann Hesse, *Siddhartha*

4. The Book of Job

5. E. Stanley Jones, *Christ and Human Suffering*

6. Peter Kreeft, *Making Sense Out of Suffering*

7. C. S. Lewis, *The Problem of Pain*

8. Frederick Sontag, *God, Why Did You Do That?*

9. Paul Tournier, *Creative Suffering*

10. Leslie D. Weatherhead, *Why Do Men Suffer?*

11. Philip Yancey, *Where Is God When It Hurts?*

43. ACADEMIA AND THE TEMPTATION OF INTELLECTUALISM

The intellectual life is not the only road to God, nor the safest, but we find it to be a road, and it may be the appointed road for us.

—C. S. Lewis

We can...pursue knowledge as such, and beauty as such, in the sure confidence that by so doing we are either advancing to the vision of God ourselves or indirectly helping others to do so.

—C. S. Lewis

As a human being, one has been endowed with just enough intelligence to be able to see clearly how utterly inadequate that intelligence is when confronted with what exists.

—Albert Einstein

Intelligence is quickness to apprehend as distinct from ability, which is capacity to act wisely on the thing apprehended.

—Alfred North Whitehead

I suspect...that men and women of outstanding intellect and gifts are particularly liable to the temptations which make human hell-fodder.

—Paul Johnson

...it is possible that a majority of the people who consider themselves well educated—that is, who have attended university, read books regularly and regard themselves as people who think seriously about the public issues of the day, and the meaning of life—would range themselves in the Promethean camp [i.e., those who believe that they can do without God], with varying degrees of consciousness and enthusiasm.

—Paul Johnson

Academic fundamentalism is...the stubborn refusal of the academy to acknowledge any truth that does not conform to professorial dogmas. In the famous "marketplace of ideas," where [supposedly] all ideas are equal..., certain ideas are simply excluded...(for example, God is not a proper topic for discussion, but "lesbian politics" is).
—Page Smith

Secularism...is at best naive, and at worst a refusal to confront life's dimension of depth.

—George Buttrick

If academic history cannot provide a man with the ultimate valuations and interpretations of life under the sun, neither is it generally competent to take them away from the person who actually possesses them....

—Herbert Butterfield

On the decisive question of the posture one should adopt towards life or the interpretation one would give to the whole human story, it would be unwise to surrender one's judgment to a scholar, any more than one would expect a scholar by reason of his technical accomplishments to be more skilled than other people in making love or choosing a wife.

—Herbert Butterfield

316

The best forms of education help students develop their minds to be sure, but they also assist them in understanding the nature and purpose of the intellect, and other human abilities, in relationship to character development and service. The mind is a wonderful gift. One can use it to understand, enjoy, and serve God and His world or as an idol in which to trust. Especially when a person receives a goodly share of mental ability, the temptation is to trust in the gift given rather than the One who gave the gift. This temptation becomes even greater as one receives growing human acclaim in the display of this gift. While a quality education should assist especially the most able students to resist the temptation of intellectualism, it should also aid all students in personal development and vocational preparation. The purpose of education should be to help us understand our Creator and His creation, and to help us to function well in the world. Thus we need to learn of God through the Bible, prayer, and other means; we need to learn of His world through the human and natural sciences; and we need to prepare for a vocation. For the Christian, vocation is not merely a job to earn money; it is that but much more, also. The Christian views vocation as a calling, a sacred mission from God to contribute to the world. Also, the best formal education creates the desire for informal, life-long learning and growing.

Some classes, books, and friends will do nothing directly to help you get a job, but they will do much to help you become a better person. This, of course, is the best form of learning. Wisdom is of greater value than knowledge, character than craft, love and kindness than skillful manipulation. What you become as a person, then, is more important than what you pursue as a career.

The formal system of thought which emphasizes the importance of the mind and reason in the search for truth is Rationalism. Some accept reason as the ultimate — even the only — source of authority in matters of opinion, belief, and conduct, and thus tend to make it their religion.

Others, such as Christian rationalists, emphasize that although reason is one very important avenue to truth and that one should take it as far as it will go, one must nevertheless, at some point employ other vehicles (e.g. experience, intuition, revelation, and faith) in a concerted effort toward understanding.

There exists a basic dichotomy between the heart, the emotions, and faith on one hand, and the mind, the intellect, and reason on the other hand. Jerusalem, the Middle Ages, and the Reformation symbolize the former while Athens, the Renaissance, and the Enlightenment symbolize the latter. The modern Christian college says that we should take the best of both worlds; in the ongoing search for understanding, scholars must embrace truth where they find it. "All truth is God's truth" is the motto; "the integration of faith and learning" is the "buzz phrase." Reason, although indispensable, is incomplete in itself, for a vital part of the truth available to us all is knowable only by God's revelation to us through the Biblical record, the person of Christ, and the ministry of the Holy Spirit.

If trusting in one's mind and pursuing knowledge only through rational processes are two forms of intellectual temptation, a third one is the compulsion to conform to the general ideological milieu of one's academic environment. As one increasingly enjoys the intellectual process and the intellectual community, it becomes tempting to indiscriminately embrace the dogmas, follow the system, and pursue the rewards of the intelligentsia. Peer pressure and the tendency toward group conformity exist for highly cerebral adults no less than for inexperienced, sometimes largely irrational teenagers. The primary focus of the last section of this essay is on how this third type of intellectual temptation can impact the Christian student in a secular institution, especially when studying on the graduate level.

In most of higher education today, the dominant thought with regard to religion is that of functional agnosticism: either one does not believe in the supernatural or one believes that such a concern should not be a subject of open, engaged discussion in academe. This was not the case before the secular revolution in higher education beginning in the late nineteenth century. Although many able Christian undergraduate colleges continue to exist, many Christian youth believe that they cannot afford to attend such private institutions with their higher tuition. Also, for the Christian student who wishes to pursue graduate study in a field other than the primarily religious disciplines of the theological seminaries, unfortunately there exist few choices other than the primarily secular institutions.

My personal reaction to graduate study in two state institutions in the 1960s was that of surprise. I had been warned that such places were intellectually beguiling and represented a severe threat to the faith of young Christian students. Therefore, I expected to find some intellectually compelling options to the Christian faith, but I found none. What I did find was rationalism, skepticism, pride, professional competition and posturing, and even sincere toleration for private belief, but nothing even close to a satisfactory alternative world view to explain the human condition and provide a basis for ultimate hope. Later I became impressed with the intellectual honesty of existentialism with its bleak portrayal of the situation of humans when limited to their own resources; but the very strength of the existentialist analysis lies in the fact that it is pre-Christian or part-Christian or even very Christian in some respects.

Secular higher education is better at critiquing Christianity—and, all the more so, Christendom, with its many foibles—than in providing a viable alternative explanation of reality. Its methods of analysis and criticism can even be helpful in aiding one's psycho-religious development as one moves beyond a largely inherited adolescent faith to a mature personally-acquired adult belief system. The critical question, of course, is whether one goes beyond critique to find a satisfactory new synthesis to affirm. Ironically, many who experienced a viable, even if simplistic, religious upbringing and then reject it during an early stage of analysis, find during a more mature stage of thoughtfulness that much of what they previously had rejected actually contains much vital truth. The poet T. S. Eliot recognized this:

> And the end of all our exploring
> Will be to arrive where we started
> And know the place for the first time.

Finally, it is of primary importance that Christian students not be unduly threatened by the views of non-Christian or even anti-Christian professors. Respect them for their technical scholarship, but do not ascribe excessive authority to their interpretations. Scholars as scholars are well-trained to ascertain the concrete facts of the past and the present, but when it comes to providing an overarching meaning to the specific data of the universe, the scholar is no more qualified than is the ordinary lay person. For example, history as pure history can neither prove nor disprove the divinity of Christ. In other words, academicians are more to be trusted when dealing with physics (i.e., the measurable) than with metaphysics (the immeasurable). And we know that it is only what lies beyond or behind the physical realm that can provide ultimate understanding and fulfillment.

QUESTIONS FOR REFLECTION AND DISCUSSION:

1. Do the risks of formal higher learning outweigh the likely benefits of the same?

2. Are scholars more independent in their thinking than is the populace at large?

3. How much more intelligent/knowledgable are you than the average person your age? What do you think about that? How much is it "tempting" to trust in your level of ability? How much do you search for wisdom as well as intelligence and knowledge? How much are humility and thankfulness a part of wisdom?

4. For a Christian, what are the most relevant factors to consider in determining when it is best to study in a Christian institution and when it is best to study in a secular one?

SUGGESTIONS FOR FURTHER READING:

1. George Buttrick, *Biblical Thought and the Secular University*

2. Paul Johnson, *The Intellectuals*

3. C. S. Lewis, "The Inner Ring" in *The Weight of Glory*

4. Charles Malik, *A Christian Critique of the University*

5. George Marsden, *The Soul of the American University*

6. William C. Ringenberg, "The Movement Toward Secularization," chapter four in *The Christian College*

7. Page Smith, *Killing the Spirit*

44. SCIENCE: FOE OR FRIEND?

If you cannot measure it, then it is not science.

—Lord Kelvin

Science means simply the aggregate of all of the recipes that are always successful. The rest is literature.

—Paul Valery

Science investigates; religion interprets. Science gives men knowledge…; religion gives men wisdom….

—Martin Luther King, Jr.

Science without religion is lame; religion without science is blind.

—Albert Einstein

Man wrestled from nature the power to make the world a desert or to make the deserts bloom. There is no evil in the atom; only in men's souls.

—Adlai Stevenson

Though many have tried, no one has ever yet explained away the decisive fact that science, which can do so much, cannot decide what it ought to do.

—Joseph Wood Krutch

The Cosmos is all that is or ever was or ever will be.

—Carl Sagan

As soon as anyone belongs to a narrow creed in science, every unprejudiced and true perception is gone.

— *Johann Wolfgang Goethe*

I distinguish between naturalistic philosophy and empirical science, and oppose the former when it comes cloaked in the authority of the latter.

— *Philip E. Johnson*

The real and enduring conflict [in the science/religion dialogue] is between rival worldviews.

— *Richard T. Wright*

The earth is the Lord's and all its fullness,...
Then the Lord God took the man and put him in the Garden of Eden to tend and keep it....an accusation was brought to him that this man was wasting his goods....So he called him and said to him, "What is this I hear about you? Give an account of your stewardship....

— *Psalm 24:1a, Genesis 2:15, Luke 16:1a-2b*

Nature, to be commanded, must be obeyed.

— *Francis Bacon*

...the ecosphere is being driven toward collapse...largely [the] unintended result of the exploitation of technological, economic, and political power. ...[its] solutions must also be found in this same difficult arena. This task is unprecedented in human history, in its size, complexity and urgency.

— *Barry Commoner*

The more we get out of the world, the less we leave, and in the long run we shall have to pay our debts at a time that may be very inconvenient for our own survival.

—*Norbert Wiener*

We are all passengers aboard one ship, the Earth, and we must not allow it to be wrecked. There will be no second Noah's ark.

—*Mikhail Gorbachev*

The previous chapter discussed ways in which the world of scholarship and thought can work against the development of faith. Of all the major academic divisions, the one that appears most threatening to modern Christians is science. That concern is the subject of this chapter.

Is there a genuine conflict between science and religion? In a way, yes. In a way, no. Ultimately no.

Historically, there have been significant periods of intellectual conflict between some or many scientists and some or many religious leaders and laity. Western science and formal critical inquiry began in Greece in the fifth and sixth centuries B.C. Western religion with its personal, ethical monotheism began over a millennium earlier with Abraham and the Hebrew patriarchs. Early Christianity, born from Judaism, could accommodate Greek science. As the Roman Catholic Church emerged as the primary institutional form of Christianity, it assumed the role of protector of ideological purity from what it perceived as threatening new ideas in science and philosophy as well as theology. Ironically the first major church controversy with regard to science was an internal conflict between late medieval Catholic scholastics like Peter Abelard, Albert Magnus, and Thomas Aquinas and conservative churchmen over the wisdom of employing reason and Aristotelian logic not only in the search for scientific understanding but also in the search for and the enhancement of faith. For Aquinas, faith and reason, including scientific inquiry, were complementary gifts from God and avenues to understanding.

The Scientific Revolution of the sixteenth and seventeenth centuries witnessed a pronounced clash between the Roman Catholic authorities and the primary scientific innovators. The church for centuries had endorsed the Ptolemic geocentric view of the universe, and when Nicolaus Copernicus in his *On the Revolutions of the Heavenly Spheres* identified the sun rather than the earth as the center of the cosmos and then was supported by the later research of fellow astronomers Tycho Brahe, Johannes Kepler, and Galileo Galilei, the church was alarmed. Still reeling from the Protestant exodus, church leaders viewed the new ideas as a further threat to their traditional teaching and authority. Consequently the church placed the Copernicus volume on its Index of Prohibited Books and sentenced Galileo to life imprisonment.

Of all the specific controversies between Science and Religion, the most intense, most widespread, and longest lasting one was that which developed from the nineteenth-century Darwinian theories of evolution. This conflict affected all major branches of the Christian faith and continues intensely to the present. If the Copernican Revolution seemed to make our earth less central among the heavenly spheres, the writings of Charles Darwin seemed to make humans less unique among the earthly life forms. Furthermore, the evolutionary theory directly conflicted with the traditional interpretation of the Genesis creation narrative and thus, by implication, raised questions about the trustworthiness of the Bible in general.

The most intense contemporary controversies in science involve less theories about the workings of nature than the establishment of ethical standards to govern the application of scientific understanding to technology, especially in the areas of nuclear energy and biomedical innovation. In this conflict the debate is not simply one between religion and science but rather one within all ethically sensitive people, including scientists. Professional and lay ethicists alike ask questions such as the following:

1. Are the new weapons of mass destruction (e.g. nuclear atomic and hydrogen bombs, and chemical and biological assault devises) so deadly and/or uncontrollable that to use them as a first strike or even at all is inherently immoral?

2. Should any limits exist upon pure or applied research in those areas most directly related to warfare applications? If so, who should impose those limits in a multi-national world? If there should be no limits, how then should we, the inhabitants of this earth, seek to save ourselves from ourselves?

3. How do we determine which medical procedures are acceptable for helping couples who desire children but are having difficulty reproducing through the normal processes?

4. How does one evaluate the costs and benefits of the highly expensive end-of-life hospital procedures?

5. Is medical intervention to alter a given person's significantly deficient genetic code for the purpose of healing disease or saving life more ethically questionable than, say, an artificial heart replacement or personality-altering medication? If so, why?

6. Would genetic engineering to aid the human race in general in living longer and more free of disease involve a usurption of the divine order?

This brief narrative of some of the historical incidents where science and religion have intersected represents less a conflict between science and religion per se and more a conflict between the interpretations, world views, and values of some scientists and the interpretations, world views, and values of some religious people. Pure science and basic Christianity, by contrast, differ rarely if at all.

There is a tendency in human nature to want to find the certain, the ultimately dependable, and the orderly in this haphazard, uncertain world. Both religion and science seek knowledge; they do, however, focus on different ways of seeking and different domains of knowing. Science studies the created natural world and what can be learned of it by means of the rational, empirical scientific method. By contrast, religion in its search, focuses on what is behind the observable world and universe. It employs such ways of knowing as intuition, deduction from nature (as opposed to the human measurement of nature), reason including logic (an important contributory rather than inherently conclusive way of knowing in the religious domain), and revelation, both general and specific; and asks questions such as: "Who or what created this world, what can we know about this force, how can or should I relate to this ultimate force, and what does this ultimate force or being say about the universal human desire to transcend death?"

Pure science is a great friend of humankind. It helps us to understand the natural world in which we live and of which we are a part. More subjectively, it helps most to appreciate the world, and for the Christian and many other theists, it facilitates a sense of awe and wonder at the goodness, beauty, and complexity of God's creation and also aids in the worship of the Almighty God.

Pure science, or science as science, has nothing to say about religion. It has no opinion on whether religion and religious study are valid domains. Individual scientists do have opinions on these religious issues, but when they think and express these opinions, they operate outside the domain of science.

Thus, in theory, science and religion do not conflict. They focus on different concerns and employ differing, albeit overlapping, methodologies; and they both agree that the goal is to find truth. Presumably their efforts are complementary. But in practice, scientists and theologians do conflict. They conflict because scientists are not precise machines but rather human beings who possess affective and rational components alike; they conflict because theologians, who admittedly operate in a subjective and mysterious domain, often, especially when acting under the umbrella of institutional authority, issue unnecessarily absolute pronouncements on complicated and unclear topics. Much of the conflict occurs then when scientists individually or in concert claim as truth more than what can be proven via the scientific method, and theologians claim as truth more than what is clearly stated in the Scriptures.

Then there is the related and awful problem of intellectual pride which inhibits the acquisition of truth as well as the development of character. How tempting it is for scientists and theologians alike to speak with undue assuredness. There is a desire to be seen as the authority, the wise one who discovers new truth and can explain almost anything. Such bold expressiveness can make lively press copy and enhance one's reputation in his or her professional group and with the public. In fact, our minds are very limited in their capacity to know. Even perfect objectivity in inquiry does not usually produce better than varying degrees of probability. Even in religion the central concept of faith implies believing in something in the face of less-than-complete certainty (see Hebrews 11:1). If certainty existed, there would be no need for faith.

At some point in this essay there must be a consideration of one of the most important ways in which science helps humanity, namely in serving as a barometer of our record as stewards of God's earthly garden. Those who take seriously the mandate in the creation and "recreation" narratives (Genesis 1:28, 9:1-2) to be fruitful in dominion over the biological order will welcome and carefully observe the emerging consensus of the best scientific data identifying areas of needed ecological correction. Hopefully, both the Christian community and society in general will respond both in personal lifestyle sensitivity and in calls for appropriate public policy reforms to allow us to live more in harmony with the long-range well-being of the physical environment in which God has placed us (on harmonious living in general, see chapter 46, "Harmony and Balance"; for prudent thinking about other future implications of present living, see Chapter 28 on "Long-Range Thinking"; and for respecting the dignity of all of created life, see chapter 18 on "The Sacredness of Life").

Human dominion over the biosphere is not a warrant to misuse or overuse nature but rather a call to assure the sustainability of our natural habitat. Conservation is not an end in itself but rather one element in the practice of human stewardship whereby we carefully balance our 1) enjoying/using, and our 2) nurturing/protecting/renewing the natural resources of God's world. If we are to obey "the whole counsel of God" (Acts 20:27b), we will not limit our spiritual concern only to evangelism and the development of personal piety but will also include in our focus the redemption and restoration of the larger social and environmental orders.

In conclusion, how then does one best bring together the worlds of science and faith? Here are a few summary suggestions:

1. As is emphasized throughout this book, seek to distinguish between primary and secondary issues. In the dialogue between science and faith, the primary issue for each individual is not what he or she

thinks about the general theory of evolution or a specific issue in bioethics but rather "is there a Creator behind the physical universe, a Supreme Being who made me and to whom I wish to relate as the foremost reality in my existence?" I suspect that most if not all scientists and lay people alike decide this ultimate issue less on the basis of data than on the basis of their personal will. The existing data is sufficient enough to choose for the idea of a maker, while it is limited enough to choose against the idea of a maker, depending upon one's disposition. One of the most amazing things about this universe is the existence of human free will.

2. In the study of origins, much ambiguity exists and therefore much humility is appropriate. Wanting to know more than you do is commendable; claiming to know more than you do is not. The more faith that one exercises in the providence and goodness of God, the Creator, the less anxious one becomes that God had to have created the world in a specific way. Similarly, it is very unwise to allow one's faith to be too closely tied to the state of scientific thinking in a given period.

3. Everlastingly rejoice in the goodness of God's creation. Evermore and in all ways seek to redeem the natural order from the effects of the Fall, both in your personal life and that of your neighbor. And remember that your neighbor, whom you are to "love as yourself," includes not only all with whom you presently share this earthly habitat, but also all who will inherit it in succeeding generations.

QUESTIONS FOR REFLECTION AND DISCUSSION:

1. Should there be any restrictions on 1) freedom of inquiry, 2) freedom of pure scientific research, 3) freedom of applied scientific research, or 4) freedom of use of scientifically produced technology? Where does a humane society place limits?

2. Is it possible to reconcile the Christian faith and Darwinian evolutionary thought?

3. What are the general privileges and responsibilities of the human dominion decrees in Genesis 1:28 and 9:1-2, and how do these apply to us in the current stage of world development?

SUGGESTIONS FOR FURTHER READING:

1. I. G. Barbour, *Issues in Science and Religion*

2. I. G. Barbour, *Religion in an Age of Science*

3. Richard H. Bube, ed., *The Encounter Between Christianity and Science*

4. Richard H. Bube, ed., *The Human Quest: A New Look at Christianity and Science*

5. William A. Dembski, ed., *Mere Creation: Science, Faith, and Intelligent Design*

6. John Houghton, *Does God Play Dice?*

7. Philip E. Johnson, *Darwin on Trial*

8. D. Gareth Jones, *Brave New People: Ethical Issues at the Commencement of Life*

9. David C. Lindberg and Ronald L. Numbers, *God and Nature: Historical Essays on the Encounter Between Christianity and Science*

10. Alister E. McGrath, *Science and Religion: An Introduction*

11. Mary Midgley, *Evolution as a Religion*

12. A. R. Peacocke, *Creation and the World of Science*

13. Nancy R. Pearcey and Charles B. Thaxton, *The Soul of Science: Christian Faith and Natural Philosophy*

14. John Polkinghorne, *The Faith of a Physicist*

15. John Polkinghorne, *Faith, Science, and Understanding*

16. William G. Pollard, *Physicist and Christian: A Dialogue Between the Communities*

17. Del Ratzsch, *Science and Its Limits*

18. W. Mark Richardson and Wesley J. Wildman, ed., *Religion and Science: History, Method, and Dialogue*

19. Norbert Wiener, *God and Golem, Inc.*

20. Richard T. Wright, *Biology Through the Eyes of Faith*

TOWARD A WORKABLE
PHILOSOPHY OF LIFE

45. HUMAN HISTORY AND THE INCARNATION

The unhappy fact is that there is more sin than virtue in the past, more criminals than saints.

—Lord Acton

History... is, indeed, little more than the register of the crimes, follies, and misfortunes of mankind.

—Edward Gibbon

Only the Word made flesh can give any sort of hope in a world as grim and ugly and hard and sordid as ours.

—Lynn Harold Hugh

The hinge of history is on the door of a Bethlehem stable.

—Ralph W. Sockman

We believe in one God, the Father Almighty, maker of all things, both visible and invisible; and in one Lord, Jesus Christ, the Son of God, only begotten of the Father, that is to say, of the substance of the Father, God of God and Light of Light, very God of very God, begotten, not made, being of one substance with the Father, by whom all things were made, both things in heaven and things on earth; who, for us men and for our salvation, came down and was made flesh, was made man, suffered, and rose again on the third day, went up into the heavens, and is to come again to judge both the quick and the dead; and in the Holy Ghost.

—Nicene Creed (325 A.D.)

...Jesus Christ... at once complete in Godhead and complete in manhood, truly God and truly man,...

—*Chalcedon Creed (451 A.D.)*

A man who was merely a man and said the sort of things Jesus said would not be a great moral teacher. He would either be a lunatic... or else he would be the Devil of Hell. You must make your choice. Either this man was, and is, the Son of God: or else a madman or something worse.

—*C. S. Lewis*

If moral virtue was Christianity,
Christ's pretensions were all Vanity....

—*William Blake*

I know men: and I tell you that Jesus Christ was no mere man. Between Him and every other person in the world there is no possible term of comparison. Alexander, Caesar, Charlemagne, and I have founded empires. But on what did we rest the creations of our genius? Upon force. Jesus Christ founded His empire upon love; and at this hour millions of men would die for him.

—*Napoleon Bonaparte*

For God so loved the world that He gave His only begotten Son, that whoever believes in Him should not perish but have everlasting life.

—*John 3:16*

Do you think it was self-denial for the Lord Jesus to come down from heaven to rescue a world: Was it self-denial? No, it was love — love that swallows up everything, and first of all self.

—*Nikolaus von Zinzendorf*

338

...God was in Christ reconciling the world to Himself,...
> —*II Corinthians 5:19a*

God clothed himself in vile man's flesh so He might be weak enough to suffer woe.
> —*John Donne*

The face of Christ does not indeed show us everything, but it shows us the one thing we need to know — the character of God.
> —*P. Carneige Simpson*

Philip said..., "Lord, show us the Father,...."
Jesus said..., "He who has seen Me has seen the Father;..."
> —*John 14:8-9*

Just as the whole of this book emphasizes both theory and practice — or belief and action, so also the two chapters of this concluding unit consider both a central focus for building one's philosophy of life (this chapter) and also an approach to applying that focus to daily living (the next or concluding chapter). For the Christian, the Incarnation is not only the center of the Christian faith; it is also the central event of all history, the entrance of God personally, even humanly, into human space and time. It is the mind of God becoming a human person with the purpose of showing us His great love, redeeming us to Himself, and further revealing the nature of God. The Divine One who made us comes to us. Of course, He has always been a God who comes (i.e. through His Spirit, through natural Revelation, through dreams, visions, and angels, and through the written Word); but his advent in the flesh was unique.

Historians date the beginning of human existence as anywhere from a few thousand to a few million years ago. They more nearly agree upon the time of the emergence of human civilization (an advanced level of human existence, usually with cities, written language, cultural institutions, settled farming, and developed governmental, technological, and economic systems) as about 3500 B.C. As historians study the past, they seek to find long-range patterns of cause and effect in human experience. Interestingly, since the beginning of history-writing, most historians have chosen political and military history as the topic of greatest significance to record. In their explaining of the human story, why should they not have found many other topics (e.g. the history of benevolence, labor, families, or religion) to be at least equally meaningful?

Those who read history have generally accepted this primary emphasis upon political and military history. Why are people in general, in the past and the present alike, so entranced with what often has been the raw and even brutal exercise of power? Is it because we are intuitively seeking a strong God-like figure to govern our lives? Is it because we are too admiring of power itself (note the writings of psychologist Alfred Adler)? Is it both? Why is it that so many leaders of what we call major civilizations have secured their hold on power by presenting themselves as God, or a god, or a descendent of God, or as someone given absolute power in their domain by God? Even what most modern Westerners would identify as the most advanced form of governance, namely democracy with its system of checks and balances, or limited power, is still based upon the self-serving power impulse whereby it is assumed that each of the many policy makers will normally advance his or her own interests. Of course, the redemptive feature of the democratic process is that it typically neutralizes rival selfishness and forces the emergence, by compromise, of something hopefully approaching the collective good (see chapter 39). Yet even under democracy as under totalitarian systems, the meek, the humble, and the benevolent-minded philosophers rarely inherit the rule of the earth.

Then there was Jesus, another historical character claiming divine powers. Given the political pattern of His day, there is little wonder that His immediate followers were expecting—even wanting—Him to be an all-powerful political ruler who would defeat the traditional oppressors of His people. But what He said was surprising, even revolutionary. He was a King, yes, but His Kingdom was not of this world; while His Kingdom operated in this present world, it ultimately transcended it. Furthermore, His weapons were not ones of physical or even spiritual force but rather ones of love and persuasion. He argued that soul force was greater and ultimately triumphed over physical force.

That the God of the universe is also the babe of Bethlehem and that He came to live amongst us to further reveal Himself to us and to give us His redemptive love, is the heart of the Christian message and hope. It is the Good News. Could we still have a Christianity if God Himself did not come from Heaven as Jesus but rather merely gave Jesus an unusual understanding of His mind and desires for humanity? Perhaps we could, but it would be a very different Christianity, one more like 1) an elevated, less-legalistic form of Judaism; 2) Islam which holds the human Jesus in very high regard as a major figure in its prophetic tradition; or 3) Confucianism with its emphasis on moral wisdom. This nonincarnational-Jesus form of Christianity, however, would have a major disadvantage compared with its counterpart world religions, namely, a fundamental problem of founder integrity, for Jesus on many occasions spoke directly or by inference of His divine nature (e.g. Matthew 7:21-23, 9:2, 16:13-18, 27:63-64, 28:18; John 6:40, 10:30, 14:6-11). If, then, Jesus inappropriately claimed Divinity, He leaves His followers with a severely, if not fatally, compromised system, for no religion is any better than its internal integrity.

Orthodox Christianity, of course, has always assumed that it was God, Himself, rather than a human emissary who came in Christ as an entrant into human history, living in the eastern Mediterranean part of the Roman Empire two-thousand years ago. That God came in human form rather than sending another prophet was unique and the ultimate expression of His passionate identification with and love for us. Ancient humanity knew something of God through internal intuition, the instruction and promptings of the Spirit of God (e. g. John 1:9; Ecclesiastes 3:11; Acts 14:16-17, Acts 17:27b; Romans 1:18-20; also see the marvelous book by Don Richardson, *Eternity in their Hearts*), and natural revelation (e. g. Psalm 19). The Old Testament Jews had their special relationship with God, including their scriptures. The Incarnation, however, brought an even larger understanding of the nature of God and His intentions toward us. Ancient peoples understood the fear of God better than the love of God. Jesus, the Christ, both by the very act of His coming as well as by His teaching and modeling sought to balance and then surpass our focus on fear with a transforming focus on love. Otherwise, wherein is the Good News? Still many of us in the Christian era continue to struggle to fully embrace the Gospel of love. Anglican cleric and counselor, Morton Kelsey, ably expressed this continuing problem:

> "...if we see the final revelation of the Bible as a vengeful, punishing, destroying, and angry God rather than Jesus, who died on the cross to reveal the unconditional love of God, then we Christians will not see love as the central reality in the universe.... And unless we truly believe that God is love, we are not likely to put forth the effort that is necessary to shape our lives by self-giving love and caring."

That God should care enough about us to come to us personally should not be surprising given what the early part of the Biblical record reveals about His character. The first of the moral attributes of God that the Bible shows, as revealed in the divine work of creation, is His love of goodness—all of His works were "very good" (Genesis 1:31). Then, when sin occurs, we learn of a second attribute, namely his mercifulness. Both are components qualifying Him as a God who can be trusted and is worthy of a response of love. Both of these attributes spring from His essential nature—He is a God of love. "God is love," John states simply.

From this God who comes in love, may we receive His gift more fully, that in turn in our years on the stage of human history, we may love more completely.

Christ's coming is central. Christ is central. Christ is victor. We are victors in Christ. Therein is our creed. Therein is our relationship. Now and forever more. Amen.

QUESTIONS FOR REFLECTION AND DISCUSSION:

1. In human history what is the relative balance between good and evil?

2. How old do you think human history to be, and how significant to you is your answer?

3. Why do history textbooks place so much emphasis upon political and military history?

4. How would your religious experience be different if you believed that Jesus was not divine?

SUGGESTIONS FOR FURTHER READING

1. Augustine of Hippo, *The City of God*

2. Donald M. Baille, *God Was in Christ*

3. John Bright, *The Kingdom of God*

4. Herbert Butterfield, *Christianity and History*

5. Robert Clyde Johnson, *The Meaning of Christ*

6. Peter Kreeft, *Christianity for Modern Pagans: Pascal's Pensees*

7. C. S. Lewis, *Mere Christianity*, Book II

8. B. B. Warfield, *The Person and Work of Christ*

9. David F. Wells, *The Person of Christ: A Biblical and Historical Analysis*

10. Charles Williams, *He Came Down from Heaven*

46. HARMONY AND BALANCE

...seek ye first the Kingdom of God...

—Matthew 6:33a

All our merely natural activities will be accepted, if they are offered to God, even the humblest, and all of them, even the noblest, will be sinful if they are not.

—C.S. Lewis

The meaning of man's life is found in obedience and intimate communion with God. ...we are not only created by God, but also by God for conscious fellowship with Him.... This is the great source of human dignity.

—Richard S. Emrich

Be still, and know that I am God....

—Psalm 46:10a

Let your gentleness be known to all men.

—Philippians 4:5a

Faith embraces many truths which seem to contradict each other.

—Blaise Pascal

Pushing any truth out very far, you are met by a counter-truth.

—Henry Ward Beecher

He who knows only his side of the case, knows little of that.

—John Stuart Mill

In the human mind, one-sidedness has always been the rule, and many-sidedness the exception. Hence, even in revolutions of opinion, one part of the truth usually sets while another rises.

—*John Stuart Mill*

Our opinions are less important than the spirit and temper with which they possess us, and even good opinions are worth very little unless we hold them in a broad, intelligent, and spacious way.

—*John Morley*

Reason, ruling alone, is a force confining; and passion, unattended, is a flame that burns to its own destruction.

—*Kahlil Gibran*

Everyday life is a stimulating mixture of order and haphazardry. The sun rises and sets on schedule but the wind bloweth where it listeth.

—*Robert Louis Stevenson*

Science says: "We must live", and seeks the means of prolonging, increasing, facilitating and amplifying life, of making it tolerable and acceptable; wisdom says: "We must die", and seeks how to make us die well.

—*Miguel De Unamuno*

A man will have to give an account on the judgment day for every good thing which he might have enjoyed and did not.

—*Rabbinic saying*

...we must seek out the recreating stillness of solitude if we want to be with others meaningfully. We must seek the fellowship and

accountability of others if we want to be alone safely. We must cultivate both if we are to live in obedience.

—*Richard Foster*

Solitude is as needful to the imagination as society is wholesome for the character.

—*James Russell Lowell*

Busyness is not of the devil; busyness is the devil.

—*Carl Jung*

It is a trick of the devil, which he employs to deceive good souls, to incite them to do more than they are able, in order that they may no longer be able to do anything.

—*St. Vincent dePaul*

...those who are in Christ share with Him all the riches of limitless time and endless years. God never hurries. There are no dead-lines against which He must work. Only to know this is to quiet our spirits and relax our nerves. For those who are out of Christ, time is a devouring beast; before the sons of the new creation time crouches and purrs and licks their hands.

—*A.W. Tozer*

There are enough hours in every day for us to fulfill God's perfect and particular will for our lives.

—*Anonymous*

If we strive to be happy by filling all the silences of life with sound, productive by turning all life's leisure into work, and real by turning all our being into doing, we will only succeed in producing a hell on earth.

—*Thomas Merton*

> *Our being is not to be enriched merely by activity or experience as such. Everything depends on the <u>quality</u> of our acts and experience.*
>
> —*Thomas Merton*

With our central focus on the Incarnate God and our victory in Him as described in the previous chapter, we can increasingly live with a settled confidence that keeps us calmly and steadily on the course of our calling without the excesses that stem from a neurotic quest for a self-defined fulfillment. In other words, proper being precedes proper doing. Harmony comes from being plugged into the power source of love, wisdom, truth, and purpose; only then can we naturally act. In the conflict between being and doing, the Christian ideal emphasizes the primacy of being—being in Christ. Doing, then, follows being—it stems from it; it doesn't create it. To start with doing in the hope of it leading to being is to accept the burden of an impossible-to-please slave driver. You can never do enough. The irony is that many—perhaps most—Christians, who should know better, in part do this. Also, many Christian organizations encourage this. God's "burden," by contrast, is "light" (Matthew 11:29-30). He simply calls us to faithfulness—not to specific results, not to human recognition. He calls us to strive toward holiness (e.g. wholeness); He does not ask us to save the whole world by ourselves. St. Dominic expressed well the desired balance between and order of being and doing: "Contemplate, and then...pass on to others the things contemplated."

With the aforementioned philosophy of being and doing in place, we increasingly move toward harmony with our mental and physical universe as we increasingly rest in our Creator and Redeemer. More and more we are freed from the compulsion toward unbalanced thinking and living. Peace and harmony stem from obedience and fellowship as we receive and return His love and continuously seek His truth and wisdom. These elements, then, are the basis for a harmonious philosophy of life; they provide a harmonizing center that judiciously arbitrates among the competing attractions and claims of life.

Adjudicating among these claims is a life-long process. It involves 1) seeking to avoid the bad; 2) finding among the good those things which, while not necessary for all, become a specific calling for you; 3) creating balance among those things which are essential for you—both those which are a part of your specific calling and those which are part of the calling for us all, and 4) seeking to avoid an overall "busyness" state of mind whereby in a given time period you try to do more than what God is asking or wanting you to do.

Few people establish a life plan that includes a balancing of good and evil—we do not want to plan for evil at all! In practice, however, such a struggle is a reality (e.g. see Romans 7:22-23) as we seek to reduce the degree of evil in our thoughts and actions. Our harmony with God, of course, is the key factor in achieving victory here. Not the least of the reasons for not doing bad things is that it steals time and energy resources from the effort to do good things.

There are so many good things that one could do in life. A large part of being a wise person is to find from the many good options those which are your specific calling. This is not always easy but it is always possible for those who are in fellowship with the One who said, "Seek and ye shall find" (see chapter 15 on "The Will of God").

Such a large part of being a balanced person is to devote neither excessive nor insufficient time and energy to each of the necessary and complementary elements of your calling. Some of these elements are unique to you (e.g. serving in a specific position during a specific period), but still need to be balanced with the many other valid demands which are common to most humans (e.g. responsibilities related to marriage, family, community, and recreation). Another model for viewing the call for balance is one that emphasizes the seemingly endless number of life situations, values and tendencies whereby one good factor competes with a contrasting second good factor, and in which victory is to be won not by the triumph of one or the other force but in the optimum blending of the two. Note the following examples:

Work and play

Activity and rest

Mental activity and physical activity

Beauty and practicality

Creation and re-creation

Thought and action

Seeking to learn all that one can and accepting the fact
that in this life, at least, one cannot perfectly understand

Fellowship and solitude

Giving and receiving

For those married, concern for the self and
concern for the partner

For those with children, loving discipline
and disciplined love

For all of us, receiving God's loving discipline
and receiving His encouragement

The nearness of God and the remoteness of God

Heart religion and head religion

Critical inquiry and positive attachment

Doubt and belief

The development of breadth and
the development of depth

Giving to those close to you and
giving to those far from you

Satisfaction and continued pursuit

Freedom and security

Freedom and accountability

Loving your neighbor and loving yourself

Geographic base and universal citizen
"No man is an island" thinking, and
 "God and you make a majority" thinking
Living in the present moment and long-range thinking
Enjoying/using and nurturing/protecting
 the natural resources of God's earth
Self-confidence and humility
Purity and unity in the Christian fellowship
Process and product in decision-making
The best ideas in support of one position and the
 most compelling ideas favoring the contrasting view
The family and the community
Professional ministry and family ministry
The individual and the country
You and me
We and them
"There is no one any more important in God's sight
 than me" thinking, and "there is no one any less
 important in God's sight than me" thinking

The problem of busyness overlaps with but is different from and often more serious than the problem of disbalance. Busyness manifests itself as a time problem but at its essence it reflects a misperception of what is good. Some people spend undue time in one area of life to receive recognition for their hard work and/or excellence in an effort to correct a wrongly perceived sense of inferiority. They need to understand that no one is inherently inferior and that to believe so is to accept a lie imposed by society or the evil one himself. The ultimate solution is to receive the sense of self-worth that comes with a realization of how completely their Maker accepts and values them, and invites them—like all others—to pursue only His specific calling which is always doable and based upon faithfulness rather than comparative results.

Others overinvest time and energy in one area that is pleasant to avoid dealing with another area that is not. If the neglected area is a necessary one, then not facing it contributes to personal disharmony and sometimes disaster. Not the least of reasons for not being too busy is that usually such hyperactivity causes our listening to God to suffer. Of course, sometimes such communion is exactly that from which the busy person is seeking to escape; a person in such a state will never be at peace.

Some forms of busyness stem from the best of intentions. Many serious-minded people continue as a habit throughout adulthood a busyness mentality learned in their formative years (perhaps from idealistic and hard-working parents or teachers). When inspired by a call to complete commitment to Christ, the goal of excellence in one's profession, or simply for a high sense of stewardship, one needs to carefully monitor the fruits of one's work patterns. Do they produce internal disharmony or strained interpersonal relations? Do they allow one to work joyously and in a serving manner in each task without a preoccupied awareness of all the other things that one must rush on to do?

Finally, we need to continually remind ourselves that the effort to achieve joy, peace, harmony, and balance is no less a part of our calling than is hard work. Harmony and vocation need to be balanced. Maybe we could even say that harmony itself is our vocation.

Let this essay and book close with the profound third verse of John Greenleaf Whittier's prayer poem, "Dear Lord and Father of Mankind":

Drop thy still dews of quietness
Till all our strivings cease;
Take from our souls the strain and stress,
And let our ordered lives confess
The beauty of thy peace
     Amen.

QUESTIONS FOR REFLECTION AND DISCUSSION:

1. How busy do you think God wants people to be?

2. How easy or difficult is it for you to say "no" to requests for your services?

SUGGESTIONS FOR FURTHER READING:

1. Anthony deMello, *The Way to Love*

2. Vernard Eller, *The Simple Life*

3. Charles E. Hummel, *Freedom from the Tyranny of the Urgent*

4. Soren Kierkegaard, *Purity of Heart is to Will One Thing*

5. Thomas Merton, *No Man Is an Island*

6. Reinhold Niebuhr, *The Nature and Destiny of Man*

7. Mark Noll, *Between Faith and Criticism: Evangelicals, Scholarship and the Bible in America*